PRAISE FOR
DIGITAL MARKET
STRATEGY

'Simon Kingsnorth has produced a book of compelling quality. So many marketers are inclined to run headlong at digital marketing with a limited amount of knowledge. Fingers get burnt and reputations can be lost forever. He has set out some brilliant guidelines for marketers of all levels which will empower them to succeed.'

Damian Ryan, digital marketer, author of *Understanding Digital Marketing, Understanding Social Media* and *The Best Digital Marketing Campaigns in the World II*

'An excellent all-in-one text for today's digital entrepreneur.'

Jonathan Gabay, keynote speaker, lecturer, brand psychologist

'Combines a detailed knowledge of digital channel management with classic marketing theory. The result is essential reading for digital marketing practitioners at all levels.'

Emma Wilson, CEO, Harvest Digital

'It's all here. An invaluable one-stop guide to navigating the discipline of digital marketing – great for newcomers and an excellent reference for the more experienced.'

Simon Fenn, co-founder, Pancentric Digital

This book is dedicated to my parents who gave me the foundation that provided me with the opportunity to work on some of the exciting projects I've been involved in. To my partner Ali for her support during the long evenings of endless typing and to everyone I have worked for and with to date as you have all helped to shape this book. It is also dedicated to those people who will create the future of this planet (and beyond).

Digital Marketing Strategy

An integrated approach to online marketing

Simon Kingsnorth

KoganPage

LONDON PHILADELPHIA NEW DELHI

First published in Great Britain and the United States in 2016 by Kogan Page Limited

2nd Floor, 45 Gee Street	1518 Walnut Street, Suite 900	4737/23 Ansari Road
London EC1V 3RS	Philadelphia PA 19102	Daryaganj
United Kingdom	USA	New Delhi 110002
www.koganpage.com		India

© Simon Kingsnorth, 2016

The right of Simon Kingsnorth to be identified as the author of this work has been asserted by him in accordance with the Copyright, Designs and Patents Act 1988.

ISBN   978 0 7494 7470 6
E-ISBN   978 0 7494 7471 3

British Library Cataloguing-in-Publication Data

A CIP record for this book is available from the British Library.

Library of Congress Cataloging-in-Publication Data

Names: Kingsnorth, Simon, author.
Title: Digital marketing strategy : an integrated approach to online marketing / Simon Kingsnorth.
Description: 1st Edition. | Philadelphia, PA : Kogan Page, 2016. | Includes bibliographical references and index.
Identifiers: LCCN 2016007169 (print) | LCCN 2016015803 (ebook) | ISBN 9780749474706 (paperback) | ISBN 9780749474713 (e-ISBN) | ISBN 9780749474713
Subjects: LCSH: Electronic commerce–Management. | Internet marketing. | Strategic planning. | BISAC: BUSINESS & ECONOMICS / Marketing / General. | BUSINESS & ECONOMICS / E-Commerce / Internet Marketing. | BUSINESS & ECONOMICS / Strategic Planning.
Classification: LCC HF5548.32 .K566 2016 (print) | LCC HF5548.32 (ebook) | DDC 658.8/72–dc23
LC record available at https://lccn.loc.gov/2016007169

Typeset by Graphicraft Limited, Hong Kong
Printed and bound by 4edge Limited, UK

CONTENTS

Bringing it all together   315

A bonus chapter, 'The future of digital', and other resources are available at the following url (please scroll to the bottom of the page and complete the form to access these):

www.koganpage.com/DigitalMarketingStrategy

ABOUT THE AUTHOR

Simon Kingsnorth is a strategic marketing leader who has built and led marketing departments and consulted to businesses across the world. He has specialized in digital for many years and run campaigns across all digital channels but also has experience running most offline channels. He has a passion for digital-first cultures but above all has a belief that integrated, client-centric strategies should be the focus for most organizations.

Simon has worked client-side for a wide range of organizations including start-ups, small and medium-sized enterprises (SMEs) and global businesses across a range of business to consumer (B2C) and business to business (B2B) industries and has also been fortunate enough to work with many leading agencies. He is a contributing author to the books *Understanding Digital Marketing* and *Understanding Social Media*.

Simon also has too many hobbies to count including photography, music and history but the things Simon is most proud of are his two wonderful boys.

ABOUT THE CONTRIBUTORS

Glen Conybeare

Glen is Chief Commercial Officer at international digital marketing agency Stickyeyes (**stickyeyes.com**). A member of the executive board, Glen is responsible for client services and is heavily involved in business development. Glen has a wealth of international client and agency-side experience, having worked in the UK, United States, Sweden and Gibraltar, and has previously held a number of senior and board-level positions at companies such as digital media agency i-level and analytics company Touch Clarity (acquired by Omniture) as well as co-founding real-time ad optimization company Cognitive Match (sold to Magnetic Inc). He lives in Leeds with his wife and two young daughters and therefore has no free time for hobbies.

Murray Cox

Murray Cox is Digital Strategy Director at Pancentric Digital (**www.pancentric.com**) in London where he helps clients make smarter digital decisions to transform their businesses. Prior to going agency-side Murray was a digital journalist in both the UK and Australia for the BBC, Australian Associated Press and the Special Broadcast Service. Murray went digital in 1998 as part of the launch team of the MSN network and has since been involved as the media and many other industries have digitally transformed. He has an MBA from Strathclyde University.

James Bourner

James is a digital advertising expert who works for the international independent agency Jellyfish. James has worked for many companies in a range of sectors and his expertise includes online advertising, digital marketing, content monetization and e-commerce. His current passion is programmatic buying.

Introduction

Welcome to *Digital Marketing Strategy: An integrated approach to online marketing*. Before we get into the meat of the book I thought that you might find it useful if we go over what it's all about.

My inspiration to write this book came from the fact that I have struggled to find supporting material and helpful tips when I have been constructing my strategies over the years. I have always been able to find guides and tips on each digital channel, on user experience, digital transformation, customer service and many more relevant subjects but there are few that bring it all together and also consider how the digital strategy should fit within your organization, no matter what it might be. I hope this book goes some way to filling that gap.

Firstly, it is worth looking at what we mean by digital strategy.

What is a digital strategy?

This is perhaps best answered with a question. Can you sum up in one sentence what you will be trying to achieve over the coming years? If not, then you don't have a strategy. If you can articulate that but you don't know how to get from where you are to your end vision, then you don't have a strategy. If you have a vision and a path to get there then you have a strategy but if that is not based on research, bought into by your leadership team and with clear deliverables then your strategy will almost certainly not be a success.

If you were to Google the word 'strategy' you would find definitions such as 'A plan of action designed to achieve a long-term or overall aim' (**www.oxforddictionaries.com**) and 'A method or plan chosen to bring about a desired future, such as achievement of a goal or solution to a problem' (**www.businessdictionary.com**). Both of these definitions are of course true, but we need to go deeper.

What we look at in this book is how to turn your great ideas and those of your team and business into one strategy that is robust, agreed and aligned with your wider business. This strategy needs to go through some clear steps to becoming something you can believe in, clearly articulate, gain advocacy for and work to as a clear plan to deliver you vision. This needs to be accomplished through these core areas:

- understand what is possible;
- understand your business and market context;
- understand your customer;
- understand the potential challenges you face;
- plan your strategy for optimal delivery;
- understand the possibilities within the relevant digital channels and touchpoints;
- measure and evolve your strategy;
- gain buy-in.

Once you have these in place you have a strategy and so this book is designed to address each of these steps.

What's the story of this book?

As mentioned above, this book will talk through each of the key steps to creating your strategy.

In Chapter 1 we look at the background of digital marketing, wider marketing and business models to ensure that the strategy you develop is based on proven techniques and models. This gives some academic perspective that is very useful in ensuring that your methods are robust.

From here, in Chapter 2 we move on to look at how your strategy must align with your business if it is to perform effectively. Working in silos is a challenge that many large businesses face but whether your business is large or small it will need to be aligned. A business that pulls in different directions runs the risk of pulling itself apart.

In Chapter 3 we look at some of the challenges that face digital marketers today. There are many challenges that can completely change the shape of your strategy and so understanding these early on is vital.

Once we have the background from these first three chapters, in Chapter 4 we look at effective planning processes and how to ensure your plan is solid and logical before we get into the detail of each channel.

In Chapters 5 to 8 we look at some of the key channels. This book is not designed to be a 'how to' guide to digital marketing and so we don't go into every channel and the detail of technical set-up, but we do focus on strategic and tactical approaches to each and what that means to your digital strategy.

In Chapter 9 we look at user experience, as this is the ultimate destination of most users, and we also examine digital transformation within your organization before moving onto wider marketing techniques in Chapter 10, such as CRM and retention and how these apply to your digital strategy.

Personalization (Chapter 11) is increasingly important and the effects of this on customer service and content strategy are examined in Chapters 12 and 13 respectively, as well as best-practice service principles and best-practice content techniques.

We look at measurement throughout the book but Chapter 14 goes into detail on tracking, measurement and analysis as well as reporting techniques to encourage knowledge sharing and continuous improvement.

In Chapter 15 we examine how we take your strategy and gain buy-in from your decision makers.

After you have covered all of these steps you should have a strategy that can withstand the tests of time, aligns with your business and is agreed by your key stakeholders, but that most importantly takes your business on a journey to delivering excellent digital progress for your organization.

A bonus chapter, 'The future of digital', and other resources are available at the following url: (please scroll to the bottom of the page and complete the form to access these):

www.koganpage.com/DigitalMarketingStrategy

How to get the most from this book

I have written this book as a guide to the strategic elements of digital marketing and it is designed to take you through the core areas and how to get the most from them. One thing I have always found when reading non-fiction books is that I just want to cut to the chase. In fact one thing I talk about in this book is that culture and technology have moved us towards a place where we demand the key information quickly.

So, whilst I hope you read the whole book and enjoy it, I have also tried to include helpful tips throughout that will help you to pull out the key elements of each topic. Below is a quick overview of some of these and how you can use them.

Chapter goals

At the beginning of every chapter you will find a set of goals. The purpose of this is to help you to understand what the chapter is trying to cover. By the end of the chapter you should have a solid understanding of all of these key points.

Key terms

At the beginning of some chapters I also include a list of the key terms used in that chapter. There is a lot of jargon in digital marketing and it is increasing all the time, but these 'key terms' sections simply help you to understand some of the more jargon-heavy chapters.

Chapter checklist

At the end of every chapter you will find a checklist that is effectively a way of checking that you feel you have a good understanding of all of the key points in the list of key areas covered at the start of each chapter. If not, you can flick back to specific sections of the chapter to refresh your memory.

Further reading

This feature contains my list of recommended reading should you wish to conduct your own deeper research into any of the specialist models, techniques or ideas discussed in this book.

Case studies

Throughout the book you will find case studies on various subjects. These really help bring the point to life (either good or bad) and I find are a great way to understand just how effective (or disastrous) digital marketing can be.

I hope these help you to get the most out of the book and you find it useful and enjoyable. Thanks for reading.

Simon Kingsnorth

What is digital marketing?

01

What we will cover in this chapter

This chapter is intended to give you a background into digital marketing, some of the established models used in constructing a marketing strategy and a focus on how they apply to digital. The key areas covered in this chapter are:

- A history of digital marketing
- The 4 Ps of marketing
- Porter's five forces
- Brand or perceptual positioning map
- Customer lifetime value
- Segmentation
- Boston Consulting Group matrix

Chapter goals

By the end of this chapter you should understand some of the key marketing and business models that will help to shape your strategy. You should have an overview of the history of digital marketing to give some perspective to your strategic plan. You should also gain an understanding of consumer behaviour, market factors, segmentation, lifetime value and the 4 Ps of marketing.

As with any book, and indeed any marketing strategy, the best place to begin is at the beginning. Digital marketing is an ever evolving and growing beast and one that continues to spread its tentacles deep into the processes that organizations have lived by for decades. That all sounds very dramatic but the truth is that it is simply aligned with the direction of travel of the modern world. Digital marketing is (or should be) a part of almost every key business decision from product development and pricing through to public relations (PR) and even recruitment. We touch on why throughout the book.

Now is an exciting time to be in digital marketing.

Digital marketing is often confused with online marketing. As we moved into the 21st century most businesses had, or were in the final throws of, developing a web presence. E-mail was commonplace and there was technology allowing people to manage this fairly easily. Customer relationship management (CRM) systems had been in place for some time to manage databases. Some companies were placing banners on websites with a similar approach to press advertising. Forward-thinking companies were working on their search engine strategy and even working with some affiliates. All of this was online marketing and, in time, online marketing teams and specialists would begin to appear.

So what has changed? The social media revolution has completely changed the internet and consumer behaviour. The penetration of broadband has increased speed, internet usage and user expectation with over 40 per cent of the world now online and over 90 per cent in many countries (Internet World Stats, 2015). Analytics has grown to the level where we can understand our consumers' behaviour in real time, including not just their usage statistics but also their demographics and even interests. Mobile has gone smart and tablets have stormed onto the scene and both of these changes have brought along apps. Touchscreen is becoming increasingly common across all devices. Google has become an enormous organization and owns search globally. TVs have gone smart and Bluetooth opens up another level of possibilities. With a naturally ageing population there is now only a very small percentage who are technophobes simply due to age. I could go on, but it is clear to see that digital is now much broader than the online channels of 15 years ago and must be embedded into everything we do. We will discuss the modern digital marketing channels in more detail in Chapters 5 to 8.

One key point that needs to be made at this early stage is that the focus of this book is on digital marketing and that the word marketing is as important as the word digital. Many organizations have moved towards creating digital marketing departments and digital departments that are separate from their marketing departments. It is crucial now, more so than ever, that digital marketing is an integral part of all marketing activities. This includes

PR, creative direction, brand, CRM, retention, product development, pricing, proposition, communications – the entire marketing mix. Creating a silo for digital activity is very dangerous and only through truly understanding the strategic benefits of fully integrating your marketing from day one will you succeed.

A history of digital marketing

Digital marketing first appeared as a term in the 1990s but, as mentioned above, it was a very different world then. Web 1.0 was primarily static content with very little interaction and no real communities. The first banner advertising started in 1993 and the first web crawler (called Webcrawler) was created in 1994 – this was the beginning of search engine optimization (SEO) as we know it. This may not seem a deep and distant past but when we consider that this was four years before Google launched, over 10 years before YouTube, and that social media was not even a dream at this point, it shows just how far we have come in a short time.

Once Google started to grow at pace and Blogger was launched in 1999 the modern internet age began. Blackberry, a brand not connected with innovation any more, launched mobile e-mail and MySpace appeared. MySpace was the true beginning of social media as we define it today, but it was not as successful as it could have been from a user experience perspective and ultimately that is what led to its downfall. Google's introduction of Adwords was their real platform for growth and remains a key revenue stream for them to this day. Their innovation, simple interface and accurate algorithms continue to remain unchallenged (although Bing have been making some good steps forward in recent years). Cookies have been a key development and also a bone of contention over recent years with new regulation and ongoing privacy debates. Whilst cookies have played a role in the ongoing privacy concerns of digital technology, they have also been a key development in delivering relevant content and therefore personalizing user experience.

Web 2.0 was a term coined in 1999 by Darcy DiNucci but not really popularized until Tim O'Reilly in 2004. With Web 2.0 there was no overhaul of technology as the name might suggest, but more a shift in the way that websites are created. This allowed the web to become a social place, it was an enabler for online communities and so Facebook, Twitter, Instagram, Pinterest, Skype and others were born. One trend that has certainly appeared in the last 10 years is an increase in buzzwords. There seems to be a new word or phrase for everything. From 'big data' to 'dark social', new terms arrive all the time. At nearly every marketing conference I attend these days there is one speaker who is trying to socialize a new phrase they have coined. Whilst these buzzwords can inspire us and open our eyes to new ways of thinking they rarely change the underpinning strategic planning of an effective marketing-led organization – and so below we will review some of the established models, with one eye on the digital perspective.

To gain a good view of the strategic side of digital marketing we review the following models:

TABLE 1.1   Marketing strategy models

Model	Summary
The 4 Ps	The established marketing model
Porter's five forces	A view of competitive positioning
Brand positioning mapping	Analysing your perceptual positioning
Customer lifetime value	Understanding true customer value
Segmentation, targeting and positioning	Understanding the customer
Boston Consulting Group matrix	Product categorization

The 4 Ps of marketing

- Product
- Price
- Place
- Promotion

There have been quite a few variations on the Ps of marketing, including the 4 Ps and 7 Ps, but for this book we focus on the core 4 Ps of marketing – often referred to as the marketing mix. They are product, price, place and promotion. So let's look at what each of these means and how they apply to digital.

Product

This may be a physical product or it may be your service proposition. The key here is that something is developed that people actually want to buy. Some businesses begin with a product and then try to force that on an audience. If there is no demand for your product and no one is interested then you will not be able to create demand.

What does this mean for digital marketing?

The key considerations here from a digital perspective are around whether your product can/will sell online. What channels are open to you for your product or proposition? Are there opportunities to make it flexible to be more appropriate for the online or mobile audiences? Does it provide real value for the consumer and is it differentiated from your competitor offerings? Is it being updated, serviced, maintained effectively to keep it strong? Are there features of it that can be added or should be excluded for the digital customer and is it fair to do this?

An example might be a music album. Three people buy an album. John buys a CD, Maria downloads the album and Robin streams it. All are different consumer behaviours and each person will use your music in a different way. John may proudly display the album on a shelf as he is a loyal fan. Maria may delete some other music from her phone to free up space for the new album. Robin may put the tracks into separate playlists in order to cultivate his collection according to genre or mood. Understanding the different motivations and usage habits for these products is vital to getting your marketing right in the digital age.

Price

Pricing is the second P and one that can be more of a science than an art. Understanding price elasticity and competitive positioning are angles to consider but we won't go into the economics of this here – the key factor is whether you are asking for a price that people are willing to pay. The 'willing to pay' element of that does of course have many factors behind it such as your brand value, online reviews, product quality and others but there are also numerous tactics that can be employed here.

What does this mean for digital marketing?

Discounts and offers are certainly not new to digital marketing but the concept of fast price comparison and the introduction of cashback and voucher sites have certainly changed consumer behaviours. Businesses can take advantage of this through affiliate marketing programmes. Affiliate marketing is where you promote your products through a third-party website in exchange for paying a commission or fee to the website when an action is taken. This is very common in the comparison, voucher and cashback space as it is very easy to directly track sales and therefore attribute value to the relationship. Commissions are often paid on sales but can be paid on click-throughs or other actions.

Affiliate marketing

Affiliate marketing has existed for a long time but has a poor reputation. This is due to a lack of clarity around measurement and genuine sales. The industry has improved greatly over the last 10 years, however there is still a need to maintain this channel and it can be resource intensive as a result. One example of this is the need to review sales reports and track them against customer acquisitions to ensure that the customers for whom you are paying for the affiliate website have joined your business. It is good practice also to ensure that your agreement with the affiliate website states that the customer must stay with you for a period of time, where this is relevant to your industry, before you pay the commission. This reduces the risk of fraudulent sales numbers.

Affiliate marketing customers will often be deal hunters, due to the nature of how they have been acquired, and so it is important to understand that they may not be the most loyal customers you have and will likely be more price sensitive than your average customer. You may need a specific CRM strategy for these customers to encourage them to stay. We look at CRM and retention in Chapter 10.

There is also an expectation in some sectors that prices should be lower online as there are no overheads. It is considered by many that selling online should be cheaper than selling from a retail outlet. One counter to this of course is that there is no need to post products from your retail outlet. Deciding how this fits with your business strategy is key. Another factor to keep in mind is that it costs less to keep a customer than to acquire a new one so retention, CRM and lifetime value are a vital part of your strategy. We examine the digital side of those in Chapter 10.

Place

Location, location, location. Building your shop in the wrong place decreases footfall and ultimately means fewer sales. Having your shop in the right place but not having the stock in the shop is even worse. Having your product in the shop in the right location but then not displaying it correctly – so people cannot find it – is also a factor of 'place'.

What does this mean for digital marketing?

All of these apply to digital marketing. You may not have a physical shop but your online shop must be easy to find – this relates back to SEO, paid search and most other digital acquisition channels. Once someone arrives is it easy to navigate and find the information and products that they want? Do you have the items in stock and is your site working correctly to dispatch them? Ultimately, if people cannot find what they are looking for then you can expect them to go elsewhere. If this happens online then you can expect them to go elsewhere much faster as speed is much more of an expectation online.

Promotion

Promotion is what most people think of when they hear the word marketing. Your TV campaign, your press advertising, your display banners. This is often the first time that people will have any relationship with your brand and sometimes, certainly in below-the-line marketing, this can be a personal relationship. As we all know, first impressions are very important so getting your promotion right is vital.

Above and below the line

Above-the-line and below-the-line marketing are terms used to differentiate between broadcast and targeted marketing techniques. Above-the-line marketing refers to mass market advertising that is often used to push specific promotional messages out to large audiences or to build your brand. Below-the-line is used to tailor your communications to individuals or segments to ensure a more powerful message. We explore personalization in more detail in Chapter 11.

Through-the-line is a term often used and this simply refers to creating an integrated approach by using an appropriate blend of above and below-the-line marketing. This is of course what we are advocating in this book. To help you further understand the split, given below is a list of marketing channels that would fall into each bracket:

- *Above-the-line*:
  - TV;
  - radio;
  - press;
  - display advertising;
  - outdoor.
- *Below-the-line*:
  - SEO;
  - direct mail;
  - paid search;
  - e-mail;
  - direct selling.

These days promotion has moved far beyond simple advertising and into dialogue. Smart marketing is much more than shouting about your product and much more about taking customers on a journey. That journey does not end at purchase either. There are many standard approaches to good-quality promotion, including being single-minded, insight-driven, integrated, communicating the features and benefits, creating a clear call to action and many others. All of these apply to the digital acquisition channels.

What does this mean for digital marketing?

One of the challenges with the digital space is that we often have limited space or time to communicate the product promotion. Where a TV advert or press advertisement may have 30 seconds to get a point across, digital will often have 100 characters or less than one second. This therefore creates a real need for impact messaging and, more importantly than anything else, a test-and-learn philosophy. No matter how much you know (or think you know) about your consumers you cannot predict every possible outcome and so being in a constant and evolving test cycle is vital to a culture of continuous improvement – something that is a key value of effective marketing.

Porter's five forces

FIGURE 1.1   Porter's five forces

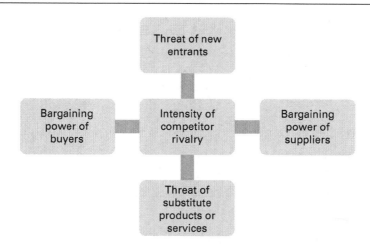

The next model worth reviewing is the five forces analysis model by Michael Porter. This is used to analyse the level of competition within an industry by utilizing industrial organization economics. The purpose is effectively to ascertain the competitive landscape and potential profitability of an industry. Any changes to these forces can directly affect an industry and the companies within it and so it is important to understand them and react to them in order to retain or gain competitive advantage. Michael Porter goes into a greater level of detail than we have space for here in his book *Competitive Advantage*, which has been used by students and businesses alike for many years in order to understand competition.

Porter's five forces are as follows:

- Horizontal competition:

  1 The threat of substitute products or services.

  2 The threat of established rivals.

  3 The threat of new entrants.

- Vertical competition:

  4 The bargaining power of suppliers.

  5 The bargaining power of customers.

Threat of substitute products or services

This first force is the existence of another similar product in another industry. An example for the digital age might be landline phones versus mobile phones or, more specifically, mobile phones versus smartphones. Were a new smartphone to be launched that charges via a pod in the home and that has specific benefits for home use, it may attract customers who have always been landline users and so this is a substitute product threat to landline providers.

There are a number of factors to consider when determining if a product is a substitute threat according to this definition. Those factors are:

- Switching cost: if the switching cost is low then there is a high threat.
- Pricing: if the other product or service is relatively low in price then again the threat is high.
- Product quality: if the potential substitute product or service is of superior quality then the threat is high.
- Product performance: if the other product is superior in performance then the threat is again high.

What does this mean for digital marketing?

This threat is ever present in the digital age as companies continue to innovate. Tablets have threatened the laptop market and phablets have in turn threatened the tablet market. Holograms, drones and many others continue to impact on more traditional and established industries and this is discussed in greater detail in the bonus chapter, available at **www.koganpage.com/ DigitalMarketingStrategy**.

Threat of new entrants

This threat is fairly obvious. A new entrant to a market can be direct competition and therefore threaten the success of an established business. There are many examples of this from the digital age, not least Google, Amazon, eBay and Twitter. Google entered the search market and quickly became the leader above many established players due to the accuracy and speed of the results. Amazon grew quickly, defeating more established players through excellent customer focus and introducing innovations in personalization that gave them a distinct advantage. Although eBay was not the first auction site it was very simple and easy to use. Finally, Twitter entered the social media space with a new micro-blogging approach that created a very simple method of sharing new thoughts and insights. It has been relatively easy for online-only businesses to enter many markets in the last 10 to 15 years. Many of the old barriers, especially capital, have been removed.

Some of the factors that can dictate the threat of a new entrant are:

- *Barriers to entry*: for example patents, regulation. High entry barriers are attractive to established businesses as they stop new businesses entering easily. Also low exit barriers help businesses to leave the industry, which is also attractive. In other words, it is easy for your established competition to leave but difficult for new competition to enter.

- *Economies of scale*: new entrants are highly likely to be smaller than established businesses and so may not be able to profitably compete on pricing.

- *Brand equity*: established businesses have brand equity – a level of trust that comes with being a recognized brand. Although it is true that new entrants do not have this, it can be quickly established with significant above-the-line marketing spend.

- *Industry profitability*: if the industry is generally highly profitable then it is likely to attract a large volume of new entrants and vice versa.

- *Government policy*: there might be government policy in place that limits the ease with which new entrants can join specific industries.

There are many other factors such as location, expected retaliation, technology and distribution and these should all be thoroughly researched and understood in order for strategy to be robust.

Barriers to entry – two examples

Financial services is a good example of an industry that has high entry barriers. There are many regulatory bodies and licensing processes in this industry and these are different around the world. It can therefore be very challenging for new businesses to gain these licences and understand all the regulations and requirements. Also staff need to be hired who have the expertise in the industry and they need ongoing training. These are all additional costs. Photography is an example of a business with very low entry barriers. To demonstrate this you could ask your friends and colleagues if any of them have a photography website and you will almost certainly find that at least one of them does. With the move to digital photography, equipment can be bought easily, techniques learnt at home and studios set up in your spare room. Anyone can become a wedding photographer or corporate photographer with minimal investment and effort.

What does this mean for digital marketing?

Specifically for digital marketing it is certainly true that new entrants are common to most markets and disruption is commonplace in the 21st century. Factors such as location, economies of scale, brand equity and technology are far less relevant for entering many industries now, for example technology businesses. Technology businesses have grown at pace in recent years and have attracted a great deal of investment as businesses look to disrupt the existing industries. In 2014 for example, funds worth US$1.4 billion were launched by London-based venture capital firms in just six months (London and Partners, 2014). Many of the businesses being invested in offer digital solutions such as marketing automation, analytics and social media. This results in the digital marketing industry being in a constant state of flux – and ensuring you keep pace with these changes is important. Attending events, maintaining strong relationships with agencies and tech companies and reading the tech news are all important ways of doing this.

Intensity of competitive rivalry

Competitive rivalry is one of the more commonly understood competitive factors and is sometimes considered the most dangerous. The distinct features and behaviours of your competition directly affect your ability to gain competitive advantage.

Alongside digital transformation there are many other factors, including:

- *The competitors themselves*: the number of competitors and their relative strength are key factors. If your industry has no industry leaders the playing field is fairly level and so competitor rivalry is increased.

- *High exit barriers*: if it is difficult to get out then more businesses will stay in, even if they are only breaking even or even losing money. Competition therefore remains high.

- *Slow industry growth*: if an industry is growing fast then all players can grow through acquisition without necessarily directly affecting the competition. All those new customers can be shared out. If growth is slow then there are no more customers but just as many companies, so to grow you need to acquire customers from your rivals.

In markets where competitive rivalry is high, we move towards 'perfect competition' or in other words a situation where everyone competes at an even level with no 'price makers', only 'price takers'. Price makers have the power to influence the price they charge, whereas price takers have no effect on the market. I would recommend more reading on Porter's five forces and generally around economic theory to understand this in greater detail.

What does this mean for digital marketing?

There are many factors to take into consideration here and the recent trend towards modernization in the form of digital transformation is one of these. Moving your business into the digital age can be a slow and expensive process for established businesses. This can certainly create a change in the competitive landscape as younger businesses are more agile. On the other hand it is equally true that the larger businesses, which of course tend to be the more established (although not necessarily), can potentially invest money and resource into creating something at scale with advanced technology that may be less available to less established businesses. Digital transformation can gain you competitive advantage and therefore reduce rivalry.

Bargaining power of suppliers

Suppliers of products or services to companies are another factor in the competitive nature of an industry. The bargaining power of suppliers directly affects the ability for companies to make a profit and therefore compete. Strong suppliers are able to control pricing and product quality, which lessens a company's ability to make profit. Weak suppliers on the other hand can be controlled or influenced more by the buyer and so the buyer can retain competitive advantage.

Some of the factors that can lead to high bargaining power for suppliers and therefore increased competition are:

- *Few suppliers*: if there are fewer suppliers than buyers then suppliers retain more bargaining opportunity.
- *Buyer switching costs*: if changing supplier is expensive then the advantage again lies with the buyer.
- *Forward integration*: if the supplier is able to produce the product or service themselves then again they are in a position of strength.

What does this mean for digital marketing?

If you are running an e-commerce operation with physical products then you may be working with a wholesaler for the supply of your goods. It is possible that your supplier may be one of very few or the only supplier of the goods that you are retailing to your customers. In this situation the wholesaler has strong bargaining power as you have limited options. This can lead to an increase in costs and therefore your profit margin. This may in turn lead to a necessity to increase prices, which may result in a decline in sales. Should more wholesalers enter the market then the competition for your wholesaler increases, which passes some of the bargaining power back to you. Another option is to look at producing at least some of the products yourself in order to remove further power from the wholesaler.

Bargaining power of buyers

The bargaining power of buyers is the final force and is simply the ability of consumers to put pressure on companies to lower prices, change their products or improve customer service. Businesses can take a number of actions to reduce buyer power: for example, engagement strategies and loyalty programmes.

Some of the factors that influence buyer bargaining power are:

- *Buyer concentration*: if there are few consumers and many companies then the buyer effectively has their choice of company.

- *Switching costs*: as with most of the other forces, switching costs are a factor. If it is easy for a buyer to switch then they retain the bargaining power.

- *Backward integration*: if buyers can produce the products themselves then they again retain the power.

What does this mean for digital marketing?

One of the best examples of how buyer bargaining power has changed in the digital age is the increased use of social media and review sites to openly rate and discuss products, pricing and customer service provided by businesses. Many consumers will include reviews within their decision-making process and will not buy products that match their requirements if the reviews from their peers are negative. This has even extended to search engines with star ratings openly displayed within results for searches such as restaurants and products, which can increase or decrease click-through rates as a result. The power of the buyer has significantly increased since Web 2.0.

Brand or perceptual positioning map

It is useful to use a brand positioning map to develop your market positioning strategy for your products or services. These maps are not, however, built from your views of your marketplace but from the perceptions of consumers and so are sometimes called perceptual maps. These maps give a clear view, albeit a little subjective, of where your brand or products sit versus your competitors, thus highlighting any gaps in the market and demonstrating where there are areas of intense competition.

Most perceptual maps are drawn with two axes, X and Y. They intersect each other in the centre and so form a cross. This is not the only way to draw a positioning map but it is by far the most common. What you choose to place on the axes is up to you and you therefore need to consider the variables in your industry and what is the goal of your research. If we were to draw a map of automotive brands using the scales of practicality and affordability (see Figure 1.2) we can see quite clearly where the direct competition lies in terms of perception and where there may be gaps in the market. This is also useful to determine where your brand is perceived to be and can help you to construct your strategy for moving your brand to where you want it to be.

FIGURE 1.2   Automotive perceptual map

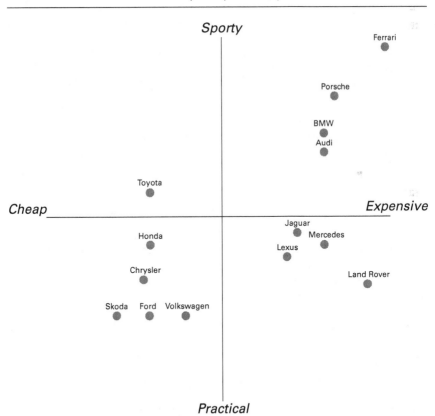

Note: The above figure is an example only and not the output of a research paper. It should not be used for decision making within the automotive industry.

As well as reviewing where your business or brand is positioned today, perceptual maps can also help you to identify opportunities for launching new brands. If the map of the automotive industry shown in Figure 1.2 were to be the output of actual research, you could decide that launching a brand that stands for sports and performance but is in the mid-price range would have little competition and so might be an opportunity. On the other hand you need to combine this thinking with the size of the market. For example, in Figure 1.2 no brands are perceived to be very sporty and very cheap so there is a gap there, but is this because that is not a profitable opportunity or because when people buy sporty cars they expect to spend money and would not trust a cheap sports car?

What does this mean for digital marketing?

In relation to positioning maps there is no specific difference between digital marketing and any other form of marketing. As mentioned at the start of this book, marketing is the key word. Brand is one of the areas where having an integrated approach is absolutely vital to success. Considering how your brand performs across all marketing considerations is essential, and whilst it is important to include digital within this, it should not have its own separate approach.

One thing that is worth bearing in mind here is that it is much easier to launch a brand today than it was in the 20th century. You can fire up your laptop at home, design a logo in Photoshop, create a website using Wordpress, create a Twitter account and build an Adwords account all in one evening. You then have a brand and it is being seen by thousands and potentially millions of people almost immediately. Whilst I would never discourage someone from launching their business or moving fast to do so, I would encourage some thought around your customer perception and competitors and this is where perceptual mapping fits in.

Customer lifetime value

Customer lifetime value (CLTV or sometimes LTV) is quite simply the value or profit attributed to a customer for their entire customer lifecycle. This can be relatively simple to calculate in some businesses and incredibly complex in others. Either way, one thing is true: there are many factors that influence it and many levers that can be pulled to alter it. Cost per acquisition (CPA) has long been used as a key metric in marketing and especially so in digital marketing due to tracking technology and the transparency of data. However, this has certainly been criticized as too simplistic a view. For example, if you know that a customer spends $100 buying a product from you that has a margin of $50 and it costs you $40 to acquire that customer then you can be happy that you have acquired them profitably. If that customer then leaves and never comes back then we have a simple model. If, however, the average customer comes back another 3.2 times and phones your call centre twice per purchase then you have additional income and expenditure for this customer that is not taken into consideration.

The CPA model continues to be used in channels such as affiliate marketing as it enables businesses to remove the risk of cost-per-click payments where conversions are not guaranteed. It would be far too complicated in most instances to ask affiliates to abide by your CLTV model as so many of the variables would be out of their control. CLTV can be used to determine which customers are the most profitable and to define segments based on this, which can then be targeted appropriately. We will look at segmentation and targeting below.

Calculating CLTV

There are several different ways to calculate CLTV but for the purpose of this book we focus on the simple approach. I would recommend understanding the different models in more detail to fully appreciate the complexities of CLTV and ensure you have a model or combination of models that is appropriate for your business. In order to calculate your CLTV using the simple method you need to have an understanding of the following two variables: 1) number of periods that a customer remains with you (customer lifetime); 2) average margin per customer in a period.

In order to help understand these variables there are some common factors that need to be understood and these are therefore also the levers that can be pulled to improve your CLTV:

- Length of customer lifetime:
  - CRM programmes;
  - member-get-member schemes;
  - loyalty schemes;
  - service levels.

- Average margin per customer:
  - repeat purchases;
  - cross-selling and up-selling;
  - returns and refunds;
  - pricing and discounts;
  - operating costs;
  - conversion rates;
  - segmentation.

The formula in simple terms is therefore as follows:

$$\text{CLTV} = \text{Lifetime} \times \text{Avg Margin}$$

To give an example of this we can look at a retailer.

This particular retailer manages to attract each customer to its store 3.9 times per week on average and those customers spend $21.69 on average during each visit. We therefore know that the customers are spending $21.69 × 3.9 = $84.59 per week. We want to understand our CLTV in terms of years so we can simply multiply by 52 to get an annual customer value of $4,399. We know that each customer has a profit margin of 10 per cent so we know that our profit per customer is actually $439. On average we know that customers stay with us for 15 years and so our CLTV is $439 × 15 = $6,585. That gives us a target figure to acquire customers. We know that we can spend up to $6,585 to acquire a customer over their lifetime.

What does this mean for digital marketing?

There are many models in digital marketing that are forced upon us. As mentioned above there are cost-per-acquisition and cost-per-click models that are very common. There are also cost-per-impression (sometimes cost-per-mille), cost-per-action and cost-per-lead models, amongst others. Whilst we are forced to use these as payment methods it is often all too easy to relax into using these as the key performance indicators (KPIs) for running the channels. CLTV is not something that can be implemented purely within one area of your business, but if this model is appropriate then it should be integrated within digital marketing as much as anywhere else. Digital marketers are blessed with exceptional amounts of data (we will look at big data in Chapter 14) so we have the opportunity to understand our customers and the variables involved in greater detail than other areas of the business. This opportunity is golden and should not be wasted.

Segmentation

Later in the book (Chapter 11) we will look at personalization, which is the ultimate goal of tailored communications and is far more possible than it was just 10 years ago. It is, however, still vitally important to understand segmentation as well. Consumers will always have similarities in their behaviours, demographics, buying patterns and other factors that enable you to group them into segments. This enables smarter, more appropriate targeting and messaging within your marketing communications. These groups will have different uses for products and varying perspectives on services. Their lifestyles will be inherently different as will be their needs, aspirations, opinions and much more.

Five common forms of segmentation – geographic, demographic, behavioural, benefit and psychographic – are listed below, including the advantages and disadvantages of each alongside how businesses use these methods.

Geographic

Perhaps the simplest of all segmentation strategies, this is quite simply the location of the individuals being analysed. Businesses that have regional retail outlets will have some focus on this but it can also prove a useful tool to understand where to target your marketing. That could be outdoor or press advertising but from a digital perspective it may inform your geo-targeting or data selection for your strategy. The disadvantage is quite simply that this is very basic and tells you next to nothing about the individuals themselves.

Demographic

A very common form of segmentation, demographics includes factors such as age, race, gender, education, employment, income and economic status. It is therefore an area of segmentation that gives a reflection of the characteristics of a group of people. Demographic segmentation is used by governments and a very broad range of organizations as it can answer questions such as 'Who can afford to buy my product?' and 'Will this group of consumers be the right age range for my product?'

The disadvantage of this type of segmentation is that there is a large assumption that people with similar characteristics will behave similarly, which is far from the truth. If someone is a French, 45-year-old factory worker who has had a poor education will they behave the same way as all their colleagues in the factory who are of roughly the same age? No. They will have different passions, hobbies and much more. To understand this in more detail we need to understand behavioural segmentation.

Behavioural

Behavioural segmentation is becoming increasingly possible. It has historically been difficult to understand consumer behaviour but in the big data world we are able to understand consumers a lot more, especially those in the digital space. This method groups consumers by buying patterns and usage behaviours. This is an excellent way of talking to individuals in a way that is highly likely to resonate with them. It is useful when talking about specific products or use occasions.

Behavioural does not of course give such a black-and-white view as demographic segmentation and therefore is not an exact science. For example, behaviour can change with your lifestyle. Divorce, children and retirement are key examples of when life changes could result in behaviour changes. It is therefore vital to be working with data that is up to date. With behavioural segmentation you have the advantage of being highly relevant to your audience whilst also running the risk of missing the mark completely.

Benefit

Something that is vital to understand in marketing, and in fact business in general, is that perception is key. How you are perceived will impact your career – we all know the clichés about first impressions. Well, this form of segmentation is based around consumer perceived benefit. Many businesses use this to understand the consumer base and to inform product development and marketing opportunities. A good example of this is the fashion industry. If you imagine retailers of coats and jackets: some consumers will look for warm winter coats for their ski holidays, some for all-weather jackets for their outdoor lifestyle, some for lightweight jackets they can wear whilst exercising, some for smart coats for work and some purely for fashion. The perceived benefit of your coat will appeal differently to each different segment, so perhaps you need to change the perception of your coat or bring out a new range to appeal to a new segment.

Psychographic

Psychographic segmentation sounds exceptionally complex but it is simply an understanding of a consumer's lifestyle. This includes studying activities, opinions, beliefs and interests. Understanding these elements can, similarly to behavioural segmentation, result in messaging and products that truly resonate with the individuals. For example, individuals may be environmentalists, Buddhists, body builders or movie lovers (or any combination of these). Creating segments on this basis creates a more 'real' view of the individuals than geographic or demographic segmentation ever could.

Personas

By pulling together the above five forms of segmentation you can create personas, as per the example shown in Figure 1.3. These are effectively descriptions of your segments. Most businesses will create between five and ten of these, as too few results in large groups that are too generic and too many can result in segments that are too small or overcomplicate the targeting approach.

FIGURE 1.3 An example of a persona

Boston Consulting Group matrix

According to Bruce Henderson, founder of the Boston Consulting Group, 'To be successful, a company should have a portfolio of products with different growth rates and different market shares' (Henderson, 1970). This model is similar to the brand perceptual model mentioned above – in that it uses a matrix. However, the Boston Consulting Group (BCG) matrix is used for a very different purpose. The model categorizes products in a portfolio into stars, cash cows, dogs and question marks (Figure 1.4) by looking at market share and market growth. This is why it is sometimes called the growth–share matrix. It is used primarily to maximize long-term value creation in a business by maximizing high-potential areas and minimizing poor performers.

Cash cows – high market share in a slow-growth environment

Cash cows are strong and safe products. They generate money steadily in a market that is not growing at any pace and, as such, do not require much investment. As a result they are highly profitable.

Dogs – low market share in a slow-growth environment

Dogs are not the strongest part of the portfolio and can in fact be damaging for a business. They tend to break even and so do not offer a great deal of benefit to the business. Businesses will generally look to reduce dogs or sell them off and should be very wary of investing money into them as returns are unlikely.

Question marks – low market share in a high-growth environment

Question marks are aptly named as they can go in either direction. They are growing rapidly but have a low share so they consume a lot of cash and do not generate a great deal. A question mark can become a 'star' if it gains market share and then even a 'cash cow' if the market slows, but it also has the potential to be a 'dog' if the market slows before it has gained momentum. Decisions around what to do with question marks must be based on extensive analysis – to invest or not to invest.

Stars – high market share in a high-growth environment

Stars generate cash due to having a strong market share but they also swallow up a lot of investment due to the high growth environment. Once the growth declines, stars become cash cows; therefore, having a range of stars in your portfolio that can become the next cash cows is an important strategy.

FIGURE 1.4   The Boston Consulting Group matrix

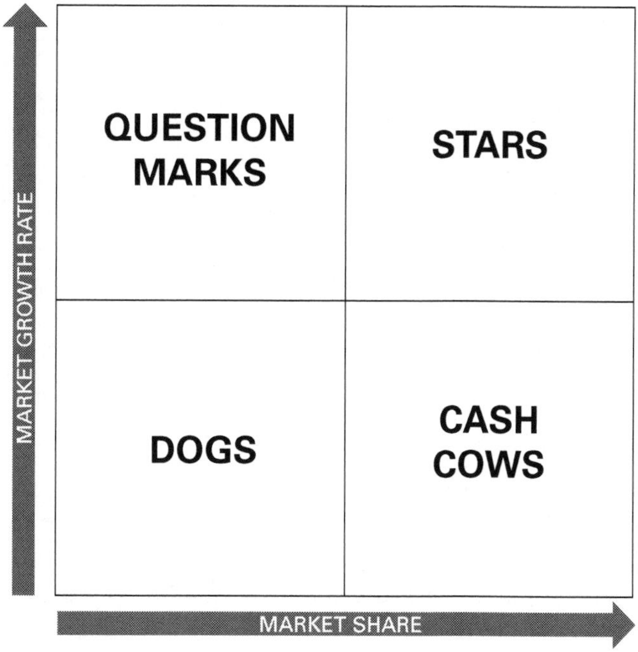

The matrix itself shows not only the position of each product but also, by utilizing the area or size of each category, the value of each product. This therefore gives a snapshot of profitability and cashflows of an organization. Ultimately, cash cows and dogs are at either end of the scale and so all business units will move to one end or the other eventually and there is a common path: question mark – star – cash cow – dog. Of course it is not the situation for most companies, or indeed the aim, to have a set of products that simply fall into one of these categories – and in fact a blend of these is important to be able to describe your portfolio as balanced:

- Cash cows exist to supply funds that can be used to invest in the future of the company.
- Stars, due to their high growth potential and high market share, are the products that build this future.
- Question marks are items to steer into your next set of stars.
- Dogs should be removed.

One key thing to remember is that the BCG matrix has complications and has been misinterpreted and misused many times, so understanding the intricacies of it and how to apply it (and indeed *when* to apply it) is crucial.

What does this mean for digital marketing?

The BCG matrix will inform which products you should be selling through which methods and channels, which will influence your overall digital strategy. You can also use it to assess your digital channels themselves and understand, therefore, whether you are applying your focus effectively. For example, is paid search a cash cow or a dog? The value of this channel is often debated and so being able to substantiate where your channels fit on the BCG matrix is a great way to communicate how your channel strategy will be managed. Moving SEO from a question mark to a star is a common goal of businesses that have poor natural search performance but understand the steps to make improvements. We will look at these channels and how to maximize them in Chapters 5 to 8.

Summary

Digital marketing has moved forward at extreme pace over the last 20 years and the way that people's lifestyles have changed in the last 20 years is arguably beyond how they had changed in the 50 years before that: the introduction of the internet, mass smartphone usage, tablets, every age group becoming digitally savvy and so on – and the pace is not slowing.

Understanding the marketing models that have been established for some time and how to apply them to your digital marketing strategy gives us a foundation to begin our strategy.

So there is a lot to think about but it is all meaningless unless we form a strategy that is integrated into our broader business strategy – so we discuss that in the next chapter.

Chapter checklist

- A history of digital marketing ☐
- The 4 Ps of marketing ☐
- Porter's five forces ☐
- Brand or perceptual positioning map ☐
- Customer lifetime value ☐
- Segmentation ☐
- Boston Consulting Group matrix ☐

Further reading

- *On the 4 Ps of marketing:*

  Perreault Jr, W D (2004) *Basic Marketing*, McGraw-Hill Higher Education. This book covers modern practical examples and best practices and pulls together the theory of the marketing mix with the strategic planning approach we discuss in this book.

- *On competitive rivalry:*

  Magretta, J (2011) *Understanding Michael Porter: The essential guide to competition and strategy*, Harvard Business Review Press

  Porter, M (2004) *Competitive Strategy: Techniques for analyzing industries and competitors*, Free Press

- *On brand positioning:*

  Riezebos, R (2011) *Positioning the Brand: an inside-out approach*, Routledge. This book discusses brand positioning in detail and looks at the different stages of positioning your brand. It is well worth a read to understand the stages of corporate identity, brand architecture, target group analysis, competitor analysis and choosing a market position.

- *On segmentation:*

  McDonald, M (2012) *Market Segmentation: How to do it, how to profit from it*, John Wiley & Sons. This book includes tips on avoiding big mistakes and determining scope, which are very helpful in the exercise of building a segmentation strategy.

- *On the Boston Consultancy Group matrix:*

  Stern, C W and Deimler, M S (2006) *The Boston Consulting Group on Strategy: Classic concepts and new perspectives*, John Wiley & Sons

References

Henderson, B (1970) [accessed 1 November 2015] The Product Portfolio [Online] https://www.bcgperspectives.com/content/classics/strategy_the_product_portfolio/

Internet World Stats (2015) [accessed 1 November 2015] World Internet Users Statistics [Online] http://www.internetworldstats.com/stats.htm

London and Partners (2014) [accessed 1 November 2015] $1.4bn of New Tech Funds Set Up in London in Last 6 Months, *London and Partners* [Online] http://www.londonandpartners.com/media-centre/press-releases/2014/140902-14bn-of-new-tech-funds-set-up-in-london-in-last-6-months

Porter, M (1985) *Competitive Advantage*, Free Press, New York

Aligning with your business strategy

02

What we will cover in this chapter

No digital strategy can work independently of the organization it is built within. Integration is vital to any successful marketing strategy. The key areas covered in this chapter are:

- Customer centricity
- Business model
- Global strategy
- Brand
- Vision
- Culture
- Research and insight
- KPIs

Chapter goals

By the end of this chapter you will understand how to align your digital strategy with your business strategy.

If there is one message to take away from this book it is that your digital strategy must not and cannot be built independently of your business strategy if it is to truly succeed. We are in the technology age and this brings new opportunities for the digital marketer every month. This means that every digital strategy evolves at pace (we will examine real-time planning in Chapter 4) and so the temptation to move your digital strategy forward independently of the restrictions that your wider organization brings can be too much to resist. In this chapter we look at how aligning to your broader business strategy is important and so this temptation must be resisted. We examine some of the areas to consider when ensuring that your strategy is aligned with your business.

Customer centricity

Many organizations claim to be customer centric, many of those include customer centricity in their values, but not all of these businesses truly make their key decisions with a customer-first mentality. So what? Why does it matter that some do and some don't? In short, it doesn't. We are not looking to define what your business strategy should be – the important consideration here is that you are honest about what your values are, as that means you can truly work towards achieving your goals.

Being customer centric, in its purest form, means making your decisions around what is best for your customers. This might mean making some financial sacrifices, reducing profits or creating work that does not directly benefit the organization. If your business claims to be customer centric then a good question to ask yourself is whether you really are putting the customer decisions ahead of the financial decisions. This is not to say that putting your financial decisions ahead of your customer decisions is a bad thing. There are circumstances where this is entirely appropriate. For example, your shareholders may demand a profit or sales target that you are not likely to achieve without increasing your prices, or you may not be able to afford the improvements that the customer demands without compromising the financial performance of the business.

According to research by Deloitte Consulting and Deloitte & Touche, customer-centric organizations are 60 per cent more profitable than those that are not and they have lower operating costs (Deloitte, 2014). This may motivate your business to take this strategy seriously but the most important thing is to ensure that your organization is open and honest about its true motivations, as this will dictate your strategy. Building a strategy that is customer centric in order to fit with the business values will create serious problems if these values are not truly lived. For example, a customer-centric strategy may involve setting up a dedicated social service team to ensure a fast turnaround to customer messages. It may involve purchasing CRM software to enable deep personalization and could also include spending money on paid search to ensure customers find the relevant pages, even if they have no commercial goals. If, however, the organization is not actually customer centric then these initiatives may well come under scrutiny for not generating financial value, but it would be too late to remove the people who had been recruited and so your strategy may gain a poor reputation amongst your stakeholders.

It is worth ensuring that your strategy is truly aligned with your genuine level of customer centricity. We will look at how to convince you stakeholders to invest in digital marketing in Chapter 15.

Business model

Your business model could be one of many and ensuring your digital strategy fits into this is crucial. Creating an aggressive e-commerce strategy for a relationship-based B2B business would not be a good fit. Likewise, leading with a pure content and social media strategy for a sales-focused retailer is highly unlikely to deliver the sales volumes you need to achieve. It is vital that you therefore fit your strategy to your business model. There are many different definitions of business model and within those there are many models. Below is a list of three common business models, some of their qualities and how they apply to your digital marketing strategy.

Mass market B2C

This model includes organizations that sell products that appeal to a broad range of consumers at an affordable price. An example of this type of business is fast-moving consumer goods (FMCG) companies. Selling a large number of products such as food, clothing or toys involves being able to attract a high volume of customers to your website and stores. This means creating awareness through above-the-line advertising, acquiring visitors and converting them into customers. This would also require a robust customer service process. Therefore all digital channels are relevant here.

Niche B2C

This model is a direct-to-consumer business that has a highly targeted service. This could include products for people living with a specific disability or products to ultra-high-net-worth individuals. Whilst this model also appeals directly to consumers, it works with a specific niche such as those in a specialist trade or ultra-high-net-worth individuals. Using broadcast media is not relevant in most of these scenarios as the majority of the viewers will not be potential customers. Creating trust and advocacy is essential, however, so a deep content strategy and first-class experience are crucial to success.

B2B

The B2B model includes organizations such as wholesalers or technology resellers that are selling directly to other businesses. Here you are dealing with other business people rather than end consumers. These business people are of course still individuals and it is important not to forget that human psychology still applies. They do, however, have very different expectations. You may be seen less as a brand and more as a supplier, which creates a very different relationship. Your customers may be more cynical or aggressive than B2C customers as they have specific objectives and goals to achieve. You may find that traditional marketing messages and sales techniques are less well received. Therefore the focus should be more on relationships through CRM, content and direct value-added discussions rather than through advertising. It is still important, however, for these customers to be able to find your site and the information they need to get to.

Within these broader business models there are of course many specific models. A B2B IT company may be a hardware product provider or a service support provider. The service model would require more of a focus on screen sharing and CRM whilst the product model would require more of an acquisition and conversion focus. A B2C model may be simply to sell products at a significant margin or simply to gain traffic in order to make advertising revenue.

Freemium

One interesting trend in business models in recent years is the freemium model. This model has grown in popularity and is essentially the method of attracting users by giving a percentage of your product or service for free and offering a more interesting, deeper experience for a price. A good example of this is the music-streaming industry with businesses such as Spotify and Deezer employing this technique. One other point here is that business models can shift and shape over time. There are many examples of this such as IBM, but there are also some more recent changes in the digital space.

Changing business models

Facebook

Facebook is a great example of a business model that has had to adapt quickly. I would imagine that even Mark Zuckerberg was surprised by the speed at which Facebook grew from being one of many college social networks to the leading global hub for a significant percentage of the world to share their lives on. The initial model of providing a network for college students had to develop a broader appeal once the growth became inevitable. As this growth took hold it was clear that costs would also accelerate and, with no obvious income, something had to be done and so the business pages and advertising models had to be developed. These shifts in the way that the business has had to change to deal with its own growth have been both significant and impressive in their speed and success. This is an excellent example of how adapting your strategy to meet the changing needs of your consumers and the evolution of your business is vital. Facebook has had to do this through the above changes to their website and user experience. We will look at this area in more detail in Chapter 9.

Google

It is hard to believe that Google spent a long time with no real income channel. The initial business model was successful by creating the best search engine in terms of accuracy and simplicity. Google became a verb as people realized that googling something would give better results than using another engine. However, a source of income needed to be developed. This is why Adwords was introduced in 2003 and that has gone on to become the foundation of the growth of every other arm of the Google we know today – a business with an incredibly diverse and profitable range of services. This has led to Google having to closely manage its brand and how it is perceived, which it has done with significant success. Their digital marketing strategy has been a minimalist approach. They promote their service and products such as Adwords and Chrome through display advertising and CRM but they do not broadcast as much as most organizations of a similar size. This is because much of their success is through word of mouth. This networking approach has been encouraged by supporting businesses that use their products, through strong and personalized customer service, networking and learning events and training materials. This personalized and deep-content digital marketing has ensured that people have trust, belief and understanding of their products, which further encourages word of mouth.

Global strategy

Globalization can be a very challenging process for any organization. It can also take some companies by surprise as they outgrow their initial local plans. This brings cultural, language, process and many other challenges. With the growth of digital, almost all businesses have an international presence through the internet even if their target audience is very localized and so some aspect of global strategy should be included in almost every digital strategy – even if that aspect is to ensure that global presence is minimized.

Culture

There are many cultural differences around the world, too many to count, and the relevant ones must be understood when building a global strategy. This can range from religious beliefs to manners and it is impossible to know what we don't know – so doing your research is important here.

For example, did you know that Mexicans celebrate New Year's Eve by eating 12 grapes at the stroke of midnight? That the colour red is lucky in China? That Suriname's land is 91 per cent jungle whereas there are virtually no trees left in Haiti? These facts can affect your copy, conversations, brand and many other factors.

From a digital perspective there are several cultural considerations. You should look at whether each region you are targeting responds well to buying online and, if not, whether your strategy should focus on thought leadership, brand awareness and directing people to your offline conversion channels. Understanding the penetration of smartphones and tablets alongside mobile coverage will also influence your strategy. For example, at the time of writing, Google's Consumer Barometer tells us that Norway has 79 per cent smartphone penetration whilst Japan, perhaps surprisingly, has only 54 per cent (Google, 2015). This could mean that moving to a responsive website is more or less of a priority for your business and you may not require the app that you have budgeted for. You will also need to understand broadband speeds and coverage as this will dictate how fast your website and off-site content will download and, therefore, the design of your assets.

Lifestyle points such as working hours and average commute times will influence your targeting and customer support programmes. Even weather, which is not cultural itself but does influence culture, is an important factor to consider as it will affect the amount of time spent indoors (near computers) and outdoors (on mobile or offline). It is also important to understand that the digital landscape may be very different in territories away from your local country. In Europe and the United States you would most likely consider Twitter at the core of your micro-blogging strategy whereas in China you would be more likely to need to look at Sina Weibo. Thoroughly researching cultural points and ensuring you are working with, or at least speaking to, local people with strong knowledge are important considerations – getting this right can be incredibly powerful and getting this wrong can be extremely damaging.

Language

Language is perhaps the most obvious consideration but one that must be considered very carefully. To give a potent example of how important this is, some organizations have been guilty of not considering language when creating their global brand and identity – leading to a name that, when translated, has been found to mean something rude in other countries. There are many examples of this and it leaves your business with four very difficult options: don't trade in that country, create a separate brand just for that country, change your brand name entirely, or do nothing and accept the damage and criticism. The prouder leaders often go for the last option, whereas option two is perhaps the most sensible. Some interesting examples of this are that Galaxy chocolate in the UK is known as Dove in many other countries; Burger King in Australia is Hungry Jack's; and T. K. Maxx is the international name for the company that is known as T. J. Maxx in the United States.

For digital marketing, language is clearly important when considering digital presence. This is not only in ensuring that our call to actions are correct and powerful but also in dealing with languages with different characters to our own. For example English, Russian, Mandarin and Arabic are all widely spoken languages but all use different characters that need to be accounted for. This can create tricky design challenges when building your site.

Payments

This is a very specific category but one that is worth highlighting as it can dramatically affect the result of your digital strategy. Payment methods are often overlooked when constructing a global strategy but it is very dangerous to assume that the world uses the same methods. Even countries that you would assume are very similar to your own may in fact be very different. One example of this is Germany where roughly 80 per cent of transactions are conducted in cash. For comparison, this figure in the United States is less than 50 per cent (Bagnall *et al*, 2014). Germans hold roughly twice the amount of cash in their wallets as people in France or Australia. This behaviour is of course vitally important to appreciate when developing an e-commerce strategy.

Brand

Your brand is one of the key parts of your business that you must align with at all times. This is understood by most people and so I am sure there is no need to spend too much time convincing you that this is the case. There are, however, some vital reasons for this that are worth examining. I often talk to people about how considering your company's brand as a person can be a powerful framework. The values of your company are like the values that you hold yourself. You may try to be polite to everyone you meet, you may be someone who wants to achieve a lot in life and you may be always looking to learn more and grow your knowledge. These values in a business could be translated as service, sales and innovation and they create the personality of your business.

Further, your brand has what non-marketers often consider a brand to be – a visual identity. What is your logo and how does it look in different scenarios? What is your colour palette? How do you design your materials? Again, this could translate into what do you look like, do you keep fit, how do you dress and what are your favourite colours? By combining your values and visual identity you create your personality and look, and therefore your brand. When you assess whether something strays from this brand you get a very easy to understand perspective about whether this feels right or not.

Values

As we have just discussed, the brand values of your organization are its personality, and having a consistent personality is important to enable consumers to understand you and therefore believe in you. Your digital strategy must therefore stay true to these values and to how they are expressed elsewhere (unless how they are expressed elsewhere is poor and you can drive improvement in those areas).

Visual identity

Your visual identity can be difficult to control and easy to compromise online and so discipline is important. There are many opportunities to stretch your logo or tweak your colour palette to fit in with another website or digital opportunity, and staying true to your guidelines is vital here wherever possible. Compromising your visual identity can create a lack of trust as you can appear less like an organization that is in control. To that point it is key to remember that your guidelines must work for digital. It is certainly less true now than it was 10 years ago, but some guidelines still are not built with digital in mind. An understanding of accessibility rules for colours, challenges around using your logo on other sites such as affiliates, and creation of logos or icons that work in limited spaces, must be built into your guidelines. Your identity may already be in use in newspapers, on television, in direct mail and on stationery. Your consumers will be seeing these in their day-to-day lives and so ensuring consistency with these is vital. In Chapter 6 we look at how consistent messaging at every step on your digital channels, such as paid search, creates a far more powerful result – and the same is true of your brand.

Innovation and pushing the boundaries is important, especially in digital, but not at the expense of a consistent face of your business as this will be detrimental to your organization as a whole.

Vision

In Chapter 4 we look at your mission and how you build your goals and objectives from this to effectively plan the delivery of your strategy. Sitting above all of this, however, is your vision. This is the statement that must embody everything your business is striving to achieve and everything it represents. Your company is likely to have a vision in place and if not you should consider whether it is appropriate for you to review this with your leadership team. This summary of what you stand for can be powerful when talking to investors, shareholders and customers alike. Whatever your company vision, it is important that every strategy within your organization fits within this vision, otherwise you run the risk of delivering something that does not align with the direction of your business.

A vision would read something like this:

'To be Earth's most customer-centric company; to build a place where people can come to find and discover anything they might want to buy online.' (Amazon)

'To bring JOY to the lives of our customers, whether they are kids or kids at heart.' (Toys'R'Us)

You can ensure that your strategy aligns with your vision by adjusting some of your goals, channels and messaging. Using the above examples your strategy could be adjusted as follows. If you were building a digital strategy for Amazon you may want to ensure that you have robust service response processes in place on social media and through other channels and you should consider everything we discussed above on customer centricity. You should also be focused on creating a deep level of personalization to be able to deliver the latter part of the vision.

For Toys'R'Us on the other hand, you would want to look at how your site can create enjoyment through the experience of accessing it and to ensure that there are activities for all ages. Understanding the needs of children as well as the adult shoppers is also important in order to be able to create a fun and therefore enticing experience.

So we can see from this that the focus for Amazon would be on personalization and service whilst for Toys'R'Us it would be on content and experience. This is of course oversimplifying the facts, but it is clear that aligning to these visions will have an impact on your strategy.

Culture

The culture of your business will likely be unique. Every business builds its own culture from the day it launches. This culture stems primarily from the decisions and behaviours of the leadership team. It also, in turn, stems from HR policy, office layout, growth plans, recruitment, location and many more factors. This culture has an effect on everything you do as an organization. Your culture may encourage your staff to be hungry for career success and willing to take risks to show they have what it takes to be the next leaders of the business. It may on the other hand simply encourage staff to be careful and try not to cause any issues and risk being fired. You may have a culture that drives towards growth and therefore a high percentage of sales-focused employees, or you may be comfortable with your market position and therefore have staff who are excellent at service and the softer skills of customer relations.

The culture of your organization will have a direct effect on your digital strategy for many reasons but some specific ones should be considered. If your business is a results-focused business then this suits channels such as paid search very well, as it is performance focused and relies on data to accurately track performance. If your culture is not performance focused then you may find that this allows more flexibility for your content strategy but this may frustrate your paid search team. If your business is highly focused on service then ensuring that social media is fully set up for customer service, has robust procedures in place, is aligned with your business processes and is fully resourced are all vital considerations. We will look at this in more detail in Chapter 12.

Whichever culture your business has it should be positive and energizing. If it is not then you should at least be trying to create that within your area.

Research and insight

Research is a driving force behind any strategy and so understanding what your data is telling you is vital to the success of your strategy. You may have a specific research function and separate insight team, both together or neither. Whatever the capabilities within your organization it is important to bring broader research into your digital strategy. Figure 2.1 is an interesting piece of digital research that clearly demonstrates that the percentage of consumers buying online is, in most countries, far beyond the percentage of businesses selling online. Understanding this data for your specific market will allow you to understand where the gaps are for your business to exploit.

The data you gain from your activity will inform future plans and tactics and even the shape of your strategy. This data, however, has one main restriction that takes two forms. This restriction is simply that it can never tell you what it doesn't know. That may sound obvious but when we look at the two forms we can begin to understand why the broader picture is vital.

First, your data cannot tell you what has not happened yet. But how can you build a strategy without understanding what is going to happen? By gaining insights into your customers' and consumers' behaviours, understanding what motivates them and how they respond to other materials, you will be able to gain an advantage that will set your strategy on a positive path from day one. Second, your data is digital and so is not tracking anything outside of your digital marketing. You may be able to use search volumes to give an indication of the success of a television advert but you cannot see directly what people thought about your creative. You may be able to see a peak in response rates when you send an e-mail about a specific product but you cannot see whether people think your competitors' products are better. By using both qualitative and quantitative research from across the organization you can understand buying patterns, interests, competitive analysis, creative feedback, customer behaviours, primary areas of dissatisfaction and many other data sets that would otherwise be unavailable to you at the start of your strategy or even when it is very mature.

FIGURE 2.1 European online shopping

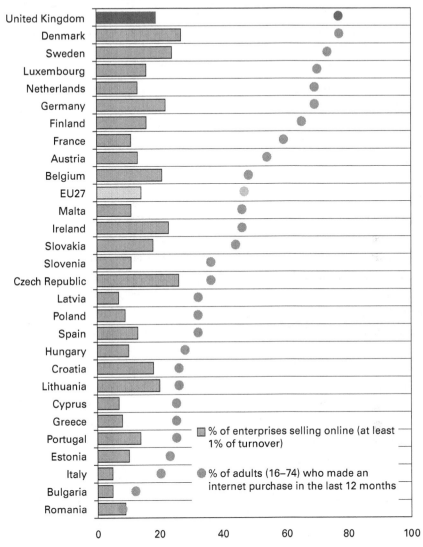

SOURCE: UK Office for National Statistics

Quantitative research is usually used when trying to gather data to validate a hypothesis or support a business case. This is the type of research that some would consider more 'real' in terms of there being a clear story backed up by undisputable facts. The limitation of quantitative research is that whilst it can give you a clear view of the 'what' it does not always tell you the 'why'. So if 100 people were to visit your website from a competitor and

300 from a news website then you will be able to make some decisions about media buying such as whether to continue your display advertising on the news website and expand to other news sites or whether to put more resource into competing with your competitors more effectively on the search channel. Without understanding why this happened, however, you cannot get to the bottom of the issue and therefore cannot understand if this will be an ongoing trend or a single peak.

Qualitative research has quite the opposite challenge. With this research method you can gain a deep understanding of the motivations and thoughts of customers and consumers. You can understand what they like and do not like about you or your marketing materials. You can understand what excites them and what really gets them down. You cannot, however, directly apply this to sales. If someone says they don't like your advertising then this does not necessarily mean that they will not buy your product.

One commonly used research method is therefore to use both qualitative and quantitative together. An example of this is to circulate a data collection method such as an online questionnaire in order to gain quantitative data from which to construct a qualitative piece of research. That research would then be gathered from the same participants and the data could tell a more compelling story.

KPIs

Key performance indicators (KPIs) are an essential method of measuring the success of your campaign. We will look specifically at this in Chapter 14. The reason for taking a quick look at this now is to ensure that, when building your reporting and dashboards for your campaign, you align the measures of success with those of the business. We have discussed that there are different business models with different objectives, visions and cultures. These will ultimately dictate what the business KPIs are – and if you are going to ensure that your strategy is accepted by your decision makers (see Chapter 15) and is perceived to be a success then you will need to be shown to be delivering what the company needs to deliver. As well as this consideration you will also need to be agile enough to align with any changes to the company's KPIs that you may not be expecting. It is entirely possible, and in fact quite common, for a business to change its primary goal, for example, from acquiring a large volume of customers to maximizing profit. This could be due to market conditions, shareholder demands or activity by the competition, amongst many other factors.

Business KPIs could come in hundreds of different forms such as customer numbers, customer satisfaction, profit, sales, retention and share price – the more top-level metrics that determine the success of a business in a given period.

Summary

In this chapter we have looked at a range of factors that must be considered if you are to align your digital strategy with your business strategy. It is vitally important that you do not build your strategy independent of the wider business, as that will give it a high chance of perceived failure or actual failure. We examined whether your business is truly customer centric, what your business model is and what traits that might create and how to work with a global strategy. We looked at your brand and vision and how they might impact your plans. We examined how the culture of your company has an impact, how research and insight can provide some vital information and how aligning to the wider KPIs of your business is vital to ensure that your story is consistent with that of the business.

In the next chapter we look at some of the barriers to your strategy and other considerations.

Chapter checklist

- Customer centricity ☐
- Business model ☐
- Global strategy ☐
- Brand ☐
- Vision ☐
- Culture ☐
- Research and insight ☐
- KPIs ☐

Further reading

- *On customer centricity*:

  Richardson, N, James, J and Kelley, N (2015) *Customer-Centric Marketing: Supporting sustainability in the digital age*, Kogan Page, London. A very relevant and interesting book on the subject of customer centricity, which examines disciplines such as knowing your company research and why companies fail through the lens of sustainability.

- *On business models*:

  Osterwalder, A and Pigneur, Y (2010) *Business Model Generation: A handbook for visionaries, game changers, and challengers*, John Wiley & Son. This handbook is not only visually pleasing but contains helpful advice on how to take many business models and implement them within your organization.

- *On brand identity*:

  Lerman, S (2014) *Building Better Brands: A comprehensive guide to brand strategy and identity development*, How Design Books. This is a great book for further reading on how to create and evolve brands. It includes positioning, as we discussed in the last chapter, experience and identity, as well as some helpful guides and powerful statements.

- *On business culture*:

  Cavanaugh, A (2015) *Contagious Culture: Show up, set the tone, and intentionally create an organization that thrives*, McGraw-Hill Professional. A great book to read for inspiration on how to do business culture. It includes step-by-step techniques on how to lead from the top to create a performance culture; something that is vital to deliver your strategy in the most effective way possible.

- *On research methods*:

  Walker, I (2010) *Research Methods and Statistics*, Macmillan Education. This covers research methods, testing hypotheses and normal distribution, amongst other more detailed research techniques, and is worth reading if you are seeking a deeper understanding in this field.

References

Bagnall, Bounie, Huynh, Kosse, Schmidt, Schuh and Stix (2014) [accessed 1 November 2015] Consumer Cash Usage: A Cross-Country Comparison with Payment Diary Survey Data, Federal Reserve Bank of Boston: Working Papers No14–4 [Online] http://www.bostonfed.org/economic/wp/wp2014/wp1404.pdf

Deloitte (2014) [accessed 1 November 2015] Customer-Centricity: Embedding it into Your Organization's DNA [Online] http://www2.deloitte.com/content/dam/Deloitte/ie/Documents/Strategy/2014_customer_centricity_deloitte_ireland.pdf

Google (2015) [accessed 1 November 2015] Consumer Barometer [Online] https://www.consumerbarometer.com/en/

Barriers and considerations

03

What we will cover in this chapter

This chapter covers some of the challenges that digital marketing faces today and how to overcome them. This is important to understand at the early stages of formulating your strategy in order to ensure that you build these considerations into your plans. The key areas covered in this chapter are:

- Technology
- Skills
- Budget and resources
- Business priorities
- Regulation

Chapter goals

By the end of this chapter you should understand some of the challenges that can surround the implementation of your digital strategy. You should also have some understanding of how to tackle these challenges and therefore ensure that your strategy is robust.

Despite what we have already said about how long digital marketing has been amongst us, it is ever evolving and this creates challenges for businesses of all shapes and sizes. One of the issues is that consumers are adapting to the digital age very quickly, but most businesses simply cannot keep up. In this chapter we examine some of the difficulties in embedding your digital strategy and the approaches that can be taken to tackle them.

When you consider that in the late 20th century consumers generally bought their products either face to face or on the phone, it is clear to understand how the digital revolution has significantly affected several areas of an established business. For example:

- New technology has meant radical changes to established systems such as customer service systems, marketing automation and information security.

- Regulations around privacy such as cookie policy and the right to be forgotten have resulted in changes to sales techniques to ensure that customers feel comfortable with the use of their data.

Long-established business cultures have had to change or suffer the consequences, including those that have been successful despite poor service and those that have led with inauthentic messaging. As completely new opportunities arrive there is inevitably a skills gap as no one exists with experience of them. A good example of this is social media. As the channel has become increasingly important it has become apparent to many businesses that a specific skill set is needed. Rearranging budgets to take advantage of new opportunities often means that something else has to suffer. If, for example, your strategy looks to take advantage of a new technology such as the launch of a new wearable, but this launch was unexpected and arrived in the middle of a budget year, then what do you cut to ensure that you maximize on the opportunity? Your business may have established priorities that are difficult to change in order to pursue unproven opportunities. For example, your company may see press advertising as a crucial channel due to a history of success in the channel many years ago. This channel may not be measured for success, but convincing the company to depart from a stalwart to delve into something that is not understood can be challenging.

In the 21st century, consumers expect sites that are available on any device with cross-device functionality and personalized experiences and they expect to be able to directly contact businesses and get a response within minutes. As I write this, most businesses are only some of the way to achieving this, if they have started at all. Many of the challenges that you will face will effectively be risks to the delivery of your strategy and so an understanding of risk is useful.

Technology

Digital marketing is of course very closely linked to technology, although it is not quite as heavily reliant on it as some may have you believe. It is often common that people outside of digital perceive it to be hand in hand with technology and, whilst that is true to an extent, it is not true that your business needs to make significant technology advances in order to take advantage of the opportunity. For example, paid search, SEO and display advertising require almost no technology internally to launch. E-mail marketing and social media require some technology but this can be bought rather than built. In order to effectively manage offline marketing channels you would also want to use technology and so the digital world from a practitioner's perspective is not always as reliant as some may think. We discuss technology, innovation, specific tools and the future throughout the book but here we look at technology from a broader perspective and view it as a challenge rather than an opportunity – in order to understand the barriers it can present.

Whenever new technology arrives it brings with it excitement and nervousness. According to the Technology Adoption Lifecycle model, by Everett Rogers, innovators will quickly take up new technology, whereas laggards will be slow (Figure 3.1). This model can also be applied to businesses with the added complexity that intention and ability to adopt do not necessarily go as hand in hand as they do for consumers.

FIGURE 3.1   Technology adoption curve

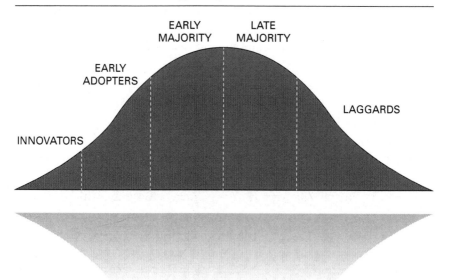

Technology developments are inevitable and have been since animals started to use tools. Never more so than in this technology age where disruption is seen by many as a positive word. Technology has always been a part of the human progress story but sometimes the mind moves faster than the hand, so inevitably we cannot always deliver the inventions and innovations that are dreamt up. One of the many concerns that stops businesses from adopting new technology is a lack of historic performance. History is strewn with failed technology and it is not always the innovators who win. There are many cases of the early adopters or even the early majority winning the battle. Apple's entry into the mobile phone market is an excellent example of a business that was not first, learnt from those that were and was able to make significant gains due to this. Closer to digital marketing we have seen many examples of businesses that have leapt into new channels and had to make the mistakes for others to learn. Social media is a fantastic recent example of this.

British Gas

In the UK, British Gas opted to run a live Q&A on Twitter with the hashtag #AskBG. However, they did this on the same day that they increased their prices. This led to British Gas being bombarded with insults and aggression from unhappy customers. This is one of many similar examples and one that businesses the world over have learnt from.

One of the main challenges within technology adoption is gaining support for the adoption. This can be a challenge as it is rare that senior leaders in a business are hungry to take significant risks, for obvious reasons. For example, convincing your decision makers to invest more heavily in mobile by building a new responsive site or an app can be a challenge due to the significant figures involved. We look at how to convince your board to invest in digital marketing in Chapter 15. Specifically for technology, one of the main routes forward is proof of concept. Reviewing competitor adoption or creating a business case is often not enough. Testing and trialling new technology in controlled, minimal risk conditions allows for a gradual implementation and roll-out programme. Of course every roll-out programme needs a roll-back plan to cover the eventuality that things may go wrong. This may not be possible for all technology but is a valuable method where possible. A roll-back plan is a process of ensuring that, should something unforeseen happen upon launch, you can quickly reset the programme back to the previous state. We have seen this in software for many years via the use of a backup and restore process. A roll-back plan is similar to this but a little broader. It is not purely technology based. You need to consider what to do not only if your technology fails but also if the market changes or there are many unfavourable reviews. This plan should be a part of the ongoing programme management agenda.

Many of the reasons that businesses do not adopt new technology are skills related, budget and resources related and business priorities related. We look at each of these below.

Skills

When new technology arrives and new consumer behaviours take hold there is inevitably a lack of experience around them. There is no data to enable planning and forecasting, no one who has an understanding of the limitations or potential of the opportunity and no case studies of best practice.

If you were launching your company's first paid-search activity you might find an experienced agency or internal candidate who could bring in excess of 10 years' experience. Someone who understands what ads work, what keyword targeting techniques to use, how to optimize and rotate the adverts, how to use location and time of day to best effect, how to use analytics tied to the ad management platform, what tagging needs to be in place to enable remarketing opportunities and so on. Were you to bring in someone who has never worked on paid search they may understand the concept of bidding on keywords in an auction style and writing ads that get a strong click-through rate but almost everything else would have to be learnt on the job or through training, which would slow your progress and give you a considerable competitive disadvantage. Advances in digital marketing also create this situation. The only difference is that you do not initially have a competitive disadvantage as everyone is in the same boat. However, the slower you are to react, the more this disadvantage becomes very real.

There are ultimately two methods for tackling skills gaps within organizations: 1) upskill the people you have – training; 2) bring in people who have the skills – recruitment.

Training

This would always be the preferred route for most companies where a team already exists. Making staff redundant and bringing in new employees is an unpleasant and costly exercise for everyone involved. There are certainly times when it can be the right route forward but it is rarely the right approach to dealing with a skills shortage. Training often comes with its own costs both in terms of paying the training supplier and lost productivity, but the value that can be gained from a full day of training can often easily justify itself versus spending a considerable time learning through trial and error. The latter approach is not only time-consuming but is also fraught with risk to your brand and commercial goals.

There are now many courses specifically for digital marketing at universities and through organizations such as the Chartered Institute of Marketing, but also from organizations such as Google. These differ in their balance of theory and practice but whatever the goal there are many options available. As well as the official training route there are low-cost opportunities for training. For example, you may well be working with one or more agencies who have expertise in the area in which you have a skills gap. You may not be working with that agency on that specific service but more often than not your partners will be willing to help you. Leaning on established relationships can therefore achieve the same as an official course – at little or no cost.

The other key consideration for training is whether you have the skills in-house already but located somewhere else within the company. Many large organizations are guilty of assuming that people within their roles are specialists at those roles and have no experience anywhere else. I have to admit that I myself have been guilty of this thinking in the past. Because someone is running press advertising or PR does not mean they have not run SEO in the past. It is worth doing an exercise to understand whether there are people in your organization who may have good knowledge to share. Do not overlook what might be right under your nose.

Recruitment

Recruitment can be a slow and expensive process dependent on a number of factors but it certainly has one guarantee – and that is that you will bring a new individual with new experience and new points of view into your business. If you get your recruitment process right then, in the vast majority of situations, this will be a very positive thing. Where new technology has arrived it is often worth seeking someone who has worked in a similar field, as there will be no existing experts. For example, as the web becomes more and more of a community we find that digital marketing techniques are increasingly moving towards a content focus. We do not try to build links – we create great content that people want to link to. We do not try to push our messages on social – we create compelling content that people find of value and want to engage with. There is therefore an increasing need for people with strong editorial skills such as those from a PR background with a digital passion. If you therefore need to build out your SEO and social channels perhaps someone from a PR background could be more appropriate than a technical expert or digital guru.

One other consideration for recruitment is that digital marketing is an evolving beast, as we have already mentioned. By the nature of society today it is absolutely true that younger people remain more digitally savvy than the older generation. Whilst it is no longer true to say that people over 60 are not tech savvy (my mother has an iPad, iPhone, laptop and countless other gadgets) it remains true that the younger generation have more of an appreciation. The line continues to move on this as well. Those teenagers who are the digital natives of today will be shamed by their lack of knowledge when the next generation comes along. I was once a programmer myself but the computers I coded on no longer exist and my five-year-old son is starting to push me for knowledge. This means that ensuring your recruitment techniques are regularly refreshed is vital. Also, ensuring that you recruit a blend of knowledgeable established senior individuals and young, digital natives will reward you with a fantastic mix of expertise and skills.

Budget and resources

Most organizations face a restricted budget in one area or another, so you are probably familiar with this barrier already. There are regularly challenges around investing in new technology or running multiple, expensive IT projects. There are also often challenges around demonstrating the value of marketing against the bottom line. In digital marketing this can be achieved a little easier than with offline channels but it is still rarely a simple exercise. It is also very common for businesses to have headcount restrictions in place or departmental salary budgets. These are often tightly controlled, especially during difficult economic conditions or when trying to invest elsewhere. It can be very difficult to grow your digital footprint without being able either to bring in the people you need or able to lean on a large number of people across your organization.

The final resource we usually find ourselves short on (and this is certainly not restricted to digital marketing) is time. Integrating technology or new methods of working can be time-consuming to say the least, not least due to having to ensure that it fits with your business goals and processes. The 21st century's biggest challenge is finding time. The success of supermarkets, mobile phones and the internet itself are largely down to the need to do more in less time – and the workplace is certainly no different.

Budget and resource constraints can often be the most frustrating of all barriers as they often seem so difficult to solve unless you have the context. There is one key to success here, one simple method to achieving your goals within these constraints – and that is to create a path to success. This combines prioritization and project management to build a process to get from A to B within the budget and resource challenges you have. To do this you can use project management techniques such as PRINCE2, Agile, Critical Path and Lean as well as the most relevant to a resource-constrained environment – Critical Chain Project Management. We will talk more about these techniques when we look at pulling our strategy together in Chapter 15. In the meantime let's have a quick look at the standard planning document developed by Henry Gantt around 100 years ago.

In simple terms, a Gantt chart shows the distinct elements of a project, their individual timelines and how they fit together to reach the project goal. They were used extensively in the United States during the First World War and have since developed into more complex versions, especially since the PC became more commonplace in businesses. Dependencies and predecessors are now commonplace within Gantt charts and there are many packages that can be used to manage your Gantt chart easily such as Microsoft Project (MSP).

The Gantt chart in Figure 3.2 shows a sample project, Project Morris, being run by 'Lulu'. This project has just three tasks and each has tasks underneath it that ensure the above level can be completed. Each task then can have a clear start and end date so that it can be tracked. You can also add dependencies to the chart to show where one task cannot be completed until another has been completed first. It is also quite common now to include a RAG (red, amber, green) status to give an immediate indication of the status of the task. In Figure 3.2 we can see that today is 11 January and everything is on track. The dashed line indicates where we are on the chart.

FIGURE 3.2 A Gantt chart

PROJECT MORRIS

Today's Date	12/01/2017

Project Manager	Lulu Kennedy
Project Start Date	02/01/2017
Project End Date	17/02/2017

ID	Tasks	Owner	Start	End	Duration	% Complete	02/01/2017	09/01/2017	16/01/2017	23/01/2017	30/01/2017	06/02/2017	13/02/2017	20/02/2017	27/02/2017
1	Task 1	Veronica	2/1/17	13/1/17	14	90%									
1.1	Sub-level 1		2/1/17	6/1/17	7	100%									
1.2	Sub-level 1		9/1/17	13/1/17	7	80%									
2	Task 2	John	16/1/17	10/2/17	28	0%									
2.1	Sub-level 1		16/1/17	27/1/17	14	0%									
2.1.1	Sub-level 2		16/1/17	20/1/17	7	0%									
2.1.2	Sub-level 2		23/1/17	27/1/17	7	0%									
2.2	Sub-level 1		30/1/17	10/2/17	14	0%									
3	Task 3	Ali	6/2/17	17/2/17	10	0%									
3.1	Sub-level 1		6/2/17	17/2/17	10	0%									

Gantt charts are of course not exclusively for projects and are useful tools when pulling together any timeline-based piece of work such as marketing campaigns, or even your overarching marketing strategy. For example, you may be launching a paid search campaign and so the tasks could be as follows:

- Task 1 – create a landing page, including sub-level tasks such as create imagery, write copy, gain sign off.
- Task 2 – ads, including writing the ads, gaining approval, uploading to the campaign.
- Task 3 – measuring success, including ensuring that tags are in place, reviewing relevant internal reporting
- ... and so on.

Business priorities

One issue that often rears its head is the need for immediate returns and a focus on the short term. You can spend months constructing an intricate strategy with solid long-term goals, quick wins and key milestones. You can achieve full buy-in to this strategy from the business and begin to put it into action. But then...

- a new competitor enters the market;
- unexpected regulation is put in place;
- the economy takes a downward turn;
- a new CEO with very different ideas is appointed.

Or a thousand other things can happen. Each of these can remove funding for a key strategic pillar, stop you from recruiting the team you need to deliver your strategy or remove the support for your strategy altogether. This is a very real challenge and one that many of us face on a regular basis. There are, however, a few things you can do to mitigate the impact, albeit you can never fully remove this risk.

It is vital that your strategy is delivered in a structured way with clear, demonstrable progress milestones. If something is delivering results and showing a very visible positive impact on your business then the chance of it being stopped or impacted by change reduces significantly. As with many other areas of business this can be as much about the presentation as the content, so ensure that you are able to tell the story. This does not mean to twist the truth but simply to ensure that your message is clear and undeniable.

It is also vital to understand fully where your business is headed and any potential challenges along that road. We have already discussed aligning with your broader business strategy (Chapter 2), and understanding it fully gives you the opportunity to have a back-up plan ready at every potential hitch. For example, if your business goal is to grow customer numbers and the business is failing to achieve its targets then how would you stop money being diverted from your web development project into direct sales and acquisition activity? How can you demonstrate that your web development project will deliver increased sales immediately? Being able to show any impact your milestones have had to date is key to success in this argument. And if your goal is gaining market share, but a big-spending competitor is making you suffer, then are you able to demonstrate the improved digital branding that your strategy is delivering and how your site is now more visible on organic search and therefore gaining digital share of voice?

There are other techniques worth using to ensure you fit with the broader business priorities, such as having a continuous improvement programme in place, including test and learn plans. These can add value to the whole business even though they do not directly show on the bottom line. Implementing this programme will enable you to highlight demonstrable improvements and their direct benefit to the business. You may also be able to receive anecdotal feedback from visitors and customers through research to support your strategy. Test and learn is a vital part of any marketing strategy. No strategy will ever be 100 per cent correct first time and so evolving your strategy is vital. It is impossible to evolve it in a structured manner without a plan – and so this should be part of your story.

Highlighting changing consumer behaviours

If we stop the long-term activity we may gain for a few months but then we will be even further behind our competition. It may also be impossible to catch up as consumers have already decided to shop where they can receive the digital experience they are looking for. Reducing digital activity or marketing in general is a dangerous path. You could trial reducing activity in specific areas if necessary and display the impact of this on the business in order to tell your story.

Quick wins

As mentioned above, these give much more appetite for those interested in the short term. If the business buys into your long-term strategy then that is great, but it is the short-term wins that will excite many of your decision makers and mitigate risks from priority changes. You should ensure that a key part of your strategy, and one that is highlighted when proposing your strategy (see Chapter 15), is quick wins. What are the immediate gains we will make from this? Patience is unsurprisingly thin in most businesses and so delivering results quickly is essential. One other concern with business priorities is that there are still many organizations that simply do not take digital seriously. Some see it as a new kid on the block, something that geeks do. This can be extremely worrying and disheartening for a strategic digital marketer. Ultimately you would not be in that organization if they did not have some belief in digital, so it is up to you to lead from the front and, as Gandhi put it, *be the change that you want to see* – I am fairly sure that he wasn't referring to digital marketing but the point remains entirely valid. Tackling this comes down to convincing your decision makers, and so in Chapter 15 we look at the psychology of decision making and how best to win these people over.

Regulation

There are many regulatory bodies in the world of marketing, from the FCC in the United States to the ASA in the UK and also many that are specific to industries, such as the APRA in Australia and CFDA in China. We cannot review each of these now and nor is it relevant to, but there are some issues of regulation that are worthwhile interrogating. Regulation is a complex area and one that has received a great deal of attention in the 21st century.

Data protection – examples of getting it wrong

Facebook

On 13 May the Belgian Privacy Commission adopted a first recommendation of principle on Facebook. Facebook has come under scrutiny many times all over the world for its use of personal data. A good example of this is their secret experiment to test the emotions of their users through manipulating news feeds, which we will return to in Chapter 11. This specific example in Belgium is around Facebook's process of tracking individuals who visit their site. Some European countries did not agree to these Facebook terms when they were introduced but Facebook's refusal to accept the authority of these countries led to further poor press for the network (CPP, 2015). Ultimately this has done little harm to Facebook to date but it is another story that is damaging for the brand, which does have some small impact on membership.

Others

- In the United Kingdom, a county council faxed details of a child sex-abuse case to a member of the public and as a result was fined £100,000 for breaching the Data Protection Act.

- In the same year a business was fined £60,000 for losing a laptop filled with personal details and unencrypted.

- In the United States Google was fined $22.5 million by the Federal Trade Commission for monitoring internet users who had selected 'do not track' from their Safari settings.

- In Australia a telecoms company was fined $10,200 and warned over privacy breaches after exposing the data of over 15,000 customers online.

Privacy and data protection

Two of the most important regulations to look at, and seemingly the most popular to discuss, are privacy and data protection. They are two sides of the same coin, so let us look at them together.

Regulations differ from country to country and sometimes from state to state. Understanding these for your global strategy is important, but more important is understanding good principles of data usage, consumer protection and security. If you build your strategy to fit consumer behaviour and demand, whilst ensuring they are safe to trade with you, then you are most likely to be aligned with any of the laws and regulations that exist around the world.

One of the hot topics here is cookie policy. In the European Union (EU) there is a law called the e-Privacy Directive (EUR-Lex, 2015). Simply put, this ensures that users have been made aware of the cookie policy and given permission for its use before the cookie is put in place. There are exemptions and the directive itself is not overly prescriptive, which gives flexibility. Implied consent is also possible, which is good news for both marketers and consumers.

An increasingly common use of data is for location purposes. There are regulations here around anonymity that are vital to understand. There are many apps now that collect location data and need to do so to function. These include apps for local weather, finding lost phones, satnav and other services, and it is not appropriate – and therefore in many cases legal – to collect data unless it is essential to provide a service. As well as being relevant and 'anonymized' you must also have permission to do this. We are all familiar with accepting these conditions when using a mobile app and I expect you will agree that you would not want it any other way.

Cloud storage is another area of concern as personal data is kept outside of the physical control of the individual. By this I mean that, whilst the individual does have a great deal of control over what is shared to the cloud, that data is not held on their device but in another location. This involves the transmission of that data and the storage in a location or locations that are unknown to the user. This therefore has a number of associated risks such as damage as the data is in multiple locations, or theft as multiple individuals are involved in the handling of the data. There is also the risk that the supplier may go out of business and then your data has a risk of not being returned or of being disposed of via an insecure method. This is important to consider when using any cloud-based services such as marketing automation or e-mail software, as well as in the broader context around your customer data.

Social media is also a concern for privacy and there have been many controversies around the policies of various social media sites as they have been trying to establish best practice in this new channel. A great deal of information can be captured as users share deep levels of information about their lives on social networks. This includes not only their interests and friends but also their locations and media such as photos and videos. Some of these items, when shared on a network, will give the rights to that network to use them, yet not every user will be aware of this. You will be able to view this information through your social insights and use it to develop highly targeted campaigns. To maintain trust it is important to ensure that your campaigns do not overtly demonstrate that you have collected more data than necessary.

There is also the right to be forgotten, which has been a significant talking point in recent years and a concept that has been agreed by the EU and other parts of the world since 2006. The cases have become more common as people have begun to share more information online, and especially as some employers have begun to research potential employees online. Many of us share things on social media that we would not want a potential employer to find, and we may also have had life events that in our past have been reported online but which no longer represent who we are. One of the challenges here is that the controlling of information in this manner may restrict freedom of speech and may start to affect the neutrality of search results. These challenges are still being worked through but it is likely that this concept will become widespread – as the damage to an individual's real life through access to irrelevant personal information can be significant.

E-mail regulation

E-mail is probably the most established digital channel and there is even discussion that it has had its day, although I do not expect it will disappear in the coming few years. As it is a mature channel, the regulation is fairly well established. Having permissions from your recipients is vital and most companies have databases with clear marketing permission flags. Collection of this permission is also fairly standardized with the opt-in and opt-out routes. How these can be implemented differs regionally and, again, I would recommend you understand the implications fully if e-mail (or data collection as a whole) is a part of your strategy. Including unsubscribe options, implementing preference centres and automating your content strategy are all routes to ensure that your recipients receive and continue to receive what is truly relevant to them. There is no benefit in sending e-mails to consumers who are not interested, simply because you can.

Viral marketing and regulation

Finally a quick look at viral marketing. This is the ultimate goal of many social campaigns and has been a buzzword in digital marketing for many years now. It is a bit of a dark art, although there are of course themes that we can extract from successful viral campaigns. The key point to remember here is that regulation, or at least guidance, exists in many regions that dictates that companies should ensure any encouragement of promotion is clearly positioned as such when asking individuals to pass on messages. This is to stop companies from using their customers to get around marketing regulations by asking them to pass on your messages for you without the necessary regulatory wording. It is important therefore that anyone passing on a message should be asked to ensure that the person they are passing it on to would be interested in the message. This in turn ensures that they are not just spamming their friends in exchange for some benefit from the company.

Successful viral marketing campaigns

The Ice Bucket Challenge (2014)

This concept swept across the world with a huge number of people taking part, or at least refusing and therefore donating, including many A-list celebrities and even the president of the United States. It raised US$98.2 million in a single month for Amyotrophic Lateral Sclerosis Association, also known as motor neurone disease and Lou Gehrig's disease, compared with $2.7 million in the same period of the previous year (Townsend, 2014). This was clearly a phenomenon, but why was it such a success?

#nomakeupselfie

This phenomenon happened as women posted photos of their faces without make-up on social media sites in order to encourage donations to female-focused charities and to charities such as Cancer Research UK. This raised £8 million for the organization in just six days, even though the charity had not started the campaign themselves. A fantastically successful campaign, but why?

Both of these campaigns are interesting as neither was actively designed by the respective organizations. They happened as the concepts caught on and evolved quickly on social media. As celebrities got involved and people challenged their friends, the fun nature of the ice bucket challenge and the challenge to the norm that the #nomakeupselfie represented took hold. The speed and depth of the success made it newsworthy, which then meant it reached people who were not active social media users but wanted to get involved.

So why did these work?

Ultimately the common themes here are charity, selflessness, simplicity, vanity, uniqueness and the use of social media. These in themselves are not a formula for success with viral marketing, but let's look at each one:

- *Charity*
  Charity is something that many people like to be involved in but it can be difficult to know which charity to give to and to actually go about starting the process. Simply being asked is not enough. You need a reason to get involved. The story of the charity itself is not enough. The story, combined with an easy route to take action, is the real goal. This

is why other campaigns such as Live Aid and Red Nose Day have been successful for so many years.

- *Selflessness*

  In today's society we all do a lot to look after ourselves. There is a good feeling that comes with helping others and most of us would freely admit that we do not do as much as we could. The opportunity to do something for others is often well received.

- *Simplicity*

  If it is difficult to understand or to take action on then it will fail no matter how strong the idea. If the message is easy to understand, the action is simple to undertake, the donations easy to make and the sharing simple to do then you have a potential viral campaign.

- *Vanity*

  This may seem odd, especially as the no make-up selfie seems to be about the exact opposite, but actually both of the above have an essence of vanity about them. Showing others how generous you are and wanting to push your activity in front of other people could be seen as a form of vanity.

- *Uniqueness*

  This is important. If your campaign is too similar to another it may gain some momentum but ultimately will never become a global phenomenon. A good example of this is the 'Rice Bucket Challenge', which quickly followed the ice bucket challenge. The concept was to donate a bucket of rice to someone in need. It didn't make any serious progress.

- *Social media*

  All of the above are of course significantly escalated by social media. The channel makes it incredibly easy to understand, watch, share and click straight through to a destination to donate online. Without social media it is likely that the above campaigns would have failed, even with a great deal more investment.

CASE STUDY   Airbnb

Background

Airbnb is a highly successful business that continues to see rapid growth and is operating in over 190 countries. Its model of allowing people to rent out their property and therefore earn an income when they are not there seems like a no-brainer to many and is an excellent example of the opportunities presented to us by using the internet as a community. According to Craig Smith of DMR, as of July 2015 Airbnb had 50 million users, half a million stays per night and was operating in 57,000 cities, which is phenomenal growth in just seven years (Smith, 2015).

Strategy

When you stop to think about the complexities of this global model, the barriers that the team at Airbnb have overcome are clear to see and they deserve a great deal of credit for it. One of these is the huge variations in laws and regulations around uses of property. Some locations do not allow people to have paying guests without licences or similar arrangements, which can result in fines or other consequences. It would not be possible to cater for all of these different scenarios, but not mentioning these issues at all could be damaging to their customers and could also create negative PR, damaging the brand significantly. Airbnb have therefore decided to include some wording within their Terms and Conditions to cover this information, thus tackling the issue globally and simply without causing any alarm.

Results

This low-key approach keeps their model working and ensures that consumers understand the regulatory concerns.

Key lessons

- When producing your digital marketing strategy it is important to understand potential barriers by researching your market thoroughly, including regulations in your territories.

- Working to employ the simplest possible solution ensures that your business, the consumers and the regulators can all have the best possible relationship.

That is all for now on the topic of regulation, but it is a deep and complex area – of which it is worth having a good understanding, so I encourage you to speak to your company's legal department and read up about this yourself.

Summary

In this chapter we discussed some of the more common challenges with implementing your digital strategy. There are of course many more, and so remaining flexible with your strategy and ensuring you plan for as many of these eventualities as possible is important. In risk management many people have adopted the terminology used by Donald Rumsfeld (the two-times United States Secretary of Defence, who is interestingly both the oldest and youngest man to serve in that position). Mr Rumsfeld spoke in a 2002 news briefing about three states of information:

> There are known knowns; there are things we know we know. We also know there are known unknowns; that is to say we know there are some things we do not know. But there are also unknown unknowns – the ones we don't know we don't know.

To give this some perspective, technology would be a known unknown – we know that technology will develop and change society and our behaviours but we do not know how. Skills would be a known known – we know the challenges that we have and that we need to train our staff to overcome these. Unknown unknowns are not listed in this chapter, for the simple reason that we cannot predict them. It is this latter category that can only be tackled by remaining as flexible and agile as possible with our strategy and delivery plans. In the next chapter we move on to looking at our planning process and how we can ensure that we account for this as much as possible.

List of types of regulatory bodies

- Advertising and marketing standards regulators
- Charity commissions
- Competition and market authorities
- Data protection authorities
- Education authorities

- Entertainment censors
- Environment agencies
- Equality and human rights commissions
- Financial services regulators
- Food standards regulators
- Gambling commissions
- Health and safety executives
- Housing regulators
- Law societies
- Medical councils
- Police and services authorities
- Social care councils
- Travel authorities
- Travel regulators
- Utilities regulators

Chapter checklist

- Technology ☐
- Skills ☐
- Budget and resources ☐
- Business priorities ☐
- Regulation ☐

Further reading

- *On risk*:

  Waring, A E (1998) *Managing Risk: Critical issues for survival and success into the 21st century*, Cengage Learning EMEA. Alan Waring explores risk assessment and management alongside specific concerns such as organizational environment, change and culture.

- *On managing budgets*:

  Sleight, S (2000) *Managing Budgets*, DK. This offers some excellent guides on managing a budget, including managing the process, identifying potential problems, tailored budgeting, writing the budget itself and ongoing monitoring. It is a useful handbook if you will be building and managing budgets for the first time or on a regular basis.

- *On regulation*:

  Lodge, M and Wegrich, K (2012) *Managing Regulation: Regulatory analysis, politics and policy*, Palgrave Macmillan. This goes into great detail on the theories, standards and enforcement of regulation as well as looking at what good looks like. If you work in a regulated environment, this is a worthwhile read.

References

CPP (2015) [accessed 1 November 2015] On 13 May the Belgian Privacy Commission Adopted a First Recommendation of Principle on Facebook [Online] http://www.privacycommission.be/en/news/13-may-belgian-privacy-commission-adopted-first-recommendation-principle-facebook

EUR-Lex (2015) [accessed 1 November 2015] Data Protection in the Electronic Communications Sector [Online] http://eur-lex.europa.eu/legal-content/EN/TXT/?uri=uriserv:l24120

Smith, C (2015) [accessed 20 December 2015] By the Numbers: 23 Amazing Airbnb Statistics, *DMR* [Online] http://expandedramblings.com/index.php/airbnb-statistics/

Townsend, L (2014) [accessed 1 February 2016] How Much Has the Ice Bucket Challenge Achieved? *BBC News* [Online] http://www.bbc.co.uk/news/magazine-29013707

Planning

04

What we will cover in this chapter

This chapter covers effective planning processes and how to apply them to your digital strategy. The key areas covered in this chapter are:

- The planning process
- The phased approach
- Goals
- Objectives and strategies
- Action plans
- Controls
- People
- Budgeting and forecasting

Chapter goals

By the end of this chapter you should understand different planning models and how to use these to create a robust plan for the delivery of your strategy. You should understand the differences between goals, objectives and action plans and be able to build resource plans. You should also understand how to manage budgeting and forecasting (Figure 4.1).

If you are reading this book I can assume you are interested in a strategic approach to digital marketing – and that is impossible without having strong planning techniques in place. Building a plan involves similar techniques to building a house. We need to understand what we are trying to build, we need solid foundations, we need to know the intricate measurements and

FIGURE 4.1   The planning process

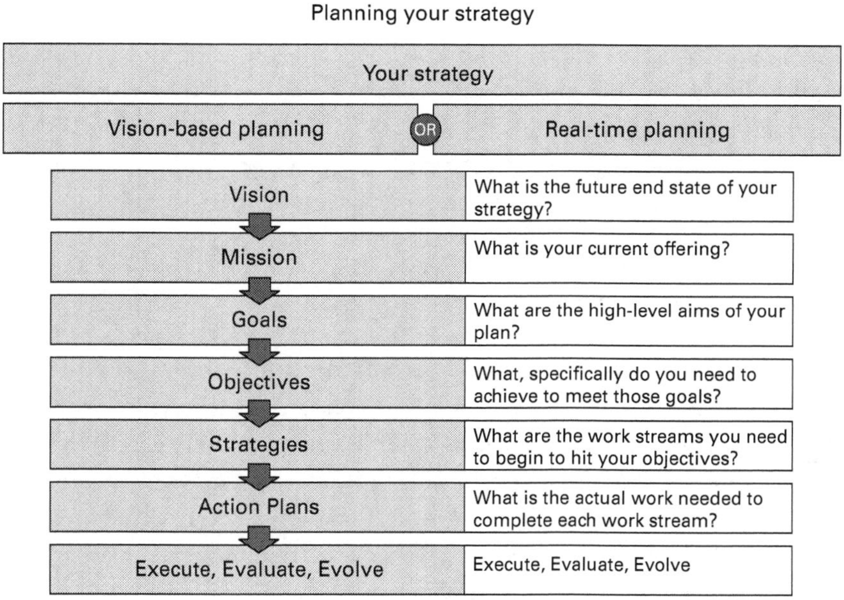

Planning your strategy

Your strategy	
Vision-based planning OR	Real-time planning

Vision	What is the future end state of your strategy?
Mission	What is your current offering?
Goals	What are the high-level aims of your plan?
Objectives	What, specifically do you need to achieve to meet those goals?
Strategies	What are the work streams you need to begin to hit your objectives?
Action Plans	What is the actual work needed to complete each work stream?
Execute, Evaluate, Evolve	Execute, Evaluate, Evolve

details of the brickwork and walls, the costs, timelines and skills of our builders. Having a plan is essential if we want our house to meet our goal. A strategy without a plan is simply an idea. Putting a plan in place for the build and delivery of your digital marketing strategy is no different and so this chapter looks at how we build a plan that clearly lays out the delivery of our strategy.

In order to deliver our digital marketing strategy we need to understand three things:

1 Where are we now?

2 Where do we want to get to?

3 How do we get there?

The first of these is answered through research, data analysis and insight, which we looked at in Chapter 2. The second is designed through the construction of a vision and mission, which we also looked at in Chapter 2. This chapter therefore focuses on the third question: how?

Digital marketing has created its own challenges here. Many digital channels can be switched on and off in real time and at a low cost and so are sometimes added into marketing campaigns and plans at the last minute. The power of effective planning, however, is in the early thinking, co-ordination and integration of the key elements of your strategy – without planning, your strategy is at serious risk of failing. Without effective planning you can spend twice as much time, money and resource trying to fix problems and find solutions, you can demotivate your people and even find yourself having to pay suppliers to help you when that should not have been needed. In extreme cases this can even lead to budgets being used up too quickly, staff resignations and your overall strategy being seriously compromised. A good planning process is essential.

In this chapter we examine some of the processes and approaches to planning that can help guide the implementation of your strategy.

The planning process

Pablo Picasso once said, 'Our goals can only be reached through a vehicle of a plan, in which we must fervently believe, and upon which we must vigorously act. There is no other route to success.' Whilst it is fairly unlikely that he was talking about digital marketing, it is certainly a point that applies here. The starting point and the key to success with planning is to have a process in place and to stick to that process. We look at the discipline of that later in this chapter, but let's start by looking at the process itself.

There are several planning models that can be used for effective planning and in this section we look at two core methods: vision-based planning and real-time planning.

Vision-based planning

Definition: the process of creating a vision and
following a clear six-stage process of delivering against it.

This method is probably the most common form of strategic planning. There are six phases to this model, beginning with creating a vision and ending with analysis and evolution where needed. This method takes you from a starting point through to a final result which may remain fluid. It is an excellent way of organizing the delivery of your strategy and helps to guide your thinking during the strategy development process. It is, however, more structured than some organizations would be willing to implement and more rigid than the real-time planning model we look at below. It also works on a future to present time frame, ie there are specific goals to be achieved by a specific point in time and this may not be relevant to every plan.

Let's look at the six stages:

1 Identify your vision statement.

2 Produce your mission statement.

3 Establish your primary goals.

4 Create specific objectives and strategies to reach each goal.

5 Implement action plans to fulfil each strategy.

6 Put the action plans into effect, evaluate and evolve.

The six stages of vision-based planning

Example A – an FMCG retailer

1 To be everyone's favourite place to buy doughnuts.

2 We provide the tastiest doughnuts in the United States to anyone, anywhere, at any time.

3 Improve brand awareness.

4 Create a social media strategy.

5 Build a viral-video marketing campaign.

6 Build the campaign, select target audience, budget, launch, test and measure.

Example B – a B2B service provider

1 To be Europe's number one IT support services supplier.

2 We offer the fastest and most reliable competitive IT support across Europe.

3 Gain word-of-mouth promotion.

4 Create a member-get-member scheme.

5 Build a personalized e-mail contact and content strategy.

6 Build the campaign, select target audience, budget, launch, test and measure.

As mentioned above, at this point you should be clear on your vision, as we have already in Chapter 2 reviewed the creation of this and how to align it with your company vision. Below we look at the mission statement and then go on to review steps three to five. Step six, the execution of your strategy, is considered throughout the book.

Mission statement

There is often confusion between vision and mission statements. The easiest way to remember the difference is that your vision statement is an expression of your desired future state, whereas the mission statement expresses your current state. With this differentiation in mind we can look at the two examples above and begin to see a clear difference. Creating this mission is important for your business but just as important for your digital strategy. Knowing what you are trying to achieve now alongside the future vision begins to clearly lay out a path that the rest of your planning process can follow.

Real-time planning

Definition: a plan that retains fluidity to your planning process
to ensure your plans are malleable to the circumstances.

The real-time model is effectively a 'casual' version of the vision-based model. This model is notable for its lack of structure and, some may even argue, its lack of a model, which is a fairly odd way to start an explanation of a planning model when we have already discussed the importance of structure. The reason this was developed, however, is because the modern world changes at pace and so building a formalized five-year plan is considered by some to be an outdated concept. The world in five years' time is likely to be very different from now, so how can such a long-term plan still be as relevant as when it was finalized? The real-time model therefore keeps the planning process 'alive' as an ongoing piece of work. It is never formally documented and so evolves continuously. It is reviewed at regular intervals, for example monthly board meetings, and therefore develops alongside real-time issues and developments within and external to the company.

The advantage is therefore that your strategy stays highly relevant and can change quickly to meet current insights. There are, however, two primary disadvantages to this approach and both ultimately come back to the lack of documentation. The first is that there is no document to share with your business. It can be extremely difficult to articulate your strategy to the wider business in this situation and so can create confusion and lack of synergy if your communication is not excellent. One way to address this is to ensure that the project lead or equivalent for the delivery of your strategy develops and manages an internal communications plan. This could involve e-mails to key stakeholders, steering group meetings, regular update seminars, internal desk drops or even launch events. The extent of this is down to the size and culture of your organization but you should never assume that people will know how the project is progressing – so great communication is essential.

Second, there is no fully formed document to share externally. Should investors or other external stakeholders wish to understand your strategy it would not look very professional only to be able to articulate this verbally from what was discussed at the last meeting. This can be tackled by ensuring that the core principles and stages of the plan are documented and the flexible elements are regularly updated and version controlled.

That is not to say that there is no structure here at all. A process of planning what the goals are and how the business aims to achieve them is still followed in a similar style to the vision-based approach we mentioned above, but you do not need to stick so rigidly to these goals for a set period of time and so are more able to retain the flexibility that this process demands. For example, the doughnut company we mentioned above would still go through the same six steps to create their plan but this may not then be documented and may evolve just a few weeks later. Should your competition launch a viral video campaign, you would change your social media plans to adapt to this challenge and perhaps create a video-based advertising campaign for YouTube that will both reach a different audience and reduce the gains your competitor makes from their video campaign.

Vision-based versus real-time example

A company decides that it wants to grow its digital footprint.

Vision-based approach

The company in question would conduct research into consumer needs and behaviours, competitor offerings and technology. An audit of the current capability would be completed and a strategy would begin to be formed. This would involve committing resources in terms of people, time and money into the work streams necessary to deliver the strategy. This would then be laid out for the following three to five years in order to ensure that those resources were ring-fenced. Perhaps the front end and back end of a website need development and so do a number of apps, so this is all planned together and committed together. Agencies and contractors may be hired to deliver this over the next 24 to 36 months. Deviating from this plan in the first two to three years would therefore involve significant loss of investment and complexity. It may also cause confusion. The end result is likely to be as per the plan and this would be a success. If, however, technology has significantly changed in that period, as we have seen many times in the past over a short period of time (the launches of the iPhone or social media, for example), then this end result may no longer be relevant.

Real-time planning approach

The company would again research and audit to establish the beginning state and desired result. Steps would then be put into place to begin moving towards this end result. This may include appointing an agency, but keeping their brief fluid and ensuring that their contract is not a long-term commitment. The goals would be based on working towards delivering the next step in the journey but perhaps not laying down any significant commitments at the early stages for what may or may not happen in year three. Decisions are made at the points that action is needed rather than a long time in advance. Should a new technology launch, or behaviours change, this plan is able to adapt to those. Therefore the back end of the website may be developed first, as it is less susceptible to consumer behavioural needs. The front end may not be scoped until the back-end work is nearing release. The apps may be the last element, as the mobile market continues to change at significant pace. This means a great deal more focus on the project from the senior leadership team, perhaps less ability to plan ahead for cost savings and a greater need for excellent communication, but it does mean that the end result is likely to be highly relevant when launched rather than risking seeming outdated.

Here is a useful comparison of the above two scenarios:

- *Stage 1*: goal – establish opportunity:
  - Vision-based: research consumers and market, internal audit, resource commitment.
  - Real-time: research consumers and market, internal audit, resource commitment.
  - The difference: no difference here. Both methods begin by understanding the current position, challenge and opportunity.

- *Stage 2*: begin development of strategy:
  - Vision-based: structure the strategy and prepare the formal document.
  - Real-time: begin test and learn.

- The difference: the vision-based approach now spends several months beginning to structure the proposal, add supporting data, creating pillars, gaining commitment from stakeholders and producing detailed financial forecasts. The real-time approach creates a loose plan and begins to test some of the assumptions in a scientific manner to shape the development on the plan.

- *Stage 3*: finalize strategy:
  - Vision-based: commit budget and finalize full five-year plan.
  - Real-time: plan for one to three years.
  - The difference: the vision-based approach would result in the above planning process being committed and bought into by all senior stakeholders (see Chapter 15). This would then become part of the business strategy. The real-time process would also need buy-in from the senior team but would be more fluid and have less of a time commitment.

- *Stage 4*: delivery:
  - Vision-based: work to plan with very limited deviation.
  - Real-time: continue to evolve and change direction as needed.
  - The difference: as the work begins there is a very clear path for the vision-based strategy to follow. The milestones must all be met and this allows full visibility of progress and clear resource management. The real-time approach has a clear beginning but must now be managed closely to create a path and direction as the strategy evolves based on the learnings, internal and external factors.

- *Stage 5*: result:
  - Vision-based: delivered as per plan but possibly now out of date and a new strategy is needed.
  - Real-time: delivered in an evolved state, which can continue within minimal work but at a higher cost.
  - The difference: the vision-based approach should accomplish its end goal and if not then the project has failed. However, if the environment has changed then the result may not be as strong as first expected and changing course can be expensive and difficult. The real-time approach should result in a more contemporary result but the path may have been more expensive and resource intensive due to the continuous reviewing and evolution of the plan.

The phased approach

Before we get on to steps three to five of the vision-based planning process it is worth quickly discussing phased planning. This refers to splitting your strategy into key development phases. These phases can be categorized into calendar-based, theme-based and business-based phasing, dependent on your strategy. There are other phasing approaches but these are some of the most common.

Calendar-based phasing

This approach is as simple as it sounds. Phasing your plan to match your calendar is one method. You could start in January, aim to have your vision completed by February, establish your goals in March etc. This type of approach is common when there is no specific delivery date in mind, no essential milestone dates or your strategy is not integrated with any other pieces of work. That does not mean that the deadlines are any less important, but you can be a little more flexible with setting those deadlines at the start of the planning process.

Theme-based phasing

Theme-based phasing is used when your strategy has specific themes that would be logical to deliver together. For example, there may be specific customer experience elements that would be powerful to be delivered together such as a new training programme and online chat technology. There could be complementary marketing channel strategies that would be far more powerful if released together, such as direct mail and e-mail.

Business-based phasing

This phasing method is focused on aligning your strategic plan with the overall business goals. Your company's strategic plan is likely to be made of key strategic pillars, which may in turn be delivering projects and change programmes. This may be less formalized in a smaller business but there will still be key areas of focus, and funding will be directed towards those. The business-based phasing approach means aligning the key parts of your plan with these pillars. This is a path of least resistance and will resonate with many senior stakeholders, but it can compromise the ideal timeline for your strategy.

Now we can come back to look at stages three to five mentioned in the vision-based planning process above. These are goals, objectives and strategies, and action plans.

Goals

Goals are high-level statements about what you need to achieve in order to deliver against your vision. Goals tend to be long term and therefore set out the underlying elements of your vision. They bring your vision statement to life by moving it towards a practical reality.

Goals need to be structured to meet a set of criteria. I call these the 4 Rs:

- **Relevant**: does it fit with your vision?
- **Resonating**: does it fit with your business's values and goals?
- **Responsive**: is it adaptable and flexible so that it can change if needed?
- **Recognizable**: is it easily understandable?

Some example goals are:

- increase sales;
- improve profitability;
- provide best-in-class customer service;
- deliver a world-class digital experience;
- hire the best talent;
- become the thought leader;
- gain market share.

You should aim to set a limited number of goals that focus on the key aims of your strategy and fit with the strategic pillars of your business. They also need to be integrated so that they fit together without any conflicting elements. Your business strategy will have goals and each goal will have objectives, strategies and action plans below it. Some of these strategies may in turn have goals that have their own objectives and so through a waterfall effect the goals of your organization are delivered.

For example, if we take the first goal above we could create a waterfall of goals and strategies that looks something like the process shown in Figure 4.2:

FIGURE 4.2   The planning flow of an organization

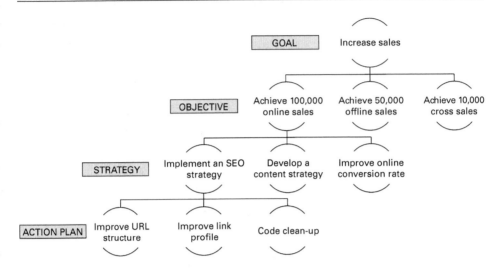

Your goals are unique in the planning process in that they require the least detail but the most thought. If your goals are not thought through then the river will be flowing in the wrong direction. How you go about meeting your goal of 'increase sales' is not something that the goal itself is concerned with. You do not need to focus on the 'how' at this stage, simply the 'what'. Your objectives and strategies will deal with how these goals are met, as we will see below. Whilst goals should be grounded in reality they do not need to be specific or be the result of thorough research. They therefore do not need to be entirely realistic. It may sound counter-intuitive to have a goal that cannot be met, but an aspirational goal can drive your business forward faster than a realistic one.

That said, there is a careful balance between being aspirational and being so unrealistic that you demotivate your people, which can compromise the delivery of your goal, especially if unrealistic goals are set regularly. If, for example, your sales goal for the year is 20 per cent above the previous year and the company has never achieved more than 10–15 per cent then this is aspirational. It feels achievable if everyone works hard and you have some luck on your side. This may stretch the team to work towards this, especially if they are incentivized to do this. If you miss the 20 per cent target but still achieve 17.5 per cent then this is still the best result your business has ever seen and a good outcome. If, however, you set the target at 40 per cent the following year and 60 per cent the year after, whilst reducing investment in the business, cancelling bonuses and reducing the workforce, then your people will begin to believe that the targets are unrealistic and this will seriously demotivate and have a negative impact on productivity. They may also openly criticize the management, which can lead to severe cultural issues and even resignations – all of which will in turn affect the delivery of your goal.

Objectives and strategies

Your objectives and strategies are where you start to build specific plans that create a journey for your overall strategy. Once these are in place we can create action plans that demonstrate the detail of how we deliver them.

Objectives

Your objectives are specific, quantifiable and time-based. They are the steps or milestones that you need to take towards meeting your ultimate goal. Many businesses use a SMART approach to creating objectives. SMART is simply a mnemonic that helps us to ensure that the objectives are well thought through and ultimately will serve their purpose. The SMART method has a number of interpretations but the 'SMART' box below outlines one of the more common ones.

SMART

- **S**pecific: no matter who were to look at your action plan it should be absolutely clear what needs to be achieved for the action plan to be met. There must be no ambiguity. Using the five 'W' questions can help here – again, there are differing interpretations of the five (or sometimes six) 'W' questions but below are those that I find the most useful:
  - Who: who will be involved in achieving the action plan?
  - Where: is a specific location involved?
  - What: what exactly needs to be achieved?
  - Why: what is this action plan going to achieve?
  - When: what is the deadline and any milestones along the way?

- **M**easurable: how will you know when you have met your action plan? It is vital that there is a clear measure so that everyone involved knows when the action plan has been hit and there is no confusion. This also allows you to understand how much progress you are making towards meeting your action plan.

- **A**ttainable: setting action plans that are realistic is crucially important. If your action plans are not attainable then you can never meet them, which ultimately means you can never reach your goals. There is no harm in setting a stretching action plan – and indeed getting the balance between too stretching and too easy is important here. Setting an action plan that does not have this balance right can also cause demotivation amongst the team working on it.

- **R**elevant: the action plan needs to be relevant to your goal. Having an action plan that does not tie in with the wider work is not only irrelevant but also a distraction from achieving your goal. Think back to the five Ws above and consider whether each of these are relevant.

- **T**ime-based: this is where the sixth 'W' comes in: 'When'. Your action plan needs a time frame and also specific milestones. As with any piece of work, having a deadline gives the action plan a much greater chance of being delivered.

If we were to take our goal of increasing sales we might create one of the following objectives: 1) increase sales of batteries through the online channel by 10 per cent to 100,000 units by the end of the sales year; 2) increase room bookings by 55 per cent to achieve 55 per cent capacity by this time next year.

These give us a target to hit and a deadline to hit it by. There is no ambiguity and it could even be more specific by breaking down into a series of objectives around the different products being sold.

If we were to take the example of the doughnut company mentioned above, their SMART objectives could be:

1 *To be everyone's favourite place to buy doughnuts*: increase footfall by 25 per cent by end of year.

2 *We provide the tastiest doughnuts in the United States to anyone, anywhere, at any time*: customer satisfaction levels on food quality at least 98 per cent for full year.

3 *Improve brand awareness*: search queries up 20 per cent within six months.

4 *Create a social media strategy*: improve engagement on Facebook by 100 per cent by December.

5 *Build a viral-video marketing campaign*: 1 million views in a three-month campaign period.

So now we know exactly what we have to do and by when – we have a simple flow. Meeting our action plans means that our strategies will deliver. If all of our strategies deliver then we will hit our goal. If all of our goals deliver then we will deliver against our mission, which is the ultimate action plan.

Strategies

The word 'strategy' in this sense refers to the specific things that we will do to meet our objective. Do not confuse this with the broader meaning of strategy that the title of this book refers to. Your strategies are the plans that spell out how you will achieve your objectives. When goals are fairly broad, strategies must be much more focused. This is where we demonstrate what we are going to do and from this we create our action plans. Without strategies your work so far will have been for nothing. Going back to our sales goal we know that we need to increase sales. In itself that does not help us a lot. Our objectives have given us something specific that we need to achieve but we still do not fully understand what we need to do to achieve that. Our strategy needs to look at the key work streams we need to implement to achieve our 100,000 sales.

What we need to do at this stage is start to look at the levers we can pull to achieve the desired outcome. For this strategy the outcome is increased sales, so what levers can we pull to achieve this? Well, let's break down the full sales funnel:

- Awareness: are consumers aware of us and our products?
- Consideration: do consumers find our brand and products appealing?
- Findable: can consumers find us if they want to?
- Informative: do consumers get the information they need from us to make a decision?
- Ease of use: is it easy for consumers to buy from us?

We should have a strong understanding of all of these factors from the research and insight work that we reviewed in Chapter 2. Each of these areas has its own internal levers, for example:

- Awareness: above-the-line marketing spend, PR.
- Consideration: proposition, brand values.
- Findable: marketing activity.
- Informative: content.
- Ease of use: user experience, customer service, conversion funnels.

These specific areas are direct contributors to the sales objective that we are trying to build our strategies for, but there are also indirect contributors. For example, customer service. Whilst providing great service to existing customers does not directly create sales it does create higher retention rates, greater repeat business, more cross-sell opportunity and word-of-mouth promotion. Each of these will directly result in increased sales and so the indirect levers are also vitally important to consider and can often be the difference between exceeding and missing objectives.

From these areas we can now build strategies such as:

- increase display advertising across highly targeted sites (awareness);
- develop a market-leading digital proposition (consideration);
- make significant SEO improvements (findable);
- develop a content strategy (informative);
- improve our conversion rate (ease of use).

Each of these strategies will need a level of detail below it to dictate how it is delivered. These are called our action plans.

Action plans

Action plans clearly define the specific pieces of work that will be done within each of the above strategies. These must not be confused with the planning processes mentioned above, or the wider use of the word 'plan' in this chapter. Ultimately this is where your strategy will succeed or fail. Action plans are where your goals, objectives and strategies come together into the hard work. At this stage, more so than any other, the detail is crucial. Planning how the work will be done, ensuring nothing is missed, working with key stakeholders, checking the legal and regulatory frameworks are in place, ensuring budgets are planned and managed accurately, selecting and managing your agencies and many more factors will be crucial to success here.

We focus on these elements throughout the book, so rather than cover all of this here we instead look at tactical delivery of the strategy. In order to create the action plan we need to review what specific tactical actions we are going to take to meet the strategy. To bring this to life we can focus on one of the strategies above that are contributing to our 'increase sales' goal. Let's look at 'Make significant SEO improvements'.

SEO can be broken down into three core areas: technical implementation, content and links. When looking at how you build your action plan for this strategy you would need to consider all three areas:

- *Technical implementation*
  - URL structure: is it optimized for the products we are looking to sell?
  - Code: does it need cleaning, are there any errors such as broken links?
  - Experience: is our site responsive? Will it be a great experience for all of our visitors?
- *Content*
  - Topic: are we producing content that covers the key areas that consumers care about?
  - Keyword: are we talking about the specific terms that people are searching for?
  - Social: is our content proving to be engaging socially?
  - Fresh: is our content of the moment?
- *Links*
  - Profile: is our link profile clean?
  - Baiting: do we have an ethically sound link strategy such as link baiting rather than link buying?

In Chapter 5 you can find more detail on how SEO contributes to your strategy; Chapter 13 covers content strategy.

---

10 steps to an effective action plan

1 Know your strategy.

2 Understand the bigger picture – your goals.

3 Be specific.

4 Create a written plan.

5 Create deadlines and milestones.

6 Ensure it is measurable.

7 Don't compromise.

8 Build in known factors.

9 Be clear.

10 Be thorough.

Controls

The above processes are very effective ways to ensure that you meet your overall business mission, but all of these are ineffective if they are not implemented and run correctly. I have seen many businesses that are excellent at this from top to bottom, but also some that are very good at the theory but fail to hit their action plans due to lack of clarity, poor communication or a fall down in the process. There are some clear disciplines and controls to have in place when building and delivering a plan that are crucial to success and they are no less important than any of the other parts of the planning process.

The most important of these controls is to implement a documented, management approach, assuming of course that you are not operating a real-time planning process (as mentioned above). This is where the Gantt chart comes in (as mentioned in Chapter 3). Using a Gantt chart to clearly illustrate the progress of each of the action plans, and therefore the strategies, gives a clear reference point at any moment for how progress is being made towards meeting the objectives and therefore goals of the business. This covers the deadline and milestone elements of the strategies. Also, implementing reporting and measurement is vital to allow monthly, weekly or even daily progress reports against the objectives. These are discussed in detail in Chapter 14 and cover the target elements of the strategies.

Reviews

Reviews are also crucial to success. A standard approach here is to implement a quarterly review, but this should be structured to fit with your strategy and business and so quarterly may not always be the appropriate time frame. These reviews should cover how each action plan is progressing against the milestones and whether targets are being met. From these reviews the strategies should be evolved. This could be the implementation of new action plans to replace failing ones, the restructure of strategies or teams or even the increase in targets due to unexpected success to date.

Risk management

Risk management is another important control. Your business and your industry will have its own risk positioning, which will be dependent on a number of factors such as regulation (we looked at this in Chapter 3). A full understanding of this dictates the plans that you produce and how you take action on them throughout their delivery. Constructing a risk matrix is a useful method of visualizing the risks that your strategies will encounter (Figure 4.3). You should familiarize yourself with the risk management techniques relevant to your company and industry.

FIGURE 4.3 A risk matrix

5	10	15	20	25	Major	
4	8	12	16	20	Significant	
3	6	9	12	15	Moderate	IMPACT
2	4	6	8	10	Low	
1	2	3	4	5	Negligible	
Remote	Unlikely	Occasional	Likely	Frequent		
LIKELIHOOD						

Contingency planning

Contingency planning is an important control to have in place. With all the best strategists, planners and best practice methods in place there still will be unforeseen factors. Macro-economic factors such as recessions are a good example of this. You cannot fully predict what will happen, so having plans in place to allow you to be flexible and implement plan B when something goes wrong is crucial. In order to build contingency plans effectively you should think through what the top 10 most likely impacts could be and how your plan might need to evolve to deal with them. This does not involve the creation of 10 new plans but simply a realistic alternative that can be built on if the situation occurs. Some examples of this are:

- A new competitor enters the market with significant impact.
- New technology is launched that our consumers would prefer to use.
- The global economy enters recession.
- There is a serious negative PR story about our business.
- New regulation is brought into force that restricts our operations.

People

A business is nothing without its people. A crucial part of planning is getting the right people working on delivering your plan. There are two key areas to consider here: skill set and resource. Do we have enough people and who should look after which part of the process?

Skill set

This really starts at the top. It is not a simple matter of ensuring that your social media experts are implanting social media correctly, it is more important to ensure that your strategists and planners are experienced and have the right mindset for the role. If this early part of the process is not conducted correctly then the rest of the strategies and action plans will be heading in the wrong direction no matter how well they are executed. For the implementation you need experts who understand their own channels but who also have an understanding of the other channels and the wider strategy. Whilst you can implement a marketing strategy with individuals working in silos, this creates a long list of issues that can be seriously detrimental to your strategy, so having people who are good communicators and leading them to behave as one team is crucial.

This brings us to the leaders themselves. For this role you must have an individual who understands each and every area of the strategy. They do not need to be a paid search expert, a research guru or a PR genius, but they absolutely have to understand what each channel and element of the strategy does, how it works and how they should fit together. Without this, the guidance will not be there for the experts who are delivering the action plans. Without guidance there is nowhere to turn for direction and that will lead your action plans off the path to success.

An interesting method of discovering the types of personality you have in your business is the Myers-Briggs model, which we look at in more detail in Chapter 15.

Resource

Quite simply, this refers to the number of hours available for delivery of the action plans. This can be quite complex and it is crucial here that the strategists have a solid understanding of what resource is available to deliver the plans. Many plans fall down due to an unrealistic expectation of the number of hours available in a team.

A good process here is to begin by allocating time to existing processes or 'business as usual' (BAU) work. For example, a team of 20 marketers may consist of one director, three senior managers, six managers and 10 executives. They work 40 hours a week. Everyone in that team has some admin to do every week such as expenses, invoicing, time management etc. The managers also have people management responsibilities such as signing off holidays, running reviews, recruiting etc. Senior managers will also have strategic plans to write, business projects to be involved with, budgets to plan, contracts to negotiate etc. The director will also have the overall department strategy, board meetings, pay reviews and other strategic projects. If we were to allocate this time at the start we would see that where we had 40 hours per week × 20 staff = 800 hours a week, we now have 35 hours a week × 20 staff = 700 hour a week. Simply through the standard BAU we have lost 100 hours a week.

We then have to look at the work that goes on within marketing that forms the foundation of keeping the department running. This may include website updates, paid search optimization, sending weekly e-mails, copywriting and uploading to the content management system (CMS) to keep our content fresh and much more. This may well take another 300 hours per week for our team, leaving us with 400 hours. We need to factor in that individuals in the team will have holiday and some sick leave, which will lose us 25 days per person on holiday and 5 days per person on sick leave during the year. This is 30 × 20 days per year = 600 days. That results in 11.5 days a week or 92 hours. So now we have just 308 hours left.

This is all hypothetical of course, but you can see how we could plan for 800 hours a week when we actually have around 300 hours a week of available resource. This kind of detailed planning is essential if you are to create realistic action plans that are deliverable.

Budgeting and forecasting

Last, but certainly not least, is the budgeting and forecasting process. This is a crucial area of planning, for obvious reasons, and there are some important techniques that can be used to ensure this process is as smooth and accurate as possible. This section deals specifically with media budgeting rather than departmental budgeting. We will therefore not be considering the running of our department, including items such as salaries, expenses, IT costs etc. We are purely concerning ourselves with budgeting our marketing spend, including items such as media costs and agency fees. Digital marketing is an area that is very transparent. Where some marketing channels may not be able to directly attribute sales or revenue, digital channels generally can. As such budgeting and forecasting accuracy expectations are high, so using solid techniques to enable you to establish this accuracy is key.

Master budget

This is a document that is often used within business to establish a budget for the coming period based on previous results. This is a static document and it would never be adjusted, no matter what results are actually seen. You therefore report against this as your master budget and, ultimately, you will be judged at the end of the year on performance against it. To produce this you will need to review historic performance of all of the key metrics such as conversion rates, engagement rates and response rates. Understanding how they have performed historically, and the trend you have seen over the previous period, will inform your view as to what to expect over the coming period. You also need to consider known macro factors such as seasonal changes, competition and regulation.

It should be noted that you can create your master budget based purely on aspirational goals if you choose, but this is likely to be inaccurate, difficult to measure against and not given credence by external parties such as analysts and investors.

Forecasting

Your forecast is a more fluid version of your budget and should be reassessed regularly. Monthly forecasts are fairly standard, especially within digital marketing where updated market and business performance can be considered in close to real time. There are several different techniques that can be used for forecasting but the most common, and the one we look at here, is the trend-based model. This technique looks at your budget alongside a 13-month rolling performance. This provides a view of your month-on-month performance and your year-on-year performance whilst showing any trends within the data and your goals from your budget. This is a fairly robust technique as it builds on solid data to make predictions. What this model does not cover, however, is any known future events.

For example, if we were to forecast our sales from paid search for August 2016 we would look back at the period from August 2015 to July 2016. We could see from this how we performed last year and see any trends since that date right up until the previous month. We can build into this our own knowledge of what has happened and we can make some predictions about August this year. But what if we know that we are repricing our products mid-month or there will be a new competitor product launching? The model does not take account for that. We therefore need to add a second element to this model.

This second element is to review the known future. If we know that a competitor is launching a new product then we need to model the effect we think that will have on our paid search channel. Have they done this before? Has someone else done something similar before? Will they promote it on paid search? Are they well known to our consumers? Are they direct competition or will we actually be less affected than we first thought? Looking at our data and making assumptions is key to being able to model this into our forecast and therefore have an accurate view of the future.

Summary

There are several planning processes that can be used to ensure that your strategy is delivered – without effective planning your strategy is unlikely to be a success. Vision-based planning enables you to have a clear, documented flow from your vision through to each individual tactical action. The real-time planning process is far less formalized and so has more flexibility. The phased approach allows you to adopt a calendar, theme or business-based structure to your timelines to ensure that you meet the integrated objectives of the business. Goals give you high-level aims that are made specific by objectives. Strategies are then formed to meet the objectives, and action plans are developed to deliver the strategies. These stages allow complete clarity at every stage of the planning process. Controls are vital to delivering your plan. Regular review, risk management and contingency planning ensure that your plans are robust. Ensuring your people have the right skill set and the correct people are put into the correct roles is essential, as is understanding in detail the resource that is available. Finally, budgeting and forecasting accuracy ensures that your strategy can be delivered within the financial resources available, so using appropriate models for these helps to ensure that this happens.

Further reading

- *On mission and vision:*

  Bowhill, B (2008) *Business Planning and Control*, JW. To understand more about mission and vision and how they apply to your organizational structure, it is worth consulting this guide by Bowhill, which has some useful insight into this area.

Search engine optimization

05

What we will cover in this chapter

In this chapter we look at search engine optimization (SEO). This includes setting up and operating the channels but with a primary focus on how to integrate them appropriately into your strategy. The key areas covered in this chapter are:

- A history of SEO
- Researching your SEO strategy
- Technical SEO
- Site structure
- Content
- Mobile
- Location
- Penalties
- Organizational structure and SEO

Chapter goals

By the end of this chapter you should understand SEO in terms of structure and technical concerns, content, mobile and location techniques. You should understand how to research your SEO strategy and how best to structure your team. You should also have an understanding of SEO penalties.

Key terms

Some of the key terms used in this chapter are:

SEO: optimizing your site for the search engine's natural results.

Natural / organic links: links that are not paid for.

Algorithm: the search engine's code used to decide how sites are ranked.

On-page: SEO factors on your website.

Off-page: SEO factors away from your site such as backlinks.

Metadata: code that tells robots about your site.

Robots: the crawlers that work their way across the internet checking content.

Keyword density: the number of repeat keywords on a page.

Tags: pieces of code attached to parts of the page to give signs to robots.

Hierarchy: the structure of your pages on your site.

Site map: a simple display of the entirety of your site.

Alt text: text associated with images to tell robots what the image is about.

Crawl: what robots / crawlers do to index sites.

Index: each search engine has an index of websites that the robots update.

Backlink: a link pointing back to your site from elsewhere.

Anchor text: the text that is visible when clicking on a link.

SEO is a digital marketing discipline that divides marketers. It is also arguably the discipline where a little knowledge really is truly dangerous, whilst a lot of knowledge is essential if you want to be able to deliver your digital strategy. This is because as soon as you have a website you are using the SEO channel whether you like it or not. If your knowledge is minimal then you might try to rank number one on a specific key term and this could cost a significant amount of money and time to achieve. However, developing a broader strategy that improves performance across a number of keywords would be far more efficient and would also reduce the risk of a penalty. Even if you have appointed a great SEO or broader digital agency you still need to ensure that you understand the fundamentals of good SEO as agencies cannot achieve success without guidance and direction from their client (despite what some may tell you).

One reason why so many digital marketers and business leaders are reluctant to embrace the detail of SEO is because they have the misconception that it is a very technical and complex discipline. Technical SEO considerations are very important, but they are just one area of SEO. If you are looking for technical detail it would be worthwhile either using online resources such as moz.com and searchengineland.com or searching for a book on technical SEO for developers. Truly strategic SEO is in fact very closely aligned to more traditional marketing techniques. If your background is in marketing then you probably already have the skills needed to implement a great SEO strategy.

It is worth noting that throughout this section only one search engine is discussed, Google. In most markets Google dominates by some margin but of course this is not the case in all. If Google is not your average customer's search engine of choice then please do consider further research than this section allows. That said, many of the principles of good SEO are actually about good content, design, user experience and other marketing principles, so good SEO is likely to work for most if not all search engines.

The final note is that when optimizing your site it is important that you do not try to learn Google's techniques and find ways to work around them to get to position one. This is a sure-fire way to cause yourself problems in either the short or medium term. SEO should always focus on optimizing for the user, not the search engine. Ultimately this is the aim of every good search engine as well – to improve the internet experience for users. If you have the same goal then you will find that your SEO strategy will be aligned to the philosophy and therefore algorithms of the search engines and you will be able to win now and in the future.

A history of SEO

SEO has changed significantly and in order to get a real understanding of how to build an effective SEO strategy it is beneficial to start with an understanding of the history of search algorithms. The analysis below is focused on Google but others have largely followed suit.

Pre-2003

Search engine algorithms at this time were simplistic, at least by today's standards. Rankings were dictated almost entirely by on-page factors such as page titles (code-based descriptions of the page), metadata (code-based descriptors of the website) and body copy, with keyword density playing a major role – the more keywords on a page, the better. Search engines were also very easy to manipulate; techniques such as creating hidden, keyword-stuffed content were very effective. The graphs in Figure 5.1 highlight the distribution of influence of each of the core factors at this time, along with the level of manipulability.

FIGURE 5.1   Manipulation levels pre-2003

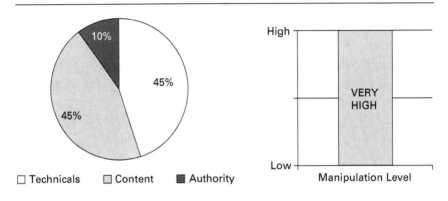

2004–11

Google's Florida update that occurred at the very end of 2003 was the first wide-reaching algorithm update. Loopholes allowing websites to spam through on-site technical work and content were sewn up, and link-based factors took centre-stage for the first time. Rankings became dictated to a large degree by link volume and particularly by the anchor text (the clickable text in a hyperlink) of links pointing back to sites. Technical optimization and content took a back seat, with relevancy assessments being made chiefly via linking anchor text. A high volume of links containing the anchor text 'used cars' would have been sufficient to deliver prominent rankings for the term, even if the quality of such links was questionable and on-site technical SEO considerations were poor. Although steps were taken by Google to improve quality considerations towards the end of this period, the algorithm remained open to manipulation. This is visualized in the graphs in Figure 5.2.

FIGURE 5.2   Manipulation levels 2004–11

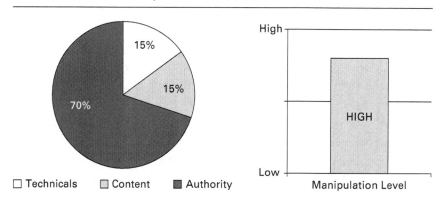

2011 onwards

Prior to 2011, cataclysmic algorithm updates capable of turning the SEO industry on its head almost overnight were a relatively rare occurrence. Typically, a major update might be anticipated every one or two years. In this respect, 2011 represents somewhat of a watershed moment for SEO. The Panda update (named after Google engineer Navneet Panda), which rolled out for the first time in February of that year, became one of the most significant and disruptive algorithm updates in Google's history. Unlike the most significant updates in the preceding years, which primarily targeted intentional breaches of Google's Webmaster Guidelines, Panda's impact was considerably broader. Specifically concerning website and content quality (as opposed to links), Panda not only impacted sites guilty of significant on-page 'spam' but also those deemed to offer a user experience low in quality or not substantially unique.

Affiliates and vertical search specialists (ie retail and travel price-comparison sites) were amongst the most affected by Panda's initial wave. The algorithm continues to evolve and remains an integral part of Google's approach to natural search, with revised iterations rolling out approximately once per month. It is widely accepted that how much (or otherwise) users interact and engage with websites they reach via Google's search results now plays a material role in how they rank. In short, Panda has assisted Google in taking its ranking mechanic from a robotic, mathematical algorithm to something much more aligned with the requirements of its human users. Going forward, it is unlikely that businesses will fare well in natural search without a robust mix of useful and engaging content (and not just of the written form), a great user experience and a compelling core proposition.

Of course, Panda is not the only 'P' word to have disrupted the SEO world in recent years. Persisting with both the 'P' and black-and-white animals theme, the Penguin algorithm was launched in April 2012. Penguin was more akin to Google updates of old, targeting link spam (paid links, mainly), however this time with much greater accuracy and impact than its many predecessors. Like Panda, the Penguin algorithm is reoccurring and ever changing, albeit on a much less frequent basis.

Crucially, the algorithm has had a profound effect in protecting its results from manipulation via unnaturally sourced links, decreasing its reliance on more manual spam-fighting techniques. Long-term, sustainable success is now highly unlikely wherever an approach heavy on paid or incentivized links with little to no value add is employed. Such an approach is far more likely to result in a Penguin penalty – a punishment that is notoriously hard to recover from.

It should be noted that links remain an important part of Google's algorithm; for the time being at least they remain a necessary ingredient for success. However, the ones that will work hardest for you are those that are unsolicited – the result of good business and marketing practice. So, whilst Panda and Penguin are entirely different propositions concerned with opposite ends of the algorithmic spectrum, their effects on SEO strategy as a whole are essentially identical. Sustainable success after their implementation can only really be achieved through a mixture of great content, experience and proposition. Indeed the SEO secret sauce has very much increased in ingredients. Technical, content and authority are all still important – but as are link profile quality, user engagement and mobile capability (Figure 5.3).

FIGURE 5.3   Current manipulation levels

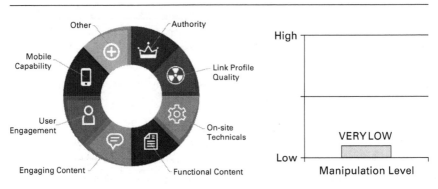

So, as we have seen above, SEO in its rawest form can be sub-divided into a number of key areas. We start here with a guide to researching your SEO strategy and then cover some of the most important considerations for a good SEO strategy: technical SEO, site structure, content, mobile and location.

Researching your SEO strategy

One of the biggest mistakes that marketers make when creating an SEO strategy is to start with the following question: 'What keywords should we be focusing on?'

This is not a bad question. In fact it is a very good question, but it should never be the first question asked. The starting point for good SEO, as we have discussed more generally, should be creating the goals and objectives for the SEO channel (for example, will SEO be your primary channel?). Once you have covered those basics the next crucial step is a thorough understanding of your customers.

Persona development

The best way to do this is to create audience personas. Consider the audience types you have and try to create no more than five distinct personas. This approach will help you considerably when you move to the next step of keyword research. Personas and segmentation are discussed in Chapter 1 but it is worth taking a quick look here at how personas apply to SEO. As we have already discussed, personas are a useful way of understanding the personality and potential behaviours of your customers. This becomes useful in SEO (and paid search) in predicting what the user may search for. As we move into the next phase of keyword research (below) this is extremely useful to understand.

If, for example, our persona is a woman in her early thirties with a young family who lives in central New York, we can start to understand some of her daily needs. We can be fairly certain that she is time poor and will want things now, so she may use words such as 'now' and 'fast'. She is likely to want something in New York as it is often harder to travel any significant distance in cities than in rural areas, so she may do a lot of searching for 'in New York' and other local terms. She will probably search for children's products and may also search for helpful tips on parenthood such as 'how much milk should I give my baby' or 'best things to do with kids at the weekend in New York'. She is still young herself though, and so it is likely she will search for babysitters, restaurants and perhaps bars and clubs. She may well buy her groceries online as it is easier than dragging the children around the local store. All of this insight that we can gain from the persona can steer our initial keyword research and we can then use the below process and evolve the campaign over time.

Keyword research

Having created personas the next job is to start to build your focus keyword list. This might seem daunting, especially as some companies have target keyword lists that run in the thousands. However, if you break down the process into the following steps the process is relatively painless:

- Step 1: create logical segments.
- Step 2: mine your data.
- Step 3: mine secondary data sources.
- Step 4: sense check.

Note that within this section we will use the term 'keyword' as a catch-all for search terms. While some searches are just one keyword, increasingly people use natural language and therefore longer phrases.

Step 1: create logical segments

Most businesses sell a multitude of products or services, some of which might well be quite diverse. So a good starting point is to split your products/services into logical segments. The good news is that if your site hierarchy is logical you have probably already done this.

Then consider each segment in detail. Which are the most valuable to you? How do customer types vary? Which should you prioritize?

Step 2: mine your data

An obvious step is to mine the data you already have. However, even in the digital world we sometimes go backwards and, sadly, in October 2011 Google implemented changes that mean it is now extremely difficult to work out the keywords or phrases that site visitors used to find a particular site. What used to be simple (check analytics) is now very difficult. This is due to Google removing the keywords returned within Google Analytics and instead simply labelling all SEO traffic as 'keyword not provided'. This has been a frustration for many digital marketers as knowledge is a crucial part of building any strategy.

However, this SEO cloud may have a silver lining, as ripping keywords directly from analytics could be self-fulfilling prophecy, ie your strategy would be too focused on what you currently rank for rather than what you could rank for. That said, it is worth looking at the data you do have. A good starting point is considering the most visited landing pages as a proxy for user intent. In addition, you may have some data from other search engines, or even historic analytics data, which can help add to the keyword set.

But do not just rely on data that is stored in hardware – brainstorming is a great way to quickly start a keyword list. To do this, review each persona and write down the keywords you think they might use. Spend no more than five minutes for each and focus on the simple/more obvious terms. Once completed, remove any duplicates and you will likely have a fairly short list. This is a good thing – these are most likely your 'halo' terms, or in other words the terms that are most commonly used and therefore have the potential to drive a lot of traffic. At this stage though you don't need to worry whether you have nailed all your halo terms, so long as you have a few the others will come out of the woodwork during the following phases.

Step 3: mine secondary data sources

By this stage you should have established some keywords. The next step is to expand that keyword set. Thankfully there are many third-party tools that can help do this. Rather than offer up a list, simply Google 'keyword research tool' or similar for the latest and greatest. Naturally, one of the best is provided by Google itself (as of course it has more data than most), the Google Adwords Keyword Planner. To access this, you will need an Adwords (Google's paid-search advertising platform) account, but you don't need to actually advertise to use the tool.

Using the tool is fairly self-explanatory, it acts somewhat like a thesaurus offering similar and related terms and, importantly, gives you an idea of the search volume. You will very quickly find that your keyword list has grown substantially. However, the quality of the data you get out is completely dependent on what you put in, so don't be tempted to skip the previous steps. There are of course other tools, both SEMRush and KeywordTool.io are well-respected alternatives.

Step 4: sense check

So now you have a big list. The temptation at this stage is to begin, but a sense check is needed. A very common mistake is to focus too heavily on the search volume: while it is important (as you don't want to pin your business hopes on a term that gets only 10 searches a month) it is only one factor. It is also important to consider the following:

1 What commercial value might this keyword have? For example 'pound/euro exchange rate' has large search volume, but if a bank were to rank number one for the term how many current accounts would get opened on the back of it? Not many. The bank might sell some currency but this term is probably not the most commercially critical.

2 What right do I have to compete for this keyword? There are very few examples of David beating Goliath in the more mature online industries. For example, the keyword 'casino' drives well over 50 per cent of natural search traffic in the online casino market and therefore trying to gain traffic in this industry is difficult without competing for this specific keyword, which is of course very competitive. If you built your site yesterday and have a small marketing budget you are best to point that resource elsewhere. Find a battle you can win and focus your attention there, at least initially.

3 Ask others. Sense check your list with others in the business. Remember: this is the foundation of your SEO strategy so it is worth spending some quality time getting it right.

Technical SEO

Whilst we will not delve deep into technical SEO, in order to understand it fully you at least need to know what the main technical elements are. This section provides a high-level overview of the main technical considerations; however, it is important to know where your strengths are and to appoint an agency to assist you if you do not have deep knowledge or resource in this area.

The tags that matter

The two most significant 'tags' that warrant attention are title tags and meta description (Figure 5.4). Neither are as scary or inaccessible as they might sound.

Title tags

The title tag is a brief description of the page content and is contained within the HTML. It is visible in search results and used by search engines to interpret site pages. Title tags should be unique, ideally less than 75 characters and

FIGURE 5.4   Tags

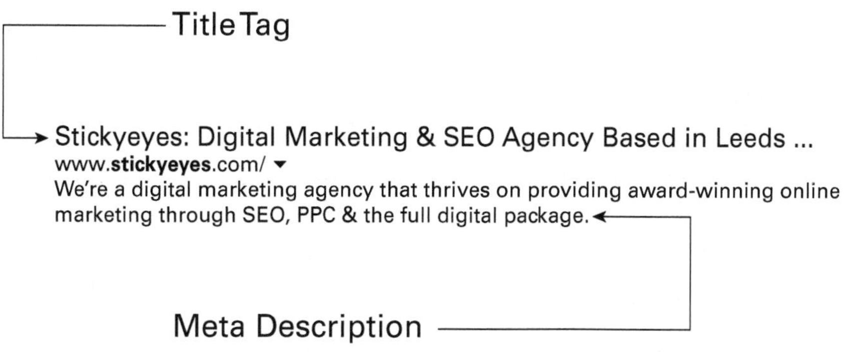

Title Tag

Stickyeyes: Digital Marketing & SEO Agency Based in Leeds ...
www.**stickyeyes**.com/ ▾
We're a digital marketing agency that thrives on providing award-winning online
marketing through SEO, PPC & the full digital package. ◄

Meta Description

have important keywords close to the front. In addition, it is generally good usability practice to include your brand at the front. As the title tag is highly visible to potential site visitors it is of course crucial to make sure it is as compelling as possible.

Meta description

The meta description is a longer description of the page content and is also displayed within the search engine results if Google feels it is relevant. No more than 160 characters are recommended – and make sure they are unique, relevant (and therefore hopefully include some of your focus keywords) and, most importantly, readable. While the meta description does not appear to influence rankings directly, a well-written one can improve click-through rate, which in turn might help drive a ranking improvement.

Site structure

As we are in danger of getting too technical we will not spend too long on this section, but hopefully we can provide enough ammunition to ask some questions of your chosen SEO expert:

- Hierarchy: your navigation flow should be logical. By this we mean that each level of your structure should sit logically below the previous level. For example, a page on your website that promotes ballpoint pens should sit underneath a page on pens, which should in turn sit under a page on stationery so that there is a logical path for a user to follow to effectively filter their way down to their destination. In other words, make sure your hierarchy uses some common sense.

- URL structure: search engines use 'robots' to interpret sites. If your URL looks something like this – **www.mysite.com/categorypage. asp?prodId=1274234** – then you are not helping the robot to work out what your site offers. The ideal is: **www.mysite.com/Stationery/ Paper/A3_Paper/Economy_A3_paper.html.**

- Site maps: create two – one for users and one for search engines. The search-engine-friendly one should be an XML site map file, which can also be submitted through Google's Webmaster Tools (see below).

- Provide alt text for images. In the HTML you can assign 'alt attributes' to help search engines interpret visual content.

- Avoid overusing Flash as it cannot always be read and therefore hinders the discovery process.

- Avoid duplicate content. Note that this means not reusing copy on other pages of your site, as well as 'borrowing' others' content. Google will penalize a site that uses a lot of duplicate content, so it is best avoided. If you cannot avoid duplicate content, do some research on '301 redirects' and the 'rel='canonical' attribute'.

- Webmaster Tools: make sure someone in your organization knows how to navigate Webmaster Tools (a Google-provided platform). Webmaster Tools help in a number of areas and are quite powerful. It is therefore also quite dangerous in the wrong hands, so proceed with caution. A summary of the main functionality available within Webmaster Tools is as follows:
  - Shows crawl errors: this is useful as a site with a lot of errors is unlikely to rank highly.
  - Allows submission of an XML site map.
  - Allows for modification of the robots.txt files (which can be used to remove URLs already crawled by Googlebot).
  - Identify issues with title and description meta tags.
  - Provide a high-level view of the top searches used to reach your site.
  - Remove unwanted site links that Google may use in results.
  - Receive notification of quality guideline violations
  - Request a site reconsideration following a penalty.

The danger mentioned above arises from the fact that these functions could enable someone to cause serious SEO issues to your site such as deleting your robots.txt file, uploading an incorrect site map or simply not being aware of serious SEO issues with the site.

Content

SEO is now much more reliant on a good content strategy. The good news is that there is no real need for a 'Content for SEO' section in this book. Chapter 13, looking at content marketing, works for SEO – as good SEO content is intrinsically linked to good content generally. It is, however, worth taking a quick look here at some specifics.

The content you need

Google uses 'robots' to try to interpret your site. It therefore stands to reason that informative content helps. While you and I can look at a picture of a bag of nails and know what it is, Google struggles (search engines are making progress on image recognition but we cannot rely on it just yet). The content that sits on your site that describes your services/products and so on is commonly referred to as functional content. It will never win any awards but it really is a crucial requirement.

A technically sound site with great functional content will go a long way, but to get real traction the site needs a degree of popularity. To help make it you will need a very different type of content: engaging content. This is content that gets attention from your target audience wherever they may be online. It can be fun (but doesn't have to be), it must be relevant and it must be on brand (for a full definition see Chapter 13). Engaging content done well will get published elsewhere and some will cite or link to your site. Each citation/link acts as a signpost to Google that you are producing something of value that others like and, as such, you might warrant a higher position in the search engines for related terms.

SEO rules for content

As we discussed earlier, the secret to SEO is not to optimize for the search engines but for your audience and this applies to content as much as any other area. If you have done your research right, you should find that you are naturally using very relevant keywords and the content you create should fly. Second, it is important to keep producing. Whilst online content will not disappear unless you delete it, Google does like to see fresh content, so ensuring an ongoing production of content is important. Finally, but perhaps most critically, you should make sure your site has a home for content. The great engaging content you produce should live on your site so that Google knows the origin and so that other sites have a reason to link back to you. This may seem obvious but, with the growth of social media, many companies have concentrated on producing content for YouTube and Twitter at the expense of the content on their own site and this can harm SEO performance.

Mobile

It is increasingly important to ensure that your site renders well on all devices. Today that really means desktop/laptop, tablet and mobile phone. The ideal approach is to create a site that is 'responsive', ie it adapts to the device being used. Although there is a lot of mystery around SEO in general there is 100 per cent clarity on this: Google actively pushes mobile-friendly sites up the rankings when a mobile device is being used. Mobilegeddon in 2015 was a major update to Google's approach to mobile rankings and it is recommended that you read more on this and the other Google updates listed above in order to have an understanding of how Google approaches these things, to gain an insight into its philosophies and to develop a view of what may happen in the future.

Location

Google loves being relevant. If I'm in Madrid and search for 'art museum' I am probably not that interested in reading about the National Portrait Museum in London. So Google includes 'local' results where it can.

Our job as digital marketers is to make sure we make it as easy as possible to let Google know where we are. A chapter could be written on local SEO but the basics are:

- Create a specific location page on your site and ensure that your location(s) (name, address, number) are all in-text so that the robots can read them.
- Create a Google page for your business.
- Get Google reviews. The tipping point for displaying reviews is around five entries, after which you should see the review stars next to your location. To achieve this, though, you may need to educate your customer base on how to leave reviews.

Reviews are an important part of today's internet and this is unlikely to change. Whilst there have been some issues with the authenticity of reviews – such as the news in 2015 that many reviews on Amazon had been produced by individuals who were paid to write them (through no fault of Amazon) – they remain an important influencing factor for shopping online. Encouraging users to visit your Google page and other review centres to leave you a review, if they are satisfied, is good practice. You will almost certainly receive negative reviews as well and it is important not to try to manipulate the result. Ultimately you need to ensure that your service is deserving of positive reviews before you begin, rather than trying to hide the negatives after they start to arrive.

Penalties

Very few marketers have not heard about Google penalties. However, very few actually understand what they really are.

There are two types of Google penalty: 1) algorithmic; 2) manual. But rather than explain the intricacies of each it is perhaps better to briefly cover how to avoid a penalty in the first place. While not exhaustive, the list below will go a long way to keeping you on the right side of Google:

- Check your backlink profile. You will need some SEO expertise to do this, but in short you need to look for the quantity of low-quality/ spammy links you have. If the ratio is high then remedial action may be needed (see below).

- Take remedial action, if needed. If you have a high proportion of links that are clearly low quality then you are advised to remove them. Of course this is not easy as it involves trying to contact webmasters who are unlikely to be that responsive. However, this is the preferred route. A last resort is to use Google's 'Disavow' process. Available through Webmaster Tools the disavow tool allows you to inform Google that you no longer want association with the site links uploaded. However, this is a very powerful and therefore dangerous tool and it would be remiss of me to try to advise on how to use it in one paragraph. In short, get expert help if you think you may need remedial action.

- Do not buy links. The significant majority of your links should be earned. Of course business is business and there may be a place for some high-quality paid placements but they should be the exception rather than the rule. There is a history of a high volume of poor-quality links being bought, when it was volume that counted. This is no longer the case and so paying someone to attain thousands of links for you will be quickly visible to Google, will add almost no value to your SEO and will give you a very high risk of a penalty.

- Check for duplicate content. If you reuse your own content or, worst case, reuse others' content, you may trigger a penalty.

- Ensure that your site is largely original content (not a mash-up of auto-generated content or adverts).

- Ensure that you do not have too many pages with thin or no content (ie few words that add little value).

- When you actively seek out links (ie coverage for the great compelling content you have crafted) make sure you are seeking them from related/relevant sites.

- Avoid unnatural anchor text (anchor text is visible text in a link, for example: cheapest sun tan lotion) – although if you are not buying links this really should not be a problem as most naturally created links will be your brand name.

- If you accept user-generated content, for example reviews, ensure that you are not vulnerable to exploitation by using the nofollow attribute. This ensures that Google will not use your link for SEO purposes and therefore will not punish you.

Organizational structure and SEO

One of the surprisingly important areas of SEO and one that is often overlooked or not implemented, due to its complexity, is organizational structure. To ensure that your SEO strategy can be fully implemented it needs buy-in and ownership from the top down. If your board of directors have the level of understanding that this section offers then you will likely be in a good place – the reason being that to do everything discussed requires multiple departments working very closely together.

CASE STUDY   MoneySupermarket

Background

The UK financial services comparison site MoneySupermarket.com (MSM) is a company that dominates most of the high-volume terms in their market. Very early on, they understood that organizational structure was key to successful SEO.

Strategy

Extracts from an interview with Ben McKay, who was then Head of Organic Performance, explains how they achieved this success:

> We have dissolved the SEO and social media teams in their traditional form, and remoulded them to be more consumer value and campaign centric – the team is now called Organic Performance. This means that the energy and talent of a wide variety of digital marketing professionals is integrated under shared KPIs... Where MSM has been most successful (from its core employees to its board) is by being very ambitious and progressive in removing organizational barriers, and thus helping consumers save money. (McKay in Devenish, 2012)

By developing a strategy that brought content, social media and SEO into one organic team the channels have been able to work much better together.

Results

This organizational change has resulted in MSM becoming perhaps the major player in the financial services space on SEO. As a result, MSM are now returned in results across an extremely wide range of topics and questions as well as having this content distributed through their social channels to a wider audience. For example, if I google 'car insurance quotes' and 'cheap car insurance' in the UK today – two high-volume terms – MSM are top on both. If I search for 'MoneySupermarket' I see 693,000 results, which is 200,000 and 300,000 ahead of their nearest competitors respectively. The numbers speak for themselves.

This has led to their dominance and is one of the major contributing factors to their success whilst their competitors have struggled in the SEO space. This is particularly important in an industry where the above-the-line marketing costs are very high amongst the major four players and a point of marketing differentiation such as this can bring overall acquisition costs down and volumes up.

Key lessons

The key learning for your strategy here is that:

- It is not just good techniques that are important, but also enabling these techniques to strengthen through better integration.

- By pulling together the teams that directly influence the result you can significantly improve performance.

- SEO, social and content are great examples of where you must align your goals and communicate highly effectively.

So, in short, SEO is perhaps the most wide-reaching digital channel and, as such, to get it right you need to consider the structure of your entire organization. In Chapter 15 we look at how to present a strategy to your board and how to influence the decision makers.

Summary

In this chapter we have examined SEO and how it applies to your digital marketing strategy. We started with a look back at this history of SEO, which is essential to understand for this channel in order to gain a perspective on the techniques that should and should not be used. We have looked at how to research your strategy and build an effective and relevant plan. We have also touched briefly on some technical elements, although we avoided going into detail here as this is not a technical manual (please see 'Further reading' for recommendations for additional study). We considered how content affects SEO and we will look at this again in Chapter 13. We also examined mobile and location implications. Finally we looked at the danger that penalties represent and optimizing your organizational structure for SEO.

In this next chapter we look at paid search – the sister of SEO.

Chapter checklist

- A history of SEO ☐
- Researching your SEO strategy ☐
- Technical SEO ☐
- Site structure ☐
- Content ☐
- Mobile ☐
- Location ☐
- Penalties ☐
- Organizational structure and SEO ☐

Further reading

- *On SEO techniques*:

  Williams, A (2015) *SEO 2016 & Beyond*, CreateSpace. This includes detailed analysis on current techniques and an SEO checklist as a tool for preparing your SEO strategy as part of your broader digital strategy.

- *On SEO tips*:

  O'Dwyer, S (2015) *500 SEO Tips*, CreateSpace. This offers a practical look at some simple actions that can be taken to maximize your strategy.

- *On technical SEO*:

  Adodra, S (2014) *SEO Expert Strategies*, CreateSpace. To gain a deeper understanding I would recommend reading this, which looks at SEO in a broader sense than purely technical SEO but it does give clear guidance for beginners and intermediates alike, which you may find helpful alongside this book.

References

Devenish, A (2012) [accessed 1 November 2015] #exclusive MoneySupermarket: We Expect to Save Consumers £1bn in 2012 [Online] https://anthonydevenish. wordpress.com/2012/10/02/exclusive-moneysupermarket-we-expect-to-save-consumers-1bn-in-2012/

Paid search

06

What we will cover in this chapter

In this chapter we look at paid search, including a background on the channel and how to refer to it, how to set up campaigns and measure and optimize your results, as well as advanced techniques and ongoing management. The key areas covered in this chapter are:

- An introduction to paid search
- Setting up a campaign
- Measurement and optimization
- Advanced paid search
- Managing paid search campaigns – humans versus robots

Chapter goals

By the end of this chapter you should understand why and when to use paid search, how to set up a campaign that is relevant to your business, how to optimize and manage the campaign and have a perspective on the advanced techniques used in order to differentiate your organization.

Key terms

Some of the key terms used in this chapter are:

PPC: 'pay per click', a term often used instead of paid search.

SEM: 'search engine marketing' – usually refers to paid search.

Bid: an auction-style bid price for your advert's ranking.

Keyword: the word people use to search.

CPC: 'cost per click' – the amount paid for every click on your ad.

Ad copy: the words that make up your ad.

Match type: the way that your keyword is matched to the phrase searched for.

Quality score: a formula that Google uses to determine your ad quality.

Publisher: a site on a network that shows ads from other organizations.

Search network: a network of sites that provide the search results.

Metrics: a measurement (see below for specific metrics).

Day parting: tailoring your campaign to days and times.

Site link: a link to a part of your website; this is one of the extension options.

Extension: these are extra functions you can add to your campaign.

An introduction to paid search

Paid search is a deceptively complex channel and one that, like many other marketing channels on and offline, takes many years to understand in detail. There are two primary reasons for this. First, paid search has more jargon and acronyms than any other form of digital marketing and so the above key terms may be useful to refer to throughout this chapter. This is ironic, considering that good marketing copywriting involves avoiding exactly this type of situation but, irony aside, it is essential to understand the language of the channel to be able to communicate your strategy effectively. Second, it is remarkably easy to begin paid search activity and to gain an understanding of the very basics but, unfortunately, very difficult to get it right and to understand the tremendous number of options and variables.

As a result, it is important that within this section we start by providing an overview of the basics of paid search (and at the same time tackle the jargon) then quickly move to measurement (as good measurement criteria reduces the risk of getting it wrong). We will of course look at measurement more generally later in the book, but as measurement in paid search is unique and crucial to success it is key that we address it here also. We then cover some of the more advanced paid search techniques and discuss whether humans or robots are best suited to managing paid search. Finally we cover how paid search can work in harmony with SEO, how the boundaries between paid search and display are blurring, and demonstrate how paid search can bring substantial rewards if done correctly.

The main paid search platform is of course Google and therefore this section focuses on the functionality provided by them. However, the others (Microsoft Bing, Yahoo, etc) follow a very similar approach.

The basics of paid search

Paid search can be quite simply defined: it is the process of bidding for potential clicks on an advert you create that is displayed within the search results pages of most search engines. However, given that this is the land of jargon, let's get to the point: it is the ads you see at the top, bottom and side of the search results page. Unlike traditional advertising, paid search is 'bought' via an auction model. For a given keyword or phrase an advertiser can place a maximum bid; the higher the bid, the higher the likelihood that the advert will be displayed in the top positions. However, one of the big attractions of paid search advertising is that the advertiser only pays each time the advert is clicked, not displayed.

This is obviously highly compelling and is perhaps the main reason why paid search has been adopted by one-man bands, multinationals and every company in-between.

What do we call the channel?

Confusingly the industry has seen fit to use different terms to describe the same thing, so let's start by clarifying this. Paid search can also be referred to as:

- PPC, or pay per click: quite a logical name, given that it very accurately describes the basic mechanics of paid search – ie you pay every time someone clicks on your ad. However, some other channels, such as affiliate and display, can use this payment method and so it can be confusing.

- SEM, or search engine marketing: SEM was once used as an umbrella term to encompass both search engine optimization and paid search, albeit mainly in the United States. Somewhat oddly the industry, again though mainly in the United States, has adopted the SEM acronym to refer solely to paid search, therefore creating a split between SEO and SEM.

- Biddable media: a newer term that covers any media you can bid on to buy. So paid search sits under biddable media.

Of all of these terms paid search is the clearest and most accurate so that is the one we use here.

Setting up a campaign

As noted above, setting up a paid search campaign is incredibly easy. However, many businesses will see this as an easy entry to digital marketing but it is important before starting to consider this: paid search can drain marketing spend very quickly and an ill-considered campaign may very well have a negative return. So this section is designed to cover the basics of getting a strategic paid search campaign set up. As per the approaches we have been discussing so far, it starts with defining your objectives and understanding your audience. We will assume that you have looked at this as part of your initial strategic planning.

Keyword research

Having set your objective and identified your audience, the next step is keyword research. In Chapter 5 there is a suggested process for this and it applies just as well to paid search. Perhaps unsurprisingly, Google's own keyword analyser (available as part of the Adwords platform) is a great tool for building out keywords. However, as with SEO, you need to pick your battles. If your budget is $500 a month, then the highly popular volume-driving or 'halo' terms are not within your budget and instead you should focus on niche or longer tail keywords that you are more likely to win the battle on. To put this into context, some of the most expensive keywords have average cost per clicks well above $50 and so you can see how quickly your budget can be depleted if your keyword research and planning is not conducted thoroughly.

Campaigns and ad groups

Google and thousands of other sources provide plenty of guidance on how to structure a paid search account. In short, you will have one or more campaigns. A campaign defines your overall budget settings and determines where your ads appear (both in terms of geography and ad networks).

If you are setting up the paid search campaign for an auto dealership, for example, you might have one campaign for cars and a separate campaign for bikes. Within a campaign you should have a number of ad groups. Think of ad groups as logical storage buckets. You would not throw all your stock into one big bucket so don't do the same with your ads. Each ad group should contain similar keywords/phrases and therefore similar products. So you might in the cars campaign have an ad group for each individual type of car you sell.

For example:

- Campaign one – cars:
  - ad group one: Fords;
  - ad group two: Toyotas.
- Campaign two – bikes:
  - ad group one: Harley Davidsons;
  - ad group two: Triumphs.

Think strategically

The keywords are the start of the user journey. This is what your user is specifically looking for. Users are individuals and want to be treated as such, therefore try to ensure that your journey is as unique as it can be. You can best achieve this by aligning your journeys to the user needs and this means creating a very large and organized set of keywords. Spending the time building out your keywords can be the difference between success and failure.

Ad copy

Paid search ad copy is an art form as you have a limited number of characters (130 including the display URL and just 63 characters for double-width languages such as Chinese, Japanese and Korean) to create something that is highly relevant and compelling. The good news is there is no limit to the number of ads you can create, so try out a few and refine as you go.

Think strategically

Following on from the section above, at this stage it is vital that your ad copy matches to the search term as closely as possible.

Ad copy

A manufacturer of socks would have a wide range of socks available, including smart socks, sports socks, casual socks and perhaps even tights. Differentiating these is vital in your ad copy to ensure maximum relevance to the user. Imagine if a user searches for 'white sports socks' and receives the following three ads in the results from three separate companies:

- Buy white socks today.

- White sports socks.

- Get cheap socks here.

Option two is returned based on the campaign set-up and is an exact match to the keyword, as the account has been built into a logical structure with deep customization to keyword type. This option is clearly a perfect match to what the user is looking for and will receive an increased level of clicks versus other ads that are returned in the same position. This in turn means that this company can bid lower in the knowledge that being returned in position two or three is fine as the relevance of their ad will ensure that they still receive the most clicks.

Match types

Once you have created your ads and defined your keyword list you need to consider match types for each keyword. In short, you can tell Google whether you want your ads to appear for just the exact keyword/phrase entered or widen it out with a number of parameters – the widest being a 'broad match', which will show your ads for the keywords/phrases requested and any related keywords. Broad matching will generate the most traffic, but by its very nature it will be less targeted and therefore performance may not be as good. In addition, broad match can very quickly get expensive. Typically most paid search experts only use broad match for an initial period of exploration to help find the keywords/phrases that convert the best.

A description of the various match types, courtesy of Google, has been included in Table 6.1. The final modifier in Table 6.1, 'negative match', is worthy of more detailed discussion as it can be very powerful. A detailed review of your ad campaign will likely show some keywords/phrases that are not a good match to the products/services you sell. If this is the case you will potentially be displaying irrelevant ads, which will affect your click-through rate (and in turn your cost per click as quality score (see below) may be affected). Removing these erroneous keywords/phrases using negative keywords is therefore highly recommended.

TABLE 6.1 Match types

Match Type	s=Symbol	Keywords for this Match Type	Your Ads Will Show on the Following Searches	Example Searches
Broad match		white socks	These words, similar words and misspelt words	buy socks
Broad match modifier	+	+white +socks	Containing these words in other orders	socks that are white
Phrase match	" "	"white socks"	This phrase and very similar ones	cheap white socks
Exact match	[ ]	[white socks]	The exact phrase and ones that are very close	white socks
Negative match	-	-white	Anything that excludes this word	black socks

Quality score

Quality score is a Google metric and is a measure of the quality of the ad. The higher the quality score, the higher your position potential. If, for example, two advertisers both have a maximum bid of $10 but one has a higher quality score, the one with the higher quality score will likely be given the higher position. Indeed, even if the maximum bid for the company with the higher quality score was $9 they may still get the higher position. Why? Because Google wants to present ads that people will find relevant and click on. The quality score algorithm is not publicly available but some of the factors that contribute to a higher score are, including how long you have been advertising, your click-through rates (CTRs) and your ad relevancy.

Search networks

Before you push your new paid search campaign live, be wary of checking the option to 'also display ads on our search network' (or similar). Checking this allows the search engine to display your ads on third-party sites that have signed up to their ad programme as a publisher. You will have very little control of where your ads are displayed and invariably performance is much lower (albeit so is the cost). The positive is that your reach is enhanced.

When looking at paid search most of us will start with the Google product, Adwords.

Measurement and optimization

As we discuss later in the book, before looking into measurement it is essential to revisit your objectives, as this will help shape the measurement criteria used. For example, if your goal is to maximize market share then acquisition metrics should not be your number one priority.

Traffic metrics

- Impression: each time your ad is displayed an impression is made. So 10 impressions = 10 views – or, more precisely, 10 'renders', as of course there is no guarantee that the user actually looks at it.
- Click: (a no-brainer) a click is a user interacting with the ad by clicking on it. The end result is a visit to your site.
- Click-through rate (CTR): usually abbreviated to CTR, this is the ratio of the number of clicks to the number of impressions (clicks/impressions). CTRs are influenced by ad position, ad copy and brand recognition.
- Cost per click (CPC): CPC is the average amount paid for a click. Of course this will fluctuate based on maximum bid levels and competitive pressure.
- Average position: the average position where your ad appears on the page (the very top of the page being first position). Bear in mind that

ad positions do fluctuate even if you are the highest bidder. Ad position is heavily influenced by your bid level but it is also influenced by quality score (see below).

- Impression share: a measure of how much of the available impressions you have captured, the maximum being position one for 100 per cent of the time.

- Quality score (QS): while not technically a traffic metric, quality score still needs close consideration as it has a direct relationship to ad position and therefore traffic potential.

Conversion metrics

- Revenue generated: simply the value of the sales made. While interesting, it is margin that really counts.

- Margin generated: margin, or gross profit, gives a more accurate view of the profitability of paid search campaigns.

- Orders: the raw number of orders made.

- Leads: for some, typically B2B or companies selling high-value products, leads are the ultimate goal. Leads might be, for example, e-mail sign-up, application completion or request for brochures.

- Conversion rate: conversion rate is the ratio of orders/leads to the number of clicks. It is as much a measure of your site's ability to convert traffic as the ad itself.

- Average order value (AOV): AOV speaks for itself and is an important metric to drill down on. Look for patterns over time and also differences in AOV for different ad groups. If one ad group has particularly low or high AOV, question why. It may be down to low/high product cost/margin but also may reflect particularly good or bad ad copy or bidding strategy.

Efficiency metrics

- Return on investment (ROI): the most common measure. While this can be a revenue measure (revenue derived/ad cost) it is better to consider profitability and use margin/ad cost.

- Cost per lead/order (CPL/CPO): given that a lead may not bear commercial fruit for some time (and indeed the end transaction might be difficult to tie back if it is made offline) CPL is a good measure of performance for advertisers not expecting direct sales.

- Lifetime value (LTV): lifetime value is an estimate of the potential value that each new customer driven will generate. While it takes some number crunching, this is a very worthwhile process. It is too easy to consider a paid search campaign a failure if the ROI does not stack up; LTV analysis is the only real way to assess whether paid search truly makes sense or not.

Test, learn, refine, test...

Having defined what you will measure, and how, the next step is to put in place a process of continuous improvement. Paid search is simple to get into and therefore it is not surprising that for most sectors the level of competition is high. Therefore an account that is working well today might start failing tomorrow if you do not put in place a process of continuous improvement.

Advanced paid search

Below I have outlined some of the more advanced paid search considerations.

Day parting

Day parting, or custom ad scheduling, allows you to control the days of the week and times of day that you want your ads to display, and also adjust the maximum bid levels based on these parameters.

Site link extensions

Site links allow you to present alternative links within your ad. In the example shown in Figure 6.1, the consumer review publication *Which?* uses site links on the ad that displays for the terms 'laptop reviews' in order to present other related links.

Star ratings

The eagle eyed will have noticed that the *Which?* ad in Figure 6.1 also has a star rating. These ratings are in fact fully automated. However, in order to show, your business needs to hit certain criteria: 1) at least 30 reviews within

FIGURE 6.1   Site links

Which?® Laptop Reviews - Compare 11 Laptop Brands

Ad www.which.co.uk/Which-**Laptop-Reviews** ▼
4.3 ★★★★★ rating for which.co.uk
Sign Up Now For Your £1 Trial!
"...Impartial reviews on all products on the market..." – This Is Money
Which? has 66,420 followers on Google+
Other Technology Reviews - Buy With Confidence - 100% Unbiased Reviews

the last 12 months; 2) an average rating of 3.5 or higher (so you will never show a poor star rating).

The rating received is an aggregate from a number of sources, both Google (such as Google Certified Shops) and third-party review sites (Google lists over 30 and they include Bazaarvoice, Bizrate, Feefo, Reevoo and Trustpilot).

Click to call

If you have the ability to take orders over the phone then adding your phone number to an ad is advised as it will drive up conversions. In most sophisticated mobiles a click-to-call button will be displayed.

Location extensions

Google is increasingly focused on providing hyper local results. The growth of mobile browsing has made this easier as location is straightforward to calculate. In addition, mobile browsers are more likely to be looking for a local solution. So if your business has physical stores, location extensions are very powerful as they allow the display of your business address, phone number and a map. On mobile devices, a link with directions to your business can be included. The starting point for displaying location information is the 'Google My Business' service, which will also help you to appear in Google Maps and organic listings.

Product list ads (Google Shopping)

Product list ads (often abbreviated to PLAs) are Google's way of shortcutting customers directly to a product. They are increasingly prominent in the search results, which is a reflection of their power to convert customers (Figure 6.2).

FIGURE 6.2   Product list ads

Shop for mothers day flowers on Google				Sponsored ⓘ
True Blue Iris	Simply Tulips - Online Flower	Pink Lady - Flower Delivery	32 British Alstroemeria	Mother's Day Flowers - ...
£25.00	**£17.95**	**£22.95**	**£24.98**	**£18.99**
Flowers Direct	eFlorist	eFlorist	ArenaFlowers...	Flowerfete

PLAs are controlled via a shopping campaign and require your product inventory to be submitted to Google Merchant Centre. What may seem on the face of it to be quite complex is in fact relatively straightforward, and if you are retailing low- to mid-cost products, it is highly recommended.

Competitive intelligence

While the various enhanced options will help you to hone your campaign it is important to remember that paid search ads are an auction. In other words, it is you versus your competitors. It is therefore crucial to ensure that you are tracking what your competitors are doing in order to make sure that you can stay one step ahead. This can be as simple as simply viewing the ads that appear when you google your key terms. However, if you depend heavily on Adwords and/or have a large budget then you will want to consider a tool that tracks ads for you. Examples are Market Defender, AdGooroo and AdThena.

These products allow you to analyse competitive data at your leisure and typically include:

- competitive ad copy;
- day parting strategy;
- split testing evidence.

As well as competitive intelligence such tools can also be used to identify brand hijacking. Brand hijacking is typically performed by an affiliate or a company selling fake goods. In short, they bid on your brand name and pass off as being your business. If you are a large advertiser, this reason alone is enough to warrant investing in an ad tracking solution.

Managing paid search campaigns – humans versus robots

All small to medium-sized enterprises (SMEs) will manage their paid search campaigns either internally or via an agency and ultimately humans will be doing all the work. However, some larger organizations use automated bidding systems. Whether this is the right route for you will depend on a number of factors but the most common reasons for considering an automated tool are:

- Tens or hundreds of thousands of products. It is unrealistic to expect humans to be able to manage a large quantity of products. Especially so when you consider stock issues and fluctuating pricing.

- Very large budget. If your monthly ad spend is measured in millions then at least some form of automation starts to makes sense.

- Your main goal is hyper efficiency. If you want to drive your cost per click as low as possible then machines are generally better (however, this can result in a much smaller share of voice-over time if not managed well).

In summary, the best combination is usually one of the following: 1) humans; 2) humans who very actively manage automated systems.

Summary

In this chapter we looked at what paid search is and how it can be integrated into your strategy. We examined the complexities of setting up a campaign and the extent of the jargon and variables that need to be understood in order to be able to optimize your campaign. We looked at the methods of measuring and optimizing your results as well as ensuring that you test and learn constantly. We examined advanced techniques and how to manage your campaign on an ongoing basis. There is a great deal of complexity in this channel and so working with an expert is essential until you are capable of running the channel yourself. It should be noted that, if you are running a large digital campaign, you may never get to the level of expertise on this channel that is necessary to run it yourself and so working with the right agency, as we have discussed, is vital.

- An introduction to paid search ☐
- Setting up a campaign ☐
- Measurement and optimization ☐
- Advanced paid search ☐
- Managing paid search campaigns – humans versus robots ☐

Further reading

- *On Adwords*:

  Rabazinski, C (2015) *Adwords for Beginners*, CreateSpace
- *On advanced paid search*:

  Geddes, B (2014) *Advanced Google Adwords*, Sybex

Display

07

What we will cover in this chapter

In this chapter we look at display advertising (often known as banner advertising), which has a rich and interesting history and future. Display was one of the first forms of online marketing and has changed significantly over time. We look at those changes, at programmatic technology, types of display advertising and how to run the channel as part of your strategy. The key areas covered in this chapter are:

- A brief history
- Programmatic advertising
- Types and formats of display advertising
- Ad servers and technological delivery
- Types of display campaign
- Planning and targeting display campaigns
- Display campaign measurement and attribution modelling

Chapter goals

By the end of this chapter you should understand the history of display and therefore some of the risks and opportunities within the channel. You should understand the technology and how this relates to planning, targeting and managing a campaign. You should also understand measurement and the key terms used in the channel. This will help you to understand whether the channel is appropriate for you and, if so, how to fit it into your strategy.

Some of the key terms used in this chapter are:

Pop-up: a display advert that pops up in front of what you are viewing.

CPM: a cost-per-thousand price (CPM = 'cost per mille').

Impression: when an advert is shown.

Assets: the creative files used for the advert.

Ad server: databases that help to co-ordinate and manage campaigns.

Programmatic: a method of automated bidding.

Retargeting: targeting a user again based on previous behaviours.

Note: there are many more terms used in display advertising and I have tried to define these throughout the chapter.

Display advertising has many different guises and many different definitions depending on whom you ask and where you are in the world. Indeed, these definitions have changed over time, as digital advertising has evolved. Display advertising sees spend levels continue to grow and, according to the IAB/PwC spend figures for the full year of 2014, the sector was worth £2.27 billion in 2014, a 26.4 per cent rise year on year (IAB UK, 2015).

FIGURE 7.1   An example of a display advert

Cheap holidays

SALE: Cheap flights to Majorca

From £69

The top 10 things to do in Majorca

Majorca is an island of the Balearics off the coast of Spain. Offering wonderful weather, short flights and a range of activities it can be a perfect get away for couples, singles and families alike.

To make the most of your time there we have compiled a list of the top ten

A brief history

The early days

Display advertising is one of the longest-enduring digital ad formats and shares ancestry with many non-digital types of advertising. Even the terminology used in some elements of the booking and delivery process indicates this. For example, an insertion order (IO), which is the document used to secure ad space in newspapers and magazines, is also the instruction to run a display campaign. In fact there is a lot of commonality with the print media and out-of-home disciplines and display adverts, especially early on in the life of digital advertising.

Three factors that display has in common with print media are:

- graphical media (imagery rather than copy based);
- uniform sizes (specific pixel sizes);
- a broadcast approach (rather than direct).

However, since the early days of display adverts being booked onto websites, for fixed periods of time, and being largely static and 'hard-coded' into the web page, things have come a long way. Display adverts now come in thousands of sizes, and they have copy that can change based on the content the ad is adjacent to, who the viewer of an individual ad is and whether a particular user has been exposed to or interacted with an advert. Animation has become a standard feature and the functionality that can exist in an ad unit is almost endless, ranging from simple form fields for data capture to content interactivity (including gamification) as well as adverts that play high-definition video content. A really interesting example of this is CBS Interactive's launch of the DVD of the movie *Inception*. The ad was placed on the Gamespot website and the site appeared to fall over to reveal a video behind it. The result of this fantastic concept was a click-through rate 247 per cent above the benchmark (Geifman, 2011).

The curse of the pop-up

One example of a route in display that is not so appreciated but still exists in some areas is the pop-up. The pop-up advert typifies the overly intrusive display format – it is totally interruptive to the browsing habits of the user and can become very annoying. Pop-up adverts are currently still seen in very specific environments and still prove effective for some advertisers. At the time of writing, the adult and gambling industries are still using pop-ups and so they are now primarily associated with the industries that are less acceptable in the mainstream. One of the primary reasons for this is because, despite clearly bringing results in certain circumstances, there is a cost to using them beyond the monetary cost of the placement. That is that they risk eroding brand equity by annoying the user and are therefore considered by many brands to be unsuitable and unusable. Brands in the adult and gambling industries are often more willing to take these risks. As a result of this association with these industries, pop-ups are now also associated with viruses and security risks, which further discourage strong brands from using them.

Beyond the first adverts

The display industry has developed at speed and this is only getting faster. There have, however, been three distinct stages to date that typify how display was planned and delivered:

1. Direct to site

Planning and buying used to be a painless and very straightforward affair. In the early commercial days of the internet, circa 1995, there were tens to hundreds of websites that made commercial sense for most blue-chip and large companies with strong advertising budgets to place adverts on. This made planning and execution relatively straightforward and a manageable task. Adverts were commonly coded straight into the website page or the creative assets sent directly to the publisher to deal with after a negotiation on price and duration. Frequently internet advertising space was given away gratis with print media bookings in the leading news and magazine titles.

2. Technology to streamline processes

The significant growth in online spend and traffic in the early 21st century was coupled with an explosion of websites fuelled further by effectiveness of search engines. This presented the display industry with several issues to overcome. First was the planning issue of having a greater, more fragmented selection of sites to run campaigns across. Established bodies such as the Audit Bureau of Circulation helped to quantify traffic volumes to sites and new measurement companies such as Hitwise, now owned by Experian, addressed the lack of independent measurement and quantification of audience that websites had.

In the earlier years media planners and buyers had an idea of where to place adverts and how many impressions were potentially available, but the next immediate problem was being certain they were actually receiving what they had bought, as no first-hand visibility of measurement was in place. This, coupled with the increased amount of work involved in booking media with each additional website, required a solution. These two issues were resolved by one of the single most important components of display advertising – the ad server. The ad server is detailed in the following section but essentially it provided a solution to these two problems:

- Simplifying the workflow. Getting creative to publishers' sites by holding a library of the different sizes and/or versions of the creative and delivering them to a publisher's website when needed. This allows advertisers to more easily work with multiple publishers and vice versa.

- Providing an independent count of how many ad impressions had been delivered by publishers for auditing and dispute reconciliation.

This set the scene for modern display advertising.

3. The rise of the ad network and the pitfalls of bad planning and bad quality

Now that there is sufficient technology in place to measure and track spend across multiple publishers, a new breed of advertising company has emerged to address the problem of the amount of work involved in making bookings. These newer and sometimes niche sites often have much lower traffic, but as they are often more specialized in their content they are as valuable as sites with much more traffic. If we picture all of the websites on the internet as being on a scale, we would find a few large websites with billions of available ad impressions per year at one end of the scale and millions of websites with only thousands of available impressions at the other end. Ad networks solved this problem for media buyers. They made the large volume of smaller sites accessible by grouping these sites into categories and delivering their clients' adverts accordingly in order to get the best results. Early on they started to employ technology to match available impressions to adverts that were contextually relevant. The pioneer was Advertising.com, still going and owned by internet giant AOL.

Programmatic advertising

Programmatic media buying and its subset real-time bidding (RTB) has gone a long way to solving the problems that display has faced. Programmatic allows buyers to assess every single ad impression as it becomes available (as a user's device is loading a web page or app) and make a decision as to whether this particular ad impression will make a positive contribution to the campaign as a whole. This can be decided based on factors that pertain to the environment that the ad is in. The advertiser can therefore assess the following factors to determine whether the opportunity is relevant:

- the website;
- the specific web page;
- the context of the article or video it surrounds;
- the location of the person looking at it;
- the time of the day, or day of the week;
- the computer operating system, mobile operating or type of device it is being viewed on;
- the propensity for that advert to be classed as 'in view' based on previous viewability rate of that ad's placement;
- the type of content the ad is next to (is it dangerous, defamatory or potentially scandalous for the advertiser to place an ad here?).

Or the known attributes of the user who is behind the screen:

- Are they known to the advertiser?
- If CRM information has been synchronized with the buying platform (known as a demand-side platform, or DSP) whether they are a frequent customer, a high-value customer, a low-value customer or someone to whom it is not worth showing adverts.
- Whether they have started to make a purchase on the advertiser's site and qualify to be shown a retargeting message.
- Their demographic, psychographic and behavioural qualities (see the section below on targeting display with data).

For example, if you are advertising televisions then the following scenarios could occur:

- Scenario A: your ad would appear on an iPhone but your website is not responsive.
  Decision: the experience would be so poor that you may harm your image –do not show the ad.
- Scenario B: your ad would be viewed by a user who regularly visits your site but never buys.

Decision: he or she is not a serious customer, just a browser – do not show the ad.

- Scenario C: the user started to buy a TV last week but dropped out of the funnel.
  Decision: a hot prospect – show a retargeting message to try to convert them on their attempted purchase.

All of these options are available to buyers across the whole of the campaign.

More importantly, the revelation for advertisers is that they now only have to buy the ad impressions they actually want. Buying targeted inventory has always enabled this to an extent but within that targeted inventory there may be people in the wrong age range, income range or gender for the advertiser's product. In the case of RTB impressions there is also the option for the advertiser to submit a bid for that single impression so it can be bought at a price point that is beneficial to the campaign goals as well.

The difference between programmatic and RTB is that programmatic provides the ability to assess impressions on an individual basis and RTB adds an auction element to some of those impressions. Programmatic impressions that are not bought by RTB are often agreed media buys with publishers to access certain targeting options or preferential rates that are unique to that publisher. These arrangements are called private marketplaces (PMPs); however, the advertiser still has the right not to buy an impression if it does not fit the immediate requirements of the campaign. The RTB element, often referred to as open exchange buying, has little restriction to entry and the targeting listed above can be applied to both. Fundamentally it is programmatic that provides this addressability that is seen in display today, by combining multiple data and decision-making options across the whole of the media campaign. The result is extremely effective campaigns.

CASE STUDY   Nestlé: improving campaign performance and effectiveness with programmatic advertising

Background

Nestlé's Dolce Gusto coffee-machine brand wished to improve the efficiency and therefore results of their display advertising. The goals were to increase awareness among new audiences and deliver a campaign with a high viewability rate (see definition below).

Strategy

Nestlé's media agency opted to deliver Dolce Gusto's campaign entirely using programmatic technology. This enabled the agency to both control the delivery of the campaign in terms of targeting it to coffee, food, appropriate lifestyle sites and also to find the target audiences on sites with less contextual relevance. Perhaps more importantly, it also enabled the agency to take data signals from Dolce Gusto's website to dictate campaign delivery. It also used programmatic technology to suppress known Dolce Gusto machine owners. These would be users who were only viewing replacement coffee capsules and parts, who were logging into the site's members' area and who had recently registered ownership of a new machine. Despite these users fitting a lot of the targeting criteria, they were excluded from being shown adverts. This simple step allowed Dolce Gusto's ad spend to penetrate further into new audiences. Additionally, the known owners were used for lookalike modelling to identify other users whose browsing habits matched those of the known customers. In the delivery of the campaign, the agency also closely watched which sites were delivering consistently high rates of viewability. These sites would be examined individually for the benefit they might bring to the campaign (highly relevant content, site quality and amount of ad placements per page).

Results

By excluding all known customers and owners of Dolce Gusto machines the campaign was able to place advertising in front of almost entirely new visitors to Dolce Gusto's website – 91 per cent of all visitors were previously unknown to Dolce Gusto during the campaign's delivery period. The campaign achieved an 84 per cent viewability rate, which was 21 per cent higher than the average rate as measured by the IAB (IAB, 2012)

Key lessons

Viewability is a measure that is more detailed than an impression in that it covers not just that an add is shown but that the ad is shown in the viewable screen.

Types and formats of display advertising

The most common form of display advertising formats are banners. These have many sizes and are constantly evolving to cope with new screen sizes and resolutions, new devices and also new ways to entice and capture the attention of web users. These are displayed in-page, which is to say that they are situated within the layout of the web page itself:

- In-page banner adverts: these are the banner adverts that are ubiquitous around the web. They come in a variety of sizes and need to adhere to strict guidelines so that they can be delivered. These adverts can also be highly customizable to what an individual user has seen or done. In-page banners are typically animated and are designed and built to specifications laid down by the Internet Advertising Bureau (IAB). If an advert simply and passively animates on a page it is almost certainly a standard in-page banner.

A display advert that does anything else becomes referred to as rich media. This is a cover-all term used to describe any display advert that is interactive in any way (such as responding to a user hovering their cursor over the creative) or does anything more than simply existing next to content as described above:

- In-page rich media: these are in-page adverts that have much more functionality or content than a standard banner. The most common examples are:
  - Video adverts: where a full video can play inside the ad creative.
  - Expandable adverts: where the ad expands to take up more (or all) of the web page if the user interacts with it. These interactions can be a mouse-over (or hover) for a period of time or a click. Some formats can expand to take over all or most of the screen (especially in mobile advertising) and that space can be used for far more than graphics – a microsite could be hosted inside the ad, for example.
  - Data capture: adverts where the user can submit their e-mail address to sign up for a newsletter or receive a reminder of a product launch date.
  - Live information: such as prices of an airline route or remaining stock levels for a heavily discounted or extremely popular product, which can be piped into advert creative from product feeds and point of sale (POS) systems.
  - Mobile ad units: these can also take control of some of the phone's features and sensors such as the accelerator and camera, which could be used to personalize or provide an element of gamification to an advert.

- In-stream: this is video creative that plays before, during or after video content on the web. Depending on this positioning, these are commonly known as:
  - pre-roll;
  - mid-roll;
  - post-roll.

Video advertising is extremely close to TV advertising in both the content and the form – ad slots are typically of a duration of either 15 or 30 seconds and it is common for advertisers to replicate their TV adverts completely. There are, as always in digital, ways to provide interactivity.

- Skippable video: since 2012 YouTube have offered an additional form of video advertising called True-View (other video providers now offer similar solutions). These adverts can be skipped by the user, which brings three big advantages over traditional in-stream placements:
  - The skippable format results in users watching the ad who truly are interested in it.
  - It takes away the content length restrictions. As the user gets the opportunity to skip the ad, the broadcaster (YouTube) is happy for the creative to be any length up to 10 minutes.
  - Pricing: the advertiser only pays for adverts that have not been skipped.

The formats and guidelines can be found on the IAB's website: **www.iab.net**.

Ad servers and technological delivery

What is an ad server?

Ad servers are a core part of the display advertising ecosystem and are used by advertisers, agencies and media owners. They are fundamentally databases but they have evolved into serious pieces of technology and their uses, although not limited to the following, include:

- storing advertising creative;
- passing correct advertising creative to publishers, networks and demand-side platforms;
- managing sequential messaging and creative iteration testing;

- creating and maintaining control/expose groups for testing and surveying;
- recording where adverts have been shown and who they have been seen by;
- storing and creating tags for distribution to publishers;
- creating and counting cookies for exposure and conversion tracking;
- providing comprehensive reporting of media activity, including attribution.

Advertisers (and their agencies), publishers and ad networks use ad servers to deliver, measure, report and verify campaign delivery. The primary function is to serve advert creative to users' browsers when the browser requests a certain web page. This request involves at least two parties but can have up to several requests in the chain. For example:

- publisher > advertiser;
- publisher > sales house > network 1 > network 2 > agency > advertiser;
- publisher > agency > advertiser.

The publisher's ad server is primarily concerned with keeping their website furnished with adverts as visitors view pages, while maximizing revenue from advertising campaigns, commonly known as yield. When a publisher has multiple campaigns running from direct bookings and bulk channels such as ad networks, the publisher's ad server will be considering:

- User: which adverts from which campaigns the user has been exposed to on their site so far this visit.
- Campaign: does the user fit any targeting criteria specified by the advertiser?
- Frequency: has the user been exposed to the specified limit of adverts for the campaign for any given period?
- Delivery: making sure that all campaigns are delivered in full.
- Yield: ensuring that the most profitable campaigns are prioritized for delivery over low-yielding ones.

As far as delivery is concerned the advertiser's ad server is more focused on:

- serving any user the correct creative if there are multiple versions, which may need to be shown to different audiences (for example, new and returning customers);

- monitoring delivery across multiple publishers or networks and programmatic elements of the campaign.

Fundamentally ad servers take control of ad campaigns and allow advertisers and their agencies to control the management of tags and pixels, track user activity and analyse advertising activity at the end of a campaign or period. However, increasingly, as advertising technology is becoming more integrated, the ad server's role is developing. This is especially true of DoubleClick™, which has been developed to bring together all of Google's marketing technology platforms.

Types of display campaign

Display advertising has many applications and purposes but below are three main purposes for display advertising: awareness, direct response prospecting and retargeting.

Awareness

This delivers brand messages or immerses customers with interactive experiences to make them aware of a brand, product or service and its benefits. It is far less accountable for providing sales in a direct response approach than the below purposes of display – awareness application of display is not intended to provide sales or be measured that way. Rich media and video are common formats for this.

How this applies to your strategy

If your business is less focused on direct sales through digital channels, such as car manufacturers or estate agents, for example, then brand awareness plays a major part in your conversion journey. Even if you are focused on high volumes of sales online you may play in a highly competitive market that therefore creates a need for awareness advertising.

Direct response prospecting

To find users for a particular product or service and aid consumers on the path to conversion, this activity seeks to find users in highly relevant areas of the web and is really the most versatile use of display. Any direct response advertiser should be using this to gain new customers. Prospecting can actually be used as a proxy for awareness as it is showing adverts to new users; however, as there is often a CPA goal it is done in a more subtle way using more cost-effective formats – mainly banner creative.

How this applies to your strategy

If your business is focused on sales then ensuring you are targeting the right customers at the right time with the right message – and therefore achieving the maximum sales volume at the lowest cost per acquisition – will be a key goal. This is where direct response display fits in. This is the area where people are most sceptical about display due to its history (as discussed above), but this history is no longer relevant.

Retargeting

This is exactly like remarketing lists for search ads (RLSA) activity in search but far more powerful as adverts can be shown to non-converting customers across the whole internet, as opposed to simply when they use a search engine. Because this uses first party data from users' actions on an advertiser's website it actually helps secure sales from all marketing, PR and promotional activity.

How this applies to your strategy

Retargeting customers can increase conversion rates from existing visitors. This can be highly targeted by following users with reminders of the products and prices they have been quoted. This can be highly effective in ensuring that your conversion rate is optimized even after the user has dropped out of the funnel. Retargeting has been given a bad reputation by some early companies who exploited it to give the illusion that their overall display activity performed better than it was. If retargeting data is mixed in as part of the overall performance data for a display campaign it can artificially inflate the click-through rate. This is due to the fact that retargeting is aimed at warm prospects whereas other display advertising is cold. It is vitally important to use advertisers' data responsibly. Retargeting with dynamic creative is very common for e-commerce advertisers, especially those operating in retail and travel sectors, where people commonly shop around for very similar versions of products.

Planning and targeting display campaigns

Now that we understand the history and key areas of display we can look at planning a campaign before going on to consider measurement. Successful display campaigns, like most other marketing channels, revolve around the simple principle of delivering the right message to the right audience at the right time. The balance and importance of these aspects can shift depending on the objectives involved, but they always play a part.

There are numerous methods for targeting display campaign delivery and some, like reporting metrics, can be specific to the creative format, site or device the user is viewing or using. There is some ambiguity when categorizing the types of targeting, but broadly methods can be put into four categories:

- Audience: targeting a group of users based on who they are and/or what they do.

- Contextual: targeting people who are viewing particular content or specific sites and apps.

- Environmental: the wider factors around delivery and the audience that do not relate to the content that the advert is adjacent to.

- Data modelled: looking at a multitude of available data points and typically using computer modelling to extrapolate audiences.

Display campaigns rarely use any of these methods in isolation but look at using combinations of targeting to deliver adverts more effectively. This is especially true of programmatic campaign delivery, thanks to technology being able to bring all of this data together. As the technology and data available to us increases in complexity, the way campaigns are planned and executed does likewise.

Planning display

At the planning stage a media plan is created that will outline how a campaign will be delivered. The plan and resulting campaign is defined by the targeting tools and data available to the industry at that time, but the plan ultimately needs to deliver the combination of websites, apps, audiences and strategies in order to reach the intended target audience and effectively achieve the campaign objective. This may be simply to reach as many of the target audience as possible or to contribute directly to sales volume.

ComScore and Nielsen are two giants of planning companies. They are able to provide you with information about where a particular audience can be found online (typically by demographic and behaviour) and what percentage of that audience can be found on particular websites. This data used to be gathered from samples and extrapolated, the same as TV, but is increasingly relying on direct data sources. These companies can be used to assess whether a campaign was delivered to the correct audience. Similar companies provide publishers and planners with more qualitative information about users, such as TGI, who provide survey-based information about the interests and habits of the consumer in order to enrich the data. Companies such as these provide a service to publishers and planners – allowing publishers to understand their audiences and therefore sell more ad inventory at a better price and allowing planners to understand where they should be buying advertising space.

Targeting display delivery

Audience data

Targeting specific audiences in display chiefly depends on considering who the user is, regardless of the content they are consuming. There are several ways of knowing who the audience is and defining who they are, what they like, what they are motivated by or interested in. There are two main types of audience data: demographical information – who they are; and behavioural information – what they do.

Demographic

This is information about a person and can be inferred from browsing habits or collected from known publicly available information such as consumer credit records.

Behavioural

This data purely observes the type of content consumed and the browsing habits of a person and makes assumptions about that user. Behavioural data tends to typify who the user is, what they are interested in and what they may be considering to purchase. For example, browse enough content about a new model of Ford family MPV car and you could be segmented into the following audiences (plus many others besides):

- new car purchaser;
- in market for new car;
- MPV driver;
- brand preference – Ford;
- parent of young family.

Each of these audiences is then made available for advertisers to target campaigns towards.

Contextual targeting

This is placing adverts next to appropriate content to ensure that the campaign is relevant. This is typically done by targeting sites and mobile apps as well as specific content or pages within sites and apps. Prior to audience data becoming commonplace, websites and apps were used as a proxy for the audience that typically make up their readership. Contextual targeting is still vitally important to advertising and it is extremely common to find part or all of a display campaign being delivered across a list of specific sites. When targeting websites it is most common to simply list sites that share commonality of content and deliver a proportion of advertising to them. This works well for specialist websites but there is a lot of traffic that exists on generalist sites. Contextual accuracy can be achieved by buying only certain sections of a website but this requires activity to be set up with each site in turn.

Keyword contextual targeting (KCT)

To address the issue outlined above keyword contextual targeting (KCT) was developed and is now commonplace on sites with a large breadth of content, but is now also adding benefit to display campaigns by expanding to all websites. KCT allows advertisers to target display advertising space on specific web pages, based on the content of that web page regardless of the site that it appears on. There are data companies who – by either working in partnership with publishers or by using technology – crawl all web content (just like Google crawls web pages to make them available via searching).

The crawled web pages are semantically analysed and categorized to ascertain the type of content on the page. Then advertisers can target display adverts to appear on pages with content that matches a small set of keywords used to define it. KCT is commonly used in both negative and positive match scenarios. An airline, for example, may use KCT to positively target or negatively suppress its adverts as related to the following:

TABLE 7.1   Example of keyword contextual targeting

Positive	Negative
Air travel	Plane crash
Holiday	Terrorist attack
City break	Air-fare increases
Business travel	Travel chaos

This is a technique also used in paid search to ensure that the terms that you want to filter out are added to your campaigns. This is important, as you can see from the examples in Table 7.1, as it reduces wasted spend on irrelevant terms and also avoids brand association with risky terms. As with most data targeting methods, the benefit has been amplified by programmatic advertising as it allows advertisers to apply the targeting criteria to the whole of a campaign's activity, across many websites as opposed to having to facilitate this with publishers on an individual basis.

Other targeting techniques

Environmental

This group of targeting options has less to do with the user's interests and media consumption but bigger levers for campaign managers to use to target activity, for factors that may be applicable to campaign delivery despite who the target audience might be.

Time-based targeting

This can be specified in order to get the most from market conditions, seasonality or consumer behaviour. Display adverts can be delivered by hour, day and month, and many advertisers up-weight activity to ensure a presence when it is most relevant to consumers. This can be especially useful for sales and events, but also the type of product. Adverts for sleeping aids, for example, may be most effective after 11 pm, whilst winter coats are likely to be more effective in October than in May.

Geo-based targeting

This is another essential tool for some advertisers. Display adverts can be restricted to very acute locations if required. In extremis, when targeting mobile devices specifically, display adverts can be targeted to within a 1 metre radius of any latitude/longitude co-ordinates. Display adverts for all devices can be targeted at village, town, city and county as well as TV and designated market area (DMA) regions. Postcodes can also be used to target display campaigns. The accuracy of geo targeting depends on the source of data used and the country in which a campaign is being delivered. In the UK, for example, although IP address is readily available information, it rarely correlates accurately to the user's location, so a combination of other factors are used for targeting desktop computers, sometimes including data from websites.

Device

The type of device that a user is currently using is also a factor. This can help delivery of the right creative format too but is sometimes brought in to help target adverts and help define users as well.

Modelling audiences

Many data points are gathered and/or used in the process of delivering ad campaigns. All of the above mentioned data sets and methodologies, when examined, can yield significant information. Lookalike and act-alike modelling are common terms that refer to a type of statistical analysis that is based in Bayesian inference logic. This is a method of trend and pattern identification and extrapolation through statistical inference. This exists as a way to extend audiences and find people who exhibit the same behaviours as known customers.

In the simplest form this involves monitoring all the audience segments that users to an advertiser's site (or customer database) belong to from a third-party data company's taxonomy. Once the highly indexing segments of the data provider's taxonomy are identified, they can be positively targeted by a display campaign. Looking at the commonality of device type, the time of day that most visits or sales occur, the sites visited and the region that sales come from are all information that can be modelled in this way. When coupled with the amount of data that is collected by advertisers from their site analytics software it can be used to look for common patterns and to find other users who exhibit the same characteristics. If not used for targeting audiences, modelling certainly provides insight and information that can help advertisers to understand campaign activity and shape it in the future.

CASE STUDY   PistonHeads: improving campaign performance with data

Background

PistonHeads.com had their own audience data but were able to improve a campaign being executed on their site by enriching this data with support from a third-party provider.

Strategy

To help power its personalization strategy by enriching its own data, and to reach out to complementary segments, PistonHeads decided to trial a rich data and dynamic segmentation opportunity with a third party – VisualDNA – a provider of psychographic audience data. VisualDNA used its analytics platform to help PistonHeads understand their audience and extend their reach. The campaign selected for this test was a lead generation for Magnitude Finance, a UK specialist in providing bespoke funding for prestige automotive vehicles.

PistonHeads split the first month of its Magnitude Finance campaign into two streams: the first using standard vertical targeting, and the second overlaying VisualDNA's segments. This split allowed the publisher to understand how the test was working versus the standard approach by having a control cell (the standard vertical targeting).

Lee Williams of PistonHeads remembers, 'The segmentation was backed by impressively rigorous methodologies, and we could really see our existing segments come to life in the data. Our editors, community manager and sales team all saw a close fit between the segments and the people that we know qualitatively on our site.'

Results

The results were startling: while the average CTR for the standard segments was 0.14 per cent, those overlaid with VisualDNA segments hit 1.15 per cent – an 800 per cent uplift. The campaign generated hundreds of well-qualified leadverts for Magnitude Finance, driving high conversion rates.

Key learning point

This example proves not only that segmentation can be very powerful, and that data itself is a valuable tool for any business, but also that implementing a programme of continuous improvement through tactical test and learn campaigns will result in an increase in performance over time.

Display campaign measurement and attribution modelling

As with all digital channels, display has a plethora of metrics and methods to measure campaign delivery, creative performance, performance against objective and, more recently, how it affects and interacts with other channels. Display advertising is widely critiqued to be the most incorrectly measured digital channel.

The most important rule when measuring any digital activity is to ensure that the metrics meet the brief by providing the relevant insights about the campaign. For example, if an advertiser is using display to increase awareness amongst a specific demographic then measuring penetration of the target audience would be a far more suitable KPI than a response-related measurement such as the click-through rate. One often overlooked fact is that, when delivering campaigns with standard banner advertising, a display campaign has more in common with its billboard and print media cousins than its digital siblings – most digital advertising is centred around eliciting a response from a user and/or reacting to an action performed by a user – paid search, for example, is both responsive to the user's query and its purpose is to gain a click from that user. Display, on the other hand, provides digital advertisers with the ability to proactively target people, and the placement of adverts and volume of delivery is controlled by the advertiser.

Display campaign objectives, and therefore measurement, should be pragmatically seen as appearing at points on a continuum of marketing activity, which leads as many users as possible to becoming customers. Different kinds of display campaigns are themselves operating in different points along that continuum, and campaigns have different objectives and measurements as a result.

An awareness campaign, tasked with informing new prospective clients about a product or service, is best measured with penetration among the target audience rather than clicks on the advert. The clicks, as a secondary metric, can help return insight about who the engaged users are and where they can be found online, which will help add insight to a campaign. Further along the continuum, closer to users becoming customers, an advertiser may be running a display retargeting campaign, where a click has more value as a way of measuring a campaign's performance.

How activity can be measured is subjective to the format and the activity being run at the time. New or bespoke ad units may have their own unique elements to measure so writing a definitive list is not possible. Ultimately all the relevant measurements and data should contribute to provide the advertiser with the full picture. Display advertising shares some metrics with other digital formats and the most ubiquitous forms of measurement and metrics in display are outlined here:

- Post-impression / post-view events: also known as 'view through' conversions or actions. This is the measurement of any conversion event (sales, visits, sign-ups etc) that happens after users have been exposed to a display advert. This activity can be tracked by the ad server, demand side platform or some analytics packages.

This is the most versatile measurement of display as it accounts for the 'halo effect' that display has by influencing users in the future. This form of measurement also helps to compare different campaign activity that happens.

- Post-click actions: also known as 'click-through conversions'. This is the measurement of everything that happens directly after a user has clicked on a display advert. Measuring post-click activity can provide valuable insight about how particular placements perform relative to others, which can be a proxy measurement for an advertiser's brand, creative or message strength.

- Search uplift: in a multichannel digital world, understanding the effects of one channel on another is important. Outside of the complex world of data-driven attribution, measurement of cross-channel activity becomes more difficult to precisely measure but can provide insight. Looking at the increase in search volumes that occur after display activity begins is a valuable indicator that a display campaign is having an effect on an advertiser's target audience.

- Increase in site traffic: as with measuring the increase in searches, looking at the increase in direct site traffic is also an applicable measurement to the effectiveness of display. The most difficult factor in measuring the indirect effects of display, at least without attribution modelling, is the delay between the beginning of a display campaign and seeing the indirect effects. These depend heavily on the type of product and how people's consideration and needs change – in extremis, both the frequency of purchase and the consideration time needed to choose a product are greatly exaggerated in the automotive sector, for example, as compared to the FMCG sector. So the effectiveness of a toothpaste campaign will see indirect results far more quickly than a car manufacturer.

  Importantly, an increase in site traffic can be focused on specific actions, such as an increase in traffic to certain areas or an increase in lead-generating forms. The measurement can be honed as well – looking at an increase in new visitors, as opposed to returning ones, is a very powerful method to ensure that advertising campaigns are delivering incremental business. A cost per new visitor is also a common metric.

- Brand uplift / recall surveys: when a campaign has a specific brand awareness objective, one favoured method of judging success is to run a survey asking users if they can recall the brand or product that has just finished its advertising campaign.

  The fundamental methodology of the campaign is a simple control/expose test that asks both the control and the exposed groups (the users who have been served an advert) whether they know of or recall the brand and product. The difference between the amounts of positive recalls that the exposed group yields versus the control group can be a measure of success of the campaign.

  This form of measurement requires consideration from the outset of any campaign, as a control group of users has to be created that display adverts need to be negatively targeted away from for the compare and contrast. It is extremely useful for advertisers that do not have any objective aside from messaging, such as government agencies, who need to be sure that their message is seen.

- Click-through rate (CTR): of all the users who have been delivered a display advert the CTR is the percentage of users who have clicked on the advert. The nature of display means that CTR is a potentially dangerous metric when used in isolation. There are a large number of clicks that are accidentally made by users. One judgement of quality of a website from an advertiser's perspective is ensuring that adverts are not too close in proximity to content – a potential problem with touchscreen technology. Therefore, despite wanting to generate clicks with a campaign, they need to be considered with other metrics that can provide the bigger picture.

- Engagement: in display advertising, engagement metrics most commonly refer to how users are interacting with an ad unit – as such, the actual event that counts as an engagement varies with the type of ad. Engagement metrics are associated with rich media – eg in an expandable banner a user expanding the ad could count as an engagement. For a click-to-play video banner, a user initiating the video would count as an engagement.

- Format-specific metrics: as rich media display formats become increasingly more sophisticated and functional the amount of measurable actions also increases. Mobile advertising typifies this, as many ad units can make use of the functions of the device within the ad unit. Therefore, calls, social shares and use of the device's location services to find a nearest store or supplier are all measurable outcomes of user engagement.

In tablet and desktop, the functionality of rich media can go further. Car manufacturers often have car configuration tools for users to choose colour, trim, engine and options on a new car. They will also have options to download a brochure or book a test drive, which are all measurable actions alongside the standard display campaign metrics.

- Return on ad spend (ROAS): this is a metric that can be broadly used to look at the effectiveness of display spend. The metric is extremely closely related to ROI calculations but looks at gross revenue generated from a campaign, or part of a campaign, as opposed to profit generated. Both ROAS and ROI are useful tools as they are easily understood by lots of client stakeholders, and allow a bipartisan look at the effectiveness of advertising tactics.

- Video completion rate: when delivering campaigns with either in-stream or in-banner video the ad server will provide reporting data about the length of time that users have been playing back the video. Normally advertisers are concerned with the number of plays that are started and then the subsequent quartiles until the end of the video, ie a report will usually detail the number of plays initiated (also called views) as well as the number of plays that reached 25 per cent, 50 per cent and 75 per cent of the advert. The most important metric is how many plays were completed. Completed views are expressed as view-through rate (VTR) and are also called completion rate. This is expressed as a percentage, exactly the same as a click-through rate in other digital medium.

- Video – cost per completed view (CPCV): the cost per completed view is an expression of how effective the delivery of a video display campaign has been. It is very effective in terms of establishing value across placements, publishers and different types of video advert (in-stream, in-banner and skippable formats) as it measures a common factor across all of the medium.

- Viewability: viewability is a new measurement for display. For each delivered ad impression the viewability rate (or in-view impressions) is calculated as a percentage of all delivered adverts in the campaign or placement. The concept is simple and is essential to the effectiveness of the campaign – the measurement of whether an individual advert made it on to the screen of a user. Virtually all web pages are longer than the screen they are viewed on and usually adverts feature all the way down a web page. Therefore, if a user does not finish reading an article, the adverts on the lower part of the page will not be seen, and will not be counted towards the in-view impressions served.

The definition of a viewable impression is that at least 75 per cent of the area of an advert has to be on the screen of the user for at least one second (this is defined by the IAB). However, the methods of calculating this vary between providers and the results of a campaign can vary wildly between different providers. Viewability is really contributing to delivering more effective campaigns as well as highlighting ineffective placements on sites. The latter point allows for publishers to start removing poor placements, which leads to nicer web pages and more effect for the remaining placements.

One key element of looking at campaign data is to make sure that the activity fulfilled the initial brief. The above metrics broadly measure effectiveness but it makes for best practice to ensure a campaign is successful by adhering to any targeting defined in the brief. If a campaign requirement was that it was to focus on central London, then there needs to be corroboration of that in the reporting. Beyond this, understanding the bigger picture is important and that is where attribution modelling can help.

Attribution modelling

For a long time advertisers did not have much more than the 'last click' model of attribution. This provides a practical and easily measurable method of measuring activity; however, it is completely ineffective at showing what happens prior to that click happening and effectively disregards any effect that activity has had prior to that on affecting a decision. Measuring success on a post-click basis may be relevant to search. However, as soon as other channels are added to the mix and a more comprehensive plan developed, which aims to influence users at multiple touch points, the contribution of these activities may not all be designed to generate clicks directly to an advertiser's site. In the early days of digital, the click was considered the primary form of measurement of campaigns.

Whatever the goal of the campaign and the metrics used to measure it, the key to successful display advertising, or indeed any channel, is using all the relevant available metrics to help paint a picture of the campaign. The metrics need to show how customers interacted with it and an idea of the marketplace being operated in, whilst also remaining focused on optimizing and refining campaign activity to deliver to the KPI.

Path to conversion reporting

As advertising technology becomes more effective at measuring and collecting data, the way that data evolves is developing too. There is now an emphasis on looking at all campaign activity and the value it brings. One key report in doing this is the path-to-conversion report. This is available to most marketers from their ad server. Where it has the visibility of each campaign component it will collate the most common sequence of exposures of advertising to people prior to them making a purchase. The most common pathways are often displayed like this:

- Display x5 adverts >> Generic Search x1 >> Retargeting x4 >> Brand searchx1 >> sale.
- Display x3 adverts >> Brand search x1 >> Sale.

A marketer will look at the top variations of the pathways in order to begin to understand where budget might need to be up-weighted and to understand the effectiveness of different channels. The path-to-conversion report is certainly valuable but attribution modelling aims to show more detail about a channel or campaign.

Summary

In this chapter we looked in detail at the history and complex journey that display has been on over the last 20 years. The channel has moved from being a simple interruptive, advertising platform to a smart, highly targeted and rich channel with a great deal of potential. The technology involved is quite complex at first but once understood can provide a wealth of data and insight for a digital strategist. In support of this point we looked at programmatic technology and real-time bidding as well as more traditional inventory purchasing. We examined types of display campaigns and how to effectively plan, target and run them. We also examined how to effectively measure success in the digital channel and the challenges that have existed and still remain today. In the following chapter we look at social media, which has some crossover with display advertising due to paid social placements that are key to distributing your content beyond your organic opportunities.

- A brief history ☐
- Programmatic advertising ☐
- Types and formats of display advertising ☐
- Ad servers and technological delivery ☐
- Types of display campaign ☐
- Planning and targeting display campaigns ☐
- Display campaign measurement and attribution modelling ☐

Further reading

- *On Bayesian inference logic*:

  Stone, James V (2015) *Bayes' Rules*, Sebtel Press

References

Geifman, A (2011) [accessed 1 November 2015] 6 Creative Display Ads That Will Inspire You, *imediaconnection.com* [Online] http://www.imediaconnection.com/content/30657.asp

Internet Advertising Bureau (IAB) UK (2012) [accessed 1 November 2015] Viewability: A New Lens for Engagement, *dg MediaMind* [Online] http://www.iabuk.net/sites/default/files/webform/user_research_documents/2012_Global_Benchmarks_Report_DG.pdf

Internet Advertising Bureau (IAB) UK (2015) [accessed 1 November 2015] Ad Ops [Online] http://www.iabuk.net/disciplines/display-advertising

Social media

08

What we will cover in this chapter

In this chapter we examine social media and its phenomenal growth since 2005. We look at the history and current state of the channel. We run through customer service and SEO concerns as well as how to build out and manage a social strategy as part of your broader digital strategy. We also examine social advertising and measurement. The key areas covered in this chapter are:

- History of social media
- Should I or shouldn't I?
- Customer service and reputation management
- The SEO angle
- Where to start?
- Types of social media
- Content
- Social advertising
- Measurement

Chapter goals

By the end of this chapter you should understand social media and the challenges and opportunities that both organic and paid social represent. You should understand how content is vital to your strategy and how to measure success on the channel. You should also be able to appreciate social advertising and its effects on SEO.

Social media is a bit of a goliath these days – omnipresent, revered and lamented in equal doses, and most definitely often misunderstood. Social media is generally defined as any website or application that enables users to create and share content, or to participate in social networking. When people think of social media, however, they often think simply of the well-known social networks (Facebook, Twitter, YouTube etc) – these are really just a small part of a much larger channel.

In this section, I try to demystify social media by starting with a brief history of where it came from and then quickly moving on to the question on most companies' lips: should I or shouldn't I (and, if so, how)? I then cover a host of different social media types in order to debunk the 'isn't it just Facebook?' theory, as well as looking at some of the social platforms that can help companies to create and publish quality social content. Finally, I cover social advertising and measurement, ending with a relevant case study.

History of social media

If you are twentysomething you might find it hard to believe that there were dark days before social media. However, you might be surprised to find that you have to go back quite a way to find these dark days. While the social media we know and love today really got started in the early 21st century it has its origins in the 1970s with the advent of bulletin board systems – essentially a method to share data, code and other information with other like-minded users. These bulletin boards were no flash in the pan, actually surviving right through to the 1990s.

In terms of the big names we still know today, it is LinkedIn that has had the most staying power, having started out in 2003 (although an honourable mention needs to go to MySpace, which was launched at the same time, but has since declined from its early success, despite efforts to rejuvenate it). While Facebook commenced life in 2004, it was a full two years later that it opened to the world (initially being focused on Harvard students, then students in general). Twitter commenced in 2006 and early users (meaning the first five years or so) will be very familiar with Twitter's 'Fail Whale', which displayed when the service went down, which it did, a lot – perhaps a reflection on how quickly the platform and social media was now growing. Interestingly, social media is one area in which Google does not have a dominant status. Google+ was the bread maker of the social media world. Lots of people had an account but very few actually used it. According to studied data compiled by Edward Morbius in January 2015 only 9 per cent of the 2.2 billion registered users had posted something (Anderson, 2015).

Should I or shouldn't I?

Regardless of Google's lacklustre (in relative terms) performance, one guarantee is that your customers, whoever or wherever they are, are likely to be using social media. According to research by Wearesocial in January 2015 there were circa 3 billion active internet users in the world (about 42 per cent of the population) and 2 billion of those were active on social media – so two-thirds of all internet users. Also interesting is that 81 per cent of those active users are active on a mobile device (Kemp, 2015). So it is doubtful that there are really any businesses who can truly say that none of their target audience are using social. Reason number one for getting involved is to be where your customers are. After all, if you owned a chain of shops and a brand new shopping centre was opened that was attracting phenomenal crowds, you would probably open up there too.

While the irrefutable fact that your audience are definitely 'on social' is a pretty compelling reason, there are others if you need further convincing (or, more likely, you need to convince your board).

Social penetration

As noted above, social is big on a global scale. However, if you are a North American or European reader you might be surprised to learn that by far the biggest social user base is to be found in Asia. According to Steven Millward at techinasia.com, China had an estimated 597 million social media users in 2013 with the top 10 sites in China having 3.2 billion users between them (Millward, 2013). Micro-blogging sites such as Sina Weibo and the lesser known Tencent Weibo use a similar model to Twitter. QZone, Pengyou, Renren and Kaixin are broader networks, in a style more similar to Facebook. There is also WeChat and KakaoTalk, which are Whatsapp-style messaging apps. This presents a significant challenge and opportunity to global businesses that have focused on the European and US networks.

Social and mobile

Social networking is very easy to do on the fly. Indeed, it is an excellent time-killer for the bus/train journey (or if you are a teenager during 'family time'). Social media is therefore ideally suited to mobile and, of course, mobile is on a similar upward trajectory. It is also important to recognize that the vast majority of social media users are engaging through apps, not through desktops or laptops. According to Statista, 80 per cent of Twitter users are now mobile and the number is similar for Facebook. Mobile and social are intrinsically linked and it is vital to appreciate this (Brandt, 2015).

Influence and be influenced

Social media allows brands to influence their customer base to a degree via brand pages. However, perhaps more importantly, it provides brands with the opportunity to be influenced. The companies that truly succeed in the social space are not those that try to own the conversation, or indeed those that just sit passively and listen. It is those that sit alongside their customers, joining the conversation and relishing the fact that they are interacting with one another. Back in 2007, Andrew Walmsley wrote an excellent article explaining just this, in which he said: 'The trialogue will influence every aspect of marketing, from product design (threadless.com) to product recommendation (tripadvisor.com), and its potency derives from the opportunity that brands now have not to talk at people, but to be a small part of billions of their conversations' (Walmsley, 2007). This still rings true today.

Customer service and reputation management

Like it or not, increasingly customers vent their dissatisfaction and indeed heap their praise online and, more often than not, via a social channel – Twitter being ideally suited to a (very) short rant or rave. However, getting customer service right in the social channel is far from easy. It requires new skills to be learned by your existing 'call centre' and demands a 24/7 presence. But perhaps most crucially it requires rapid response. Customer expectations on response times have shifted dramatically. Days have turned into hours and hours into minutes. But those that are prepared to accept this shift can profit.

CASE STUDY   KLM

Background

The airline KLM is an excellent example of a business that has mastered customer service and reputation management. KLM flies to 67 countries around the world and so needs to supply global service to a wide range of customers. It is a long-established business and it is quite rare for organizations with so much history to lead the way in areas such as social media. Indeed, as with many of the world's biggest success stories KLM has learnt to fail before it learnt to succeed.

Specifically in the soccer World Cup when, after the Netherlands beat Mexico, they tweeted 'Adios Amigos' – KLM being a Dutch company. This received 90,000 responses of which 70 per cent were negative.

Strategy and results

Specifically for service, KLM has put numerous tactics into place that have helped them to gain real strength in the social service arena. These include a risky approach of answering all questions in public, no matter how negative. This focus on service has created strong results, which they have taken the unusual approach of broadcasting. KLM has even gone as far as emphasizing, during on-board announcements, their one-hour response time to social media questions. The fact that they can also cover 13 languages and have an average response time of 22 minutes has also likely helped them to generate €25 million a year in sales from social media alone (Moth, 2014).

Key lessons

- Whilst there are risks in social media, there are also huge gains to be had if you focus on it.

- Having strong principles and procedures that are followed and committing to these can offer significant gains.

- However, it is also worth being aware that publicly promoting these principles and procedures before they are robust, or when you are not fully committing the resource to deliver them, is dangerous and must be avoided (we will look at this again in Chapter 12).

Social and the power of word of mouth

Social has immense untapped potential for brands if they can use it to generate mass word-of-mouth recommendation. First and foremost, social is about the power of the network – as people trust the people they know more than they trust any advertising in the world. Social recommendations and the resulting word of mouth can help turbocharge your marketing.

The SEO angle

Much has been written about how social media can help with natural search rankings. Some suggest that there is a very strong link, others (including this author) suggest that the link is there but it is not a huge signal in Google's current algorithm. However, you will do well to find someone who believes that there is absolutely no link. Perhaps discussed less but very pertinent is that social media is increasingly being used as a discovery tool. It is not uncommon for around 30–40 per cent of web traffic to be driven from social channels. Why? Because people are increasingly using social filtering (ie things tweeted/posted by their friends/connections) as a means of discovering content and brands as well as search engines. For example, prior to the explosive growth of social media since 2007, most internet users would search, primarily through Google, to find something online. Since then, social media has created an increase in the interactions we make with each other on a daily basis and, as a result, we are now far more interested in the recommendations and insights we receive from our network than from internet advertising. Our networks may even include the brands themselves. These recommendations and insights can in turn steer our brand awareness and consideration.

Where to start?

Most companies who decide they want to embrace social media stall almost immediately – where to start?

As we have discussed throughout the book, your goals on social media, like any other channel, must align with your overall strategy. Specific considerations for social media could be: what are your high-level goals for the channel? What should be your tone of voice? How will you participate? How will you respond? In what languages? On what time zone?

All these questions are crucial, but the single most important thing you can do when setting a social media strategy is to start by listening. Social media monitoring tools such as Brandwatch, Radian 6 and Social Bakers are indispensable if you want to really understand what people are saying and how they respond to different content/messages.

Having listened and learned you can then start to form what you want to both be and do on social before jumping in. It is absolutely crucial to get your social personality right. It should reflect your customers while also still being true to your brand.

Social personality is a term used to define how you represent yourself on the social networks. The simple truth here is that your social personality should be entirely consistent with your brand personality elsewhere. Your brand is your personality and, in the same way that you would not expect your friends to have different personalities depending on where they are, you would not expect a company to have different personalities on different channels. Being consistent and authentic to your brand is essential on social media. Many businesses try to fit in to the channel rather than fitting the channel to their business. This is a mistake. We looked at brand in Chapter 2, so reviewing this is worthwhile here.

Types of social media

To truly understand social media you need to get a handle on the numerous different types. However, this is not, I'm afraid, as easy as it might seem. There are literally thousands of social sites, apps and platforms, and therefore classifying and cataloguing them is incredibly difficult. Add to this that there are probably 10 new social sites/apps created every day – and also that today's popular platform is tomorrow's dud – and this is a bit of a minefield. So in this section I try to cover the main types of social media and list just a few of the (current) big players.

Social networking

When most people think social they think of sites such as Facebook, which allows users to post most forms of media and share with a close group of friends or, if they prefer, the whole world. Typically these sorts of sites are categorized as true 'social networks' but the term should be used in a much broader sense. Some social networks in fact encourage face-to-face interaction, Meetup (**www.meetup.com**) being one example, and numerous 'friend finder'/dating applications being others. If your business operates within these markets then you could investigate potential opportunities such as advertising or even sponsoring events, which could be online or even offline.

For your digital strategy these networks can offer significant brand awareness opportunities and direct conversion campaign opportunities. Facebook, for example, offers paid campaigns, company pages and even insights to provide analytics on performance. These networks are probably the broadest in terms of opportunity.

Blogs and micro-blogging

Blogging is hugely popular. However, the vast majority of blogs are not! While some bloggers have hundreds of thousands of followers, the majority are small hobby sites for close family and friends. The proliferation of blogs is due in part to the relative simplicity of setting one up. Blogging platforms such as Blogger and Wordpress are hugely popular and the majority of domain registration companies will happily bundle in a blog with your domain purchase. While some blogs are global phenomena, for example the Huffington Post typically receives over 100 million monthly visitors (Huffington, 2014), even these pale into insignificance compared to the largest micro-blogging platform, Twitter, which at the time of writing had 320 million active users sending 500 million tweets a month (Twitter, 2015).

Both types, of course, have different purposes and need to be considered differently by marketers. Twitter is great to push out pithy messages and indeed to receive them from your customers. Blogs allow for more detailed consideration and can therefore wield quite considerable power over potential customers. For example, positive reviews on technology, such as on Tech Radar or Pocket-Lint, can have a significant impact on sales. Blogs can offer an opportunity to organizations that have rich content to share or have products and services that can be promoted to highly relevant blog sites. Micro-blogs such as Twitter and Sina Weibo can offer a great deal of advertising potential to an audience that is limited on time and looking for interesting content to share and absorb.

Visual media sharing

A number of social platforms have been developed that focus on visual media, the most ubiquitous being video-sharing site YouTube; popular photo or image-sharing sites include Pinterest, Flikr and Instagram. A more recent phenomenon is short bite-sized video or images, the 'Twitter of video' if you like. Two good examples are SnapChat, where the user 'snaps' a photo or a video, adds a caption, and then sends it to a friend – the twist being that the image/video disappears after a few seconds) – and Vine, which creates short, looped video clips. Being able to create adverts that fit with the visual medium is highly relevant for some businesses in areas such as media and fashion, although not relevant for others. We should expect to see more opportunities in this space in the coming years as these social sites expand even more.

Professional networking

Professional networking sites are, as the name suggests, largely for the business or academic world. LinkedIn is the most known and has replaced many people's rolodex of business cards, the huge benefit being that LinkedIn contacts remain up to date regardless of the number of job switches a person may have. With 350 million registered users it is also a recruiter's dream and has, perhaps inadvertently, helped mobilize the workforce. This can therefore be useful for building your digital team or even sourcing your agency. Also within this category are a number of document-sharing sites, for example Slideshare and Docstoc, which are both useful for publishing more formal content and researching an opportunity. These can play a part in your content strategy (see Chapter 13). Here the opportunity is not only to attract new employees but also to disseminate content to other professionals. This can be particularly advantageous in the B2B space, where being a thought leader and gaining trust are vital to success.

Reviews and ratings

Reviews and ratings sites answer a very basic human need – peer approval. We don't like to make mistakes when purchasing goods and services and, in this, peer reviews have always been important. The internet has allowed us to expand our 'peer set' on a global scale, thanks to the plethora of review sites and platforms. One of the best-known review sites is TripAdvisor, which covers over 4.5 million accommodations, places and attractions and operates in 45 countries.

The power of consumer reviews has encouraged brands to offer customers the ability to review their products/services on-site. Third-party platforms such as Trustpilot and Reevoo have been created to fill this demand.

Forums

Forums are often considered a little outdated and some of the younger social media professionals might question their inclusion here. However, there are still many highly active forums, albeit usually part of a larger site. Two great examples are Netmums and PistonHeads. Although the former is clearly focused on babies and the latter on cars, it is important not to pigeon-hole forums. Consider, for example, the following posts:

FIGURE 8.1   Forum post Example 1

exhaust making rattling noises

Hi, When i am driving i can hear a rattling noise which i assume is the exhaust. It does not start off like that, only sometimes. The exhaust does not feel wobbly. It seems to be when i am braking or slowing down. Is it likely to just drop off or could it be something else? I get it serviced every year and it was only done in Sept 07. Could it be that or someting else? Any ideas????

thanks,

FIGURE 8.2   Forum post Example 2

Author	Discussion
	🗨️quote 🗨️quote all [news] [report]
Original Poster ◄ 243 posts 97 months	With my 11 week old daugher consuming all my spare time, I am not training anywhere as much as I would like. This has led me to consider ways in which I can train with her (when she is a little older). Has anyone used a running pram before, and if so what are your thoughts/recommendations? Initial thought is that it will be strange running with my arms out rather than swinging to my side but I am sure you get used to that? Also I'm 6'3" – is there plenty of space to swing my long legs? Thanks PH!

Perhaps surprisingly, Example 1 is from Netmums and Example 2 is from PistonHeads, demonstrating that forums are more about a collection of like-minded individuals who might well drift off the central forum topic.

These forums provide an opportunity for your business to engage directly with customers and prospects alike, if you can add genuine value to the conversation. Cynically stepping into the middle of conversations with advertising messages, however, will result in negative brand sentiment as well as potentially resulting in being banned from the forum and even re-ceiving negative PR. If nothing else, forums can be a great way to monitor overall brand sentiment and understand any concerns or complaints.

Content

Discovering great new content is increasingly difficult in a world dominated by big media brands and the vast quantity of new content added every second to the web. To help solve this issue a number of content curation services have been created, the vast majority of which leverage the power of the crowd to perform the curation. Storify is a good example of a more commercially focused platform; pitched more to businesses than individuals, it allows for collaboration as well as curation. Reddit is a good example of a very broad platform that is perhaps more consumer than business focused.

Social publishing

With the vast quantity of social platforms at your disposal (and, of course, at the disposal of your customers) the job of managing the publication of your social messages is quite daunting. However, as with everything in the social world we are spoilt for choice when it comes to social publishing platforms. Two of note are Hootsuite and Buffer. Hootsuite syncs with Facebook and Twitter and is also fairly capable on other major platforms too. It allows scheduling of posts, team collaboration and, as one of the most widely used publishing platforms, is well supported. It is squarely pitched at community managers and does a great job of providing user interaction stats. It therefore has value from a customer service perspective as well. Buffer's attraction is the sophistication and simplicity of its user interface. One look at your homepage and you will get all the basic questions answered. While Buffer does not quite have the analytics depth that Hootsuite does, it is an excellent tool for those keen to jump in quickly – as it is certainly simpler to master.

Social advertising

For years many esteemed digital marketers suggested that social (in particular, Facebook) and advertising were simply not compatible, the rationale being that when on Facebook users' mindsets were not generally in shopping mode. As it turns out they (and I include myself in this) were wrong. The problem was not that Facebook's audience had a lack of appetite, the problem was Facebook's layout. In short, the ads were way too easy to ignore and in 2013 Facebook took the brave step of including them in the main news feed. Predictably there was a massive backlash (as there had been, and will be in the future, for all major redesigns) but this time Facebook had got it right commercially (and as the platform is so ubiquitous the majority of those who said they would leave the platform just went quiet for a while).

The placement of ads made a difference, as did the targeting, which allows advertisers to create 'look-a-like' groups based on their current customer base. The mix of better targeting and better ad placement has worked wonders for advertisers and, of course, Facebook's bottom line.

It is worth remembering, though, that social ads should not necessarily be duplicates of your direct response display ads. Social can absolutely be a direct response channel and indeed is well suited as such for some verticals (fashion, for example). However, the platform is also great for more engaging or even experimental ads – think awesome content that gives users something to share and advocate, not 'just an ad'. Finally we have also seen a growth in social advertising platforms to help advertisers spread their message through multiple sites, the most notable being Kenshoo, Marin and Nanigans.

Measurement

The first question to answer when considering measurement approach is what to measure. It is important to think beyond fans or views – while these metrics are interesting the real value is in the quality of the engagement:

- Volume and reach: the quantity and penetration of touchpoints with potential customers.
- Engagement and quality: the quality of interaction with potential customers.

Measuring volume and reach

Typical volume/reach metrics are:

- Brand volume: volume of brand and brand product mentions.
- Market reach: volume of fan/Twitter/subscriber followers (and their followers).
- Twitter followers: volume of Twitter followers on a brand's Twitter profile.
- Facebook fans: volume of Facebook fans on a brand's Facebook page.
- YouTube views: volume of YouTube video views.

And, of course, you can roll out this approach to other platforms that you/your customers are active on.

Measuring engagement and quality

Typical engagement/quality metrics are:

- Brand conversation: the number of times that individuals are talking repeatedly about a brand, as well as comments and replies on the main social profiles.
- Content dissemination: an aggregated value that measures how brands have engaged with their audience across all the main

platforms (to measure whether there is a bias to one or more platform).

- Twitter engagement: the number of posts, shares or retweets related to the brand.

- Facebook engagement: the number of posts or shares related to the brand.

- YouTube engagement: the number of shares of videos and subscribers to the brand channel.

- Overall sentiment: high volume/engagement is one thing but you also need to measure the sentiment: 100,000 comments sounds good, but if 99,000 are negative then you have a problem. All good social media monitoring tools will help measure sentiment.

Creating a social media dashboard

The above metrics require some work to piece together. Tools such as Brand-watch (or other social media monitoring tools), Facebook Insights, Google Analytics, Topsy (**http://topsy.com/**) will help, but the key is to glue all this data together into a social media dashboard that is meaningful to your business.

This starts, of course, with your objectives – if you know what you expect to achieve from social then you know what to measure.

CASE STUDY Motors.co.uk – Motors' Most Deserving Student

Background

Motors.co.uk are one of the UK's leading names in the used-car industry.

Strategy

Motors.co.uk wanted social exposure but did not want a tick-box exercise, so worked with the digital marketing agency Stickyeyes to create a campaign that would truly stand out. The target audience for their campaign was students – a group that has been hit particularly hard by rising insurance premiums, fuel prices and, of course, tuition fees. Motors wanted to address this by rewarding one particularly deserving student, not only to help them get behind the wheel but also to get on with their studies. So the search for Britain's most deserving student began.

The prize on offer? A fully insured car and a £1,000 donation to the university cause of their choice.

Initially the message was spread by contacting universities and higher-education institutions across the UK. This initial groundswell was then complemented by leveraging Motors' own social channels as well as participating universities. As the campaign awareness grew the mainstream media became interested, including BBC Radio. Throughout the campaign, Motors published a wealth of content that told the unique and heart-warming stories of each and every one of the finalists.

The winner, PhD student David Moorhead from the University of Bedfordshire, had a story that stood out to the judges. After leaving secondary school having been labelled as 'stupid', he later discovered he was dyslexic and dyspraxic. This motivated him to pursue his dream of achieving a PhD. As well as the stresses and strains of his studies, David also travelled across the country every week to care for his unwell daughter. His £1,000 was donated to the university to purchase Claro software, which will help dyslexic students in the future.

Results

With social mentions increasing from an average of five per day to 52 per day (a 940 per cent increase) and more than 50 pieces of detailed media coverage, the campaign was able to reach out to an audience of 14.5 million people.

Key lessons

- The Most Deserving Student campaign succeeded in introducing Motors.co.uk to a brand new audience.

- The campaign raised awareness not only of the Motors brand, but also of a number of charities and good causes that were being supported by many of our nominees.

Summary

This chapter looked at the history of social media and its meteoric rise in society. We examined how it fits into your digital strategy and some of the challenges with both organic and paid activity. We looked at how customer service is now an important part of your social media strategy (we will revisit this in Chapter 12). We also looked at how SEO is affected by the signals received from your social media activity, as well as the types of social channels available and how each can play a part in your strategy, plus how content is key (we will revisit content in Chapter 13). Advertising and measurement have also been examined in order to understand how to grow beyond your natural content distribution and how to measure success. Now that we have examined some of the key digital channels, in the next chapter we look at the destination that you are sending these users to – your website.

Chapter checklist

- History of social media   ☐
- Should I or shouldn't I?   ☐
- Customer service and reputation management   ☐
- The SEO angle   ☐
- Where to start?   ☐
- Types of social media   ☐
- Content   ☐
- Social advertising   ☐
- Measurement   ☐

References

Anderson, K (2015) [accessed 1 November 2015] How Many People are Publicly Using Google Plus? [Online] http://kevinanderson.nl/how-many-people-are-publicly-using-google-plus/

Brandt, M (2015) [accessed 1 November 2015] 80% of Twitter's Users are Mobile, Statista [Online] http://www.statista.com/chart/1520/number-of-monthly-active-twitter-users

Huffington, A (2014) [accessed 1 November 2015] 100 Million Thank-yous to Huffposters, *Huffington Post*, 15/09 [Online] http://www.huffingtonpost.com/arianna-huffington/100-million-thank-yous-to-huffposters-around-the-world_b_5822998.html

Kemp, S (2015) [accessed 1 November 2015] Digital, Social & Mobile Worldwide in 2015, *Wearesocial* [Online] wearesocial.net/tag/statistics

Millward, S (2013) [accessed 1 November 2015] Check Out the Numbers of China's Top 100 Social Media Sites, *TechInAsia*, 13/03 [Online] https://www.techinasia.com/2013-china-top-10-social-sites-infographic

Moth, D (2014) [accessed 1 November 2015] KLM: We Make €25m Per Year From Social Media, *Econsultancy*, 12/11 [Online] https://econsultancy.com/blog/65752-klm-we-make-25m-per-year-from-social-media

Twitter (2015) [accessed 1 November 2015] [Online] https://about.twitter.com/company

Walmsley, A (2007) [accessed 1 November 2015] Andrew Walmsley on Digital: Democracy Overpowers Deific Brands, *Marketing Magazine*, 13/06 [Online] http://www.marketingmagazine.co.uk/article/664221/andrew-walmsley-digital-democracy-overpowers-deific-brands

User experience and transformation

09

What we will cover in this chapter

In this chapter we look at user experience (UX) and how the thinking behind this can be applied on a grander scale to drive digital transformation.

The key areas covered in this chapter are:

- User experience
- Digital transformation

Chapter goals

By the end of this chapter you should understand digital transformation, UX and some of the key methods to ensuring that users of your website get the best possible experience. You should also understand roles and responsibilities and relevant research techniques. This will ensure that your digital destination – your website – maximizes the potential of the traffic you are going to generate from your strategy and that your business will be best positioned to take advantage of it.

User experience (UX)

Since 2011 UX has become more and more central to the creation and optimization of digital properties. In fact, its rise mirrors the web's own development from a largely static one-way communication platform to the interactive, immersive and mobile internet we recognize today.

Wikipedia gives a lovely definition of UX in a rich snippet amid Google's search results: 'The overall experience of a person using a product such as a website or computer application, especially in terms of how easy or pleasing it is to use.'

Google's rich snippet on UX

A rich snippet is a piece of structured data that Google can read and insert into your search results. This could be product information, reviews, price, availability, recipes, event times and locations or app information. These give the user greater information to make a decision and give your results more stand-out.

Roles and responsibilities

As a relatively new discipline, those working as UX designers or architects come from very varied backgrounds. Some come from the creative or visual side, others from a more technical HCI (human computer interface) background and others have been product designers or even building architects. The more purist UX designers (UXDs) are those who have come through working in the digital experience sphere for many years. The advantage that this set of UX experts have is that they were historically focused on understanding the important truth that accounting for the context of a user is crucial to the delivery of successful products, services or experiences. A simplistic interpretation is that the UXDs lay out the building blocks of the internet by defining what a website or application is going to do and how it is going to do it – in terms of the interactions that will be necessary to satisfy users' needs.

Alongside the UXDs, designers will define the look and feel, while business analysts and developers will worry about the functionality and how it will be delivered. Effectively, UXDs do the 'why', creative designers do the 'what' and developers do the 'how'. Project managers will then often be involved to ensure that the work meets its milestones and deadlines – through this method the team remains focused on the problem that the software or site is trying to solve. However, firm distinctions between these disciplines are increasingly hard to arrive at. The default methodology for making things happen in agencies is through Agile software development methods. This is a move away from more traditional sequential development, which was slower and less able to react to change. Agile emphasizes collaborative working, where the different disciplines sit next to each other to ease communication and speed up the pace of delivery.

Agile also demands a continual re-evaluation of priorities in light of the time available and the code that has already been developed. Agile projects are delivered in sprints (short blocks of time, typically one to three weeks) with the goal that working code is released at the end of each sprint in order to maintain focus on what is important. The Agile Manifesto was first released back in 2001 (see agilemanifesto.org for more detail) and was borne out of frustration at numerous large IT projects failing because of requirements changing during the course of the project's life. The iterative nature of Agile means that course corrections can be made more easily. Many digital agencies make a virtue of the multidisciplinary, amalgamated teams used on Agile projects. It is ultimately the shared responsibility of the Agile team to consider the user's context, although that responsibility typically falls most heavily on the shoulders of UXDs and strategists.

The importance of context

Context has become vitally important because of the proliferation of devices that people use to access the internet, and the fact that digital is becoming the primary channel for so much of our lives. Understanding how, where and when your users are interacting with you is vital to providing them with the best experience. We can no longer assume that because we have built a great website we will satisfy all users. Mobile users will have a different view, will interact through touch rather than a keyboard or mouse, may be interrupted by calls or messages and are more likely to be looking to absorb content rather than make a purchase, as compared to a desktop user. Appreciating these context differences is crucial to creating a great experience.

We work on the internet. We buy on the internet. We communicate on the internet. We entertain ourselves on the internet. We find love on the internet. We book holidays, tell stories and manage our finances on the internet. We get things done on the internet. US research house Forrester issued a report in March 2014 entitled 'The Future of Business is Digital' (Forrester, 2014). In itself that title is nothing groundbreaking, of course, but the message from the report is clear: 'You must harness digital technologies, both to deliver a superior customer experience and to drive the agility and operational efficiency you need to stay competitive.' Ernst & Young went further in a report called 'The Digitisation of Everything' (Ernst & Young, 2011): 'The real imperative in a world where "everything" is digitised is that businesses need to pursue innovation to disrupt their business model before the competition does. Without innovation strategies, companies will lose their competitive advantage in an increasingly commoditised world.' The context of most companies can therefore be seen to be inherently digital, while the context of customers and consumers is perhaps more complicated.

In the days of what Seth Godin, author of *The Purple Cow* (Godin, 2005), calls the TV industrial complex, marketing was relatively straightforward. Godin's premise is that you paid for some advertising and you blasted your message at people. They consumed that message passively as there was no return path, and you could hit millions of people at once because there was a limited number of outlets or channels available to you as the marketer. The death of the TV advert has been predicted many times, but it has yet to happen. However, TV commercials do need to work so much harder than before in order to cut through in the multiscreen world. Broadcast advertising and offline channels still have a very valid role to play in brand building and direct response marketing. Indeed the integration of digital and offline is the real key to success in today's world, but it is entirely correct that these channels are not what they used to be. At this stage I'd like to ask you a few questions. When did you last watch TV? When did you last watch terrestrial, scheduled TV on your living room TV without a laptop, tablet or mobile device in your hands at the same time? Were you watching a previously recorded show, streaming something through Netflix, or watching a movie you downloaded? Do you pay a subscription for that or did you purchase the show? Did you watch adverts before or during the show? Were you watching on a TV, tablet, phone or another device? Could you click on those adverts and could you fast forward through them?

Context has become very complicated and very important to consider. And that brings us back to user experience. The role of UX can be seen as mediating between the company that wants its customers or prospects to take a particular action, and those customers who just want to solve a problem (in the broadest sense). Therefore, optimizing your UX across all touchpoints is crucial as it will be a deciding factor in making it possible to achieve your digital marketing strategy goals.

So there are two important ways to think about context for relevance: what you, as a service provider, know about your customer (who they are, where they are, their point in the customer journey, their past interaction history etc) and what your customer thinks about you in their context as a digital customer (ie they are used to the intuitiveness of Facebook and Google and therefore will not forgive you for delivering a poor experience). Understanding the user's context is therefore crucially important for service providers. Making assumptions rather than working from a position of knowledge is a dangerous choice to make and one that can be extremely difficult to unpick later. With an understanding of context, you can prioritize particular features and content. Is it safe to assume, for example, that someone browsing McDonald's website on their mobile device just wants to know where the closest branch is? Do they actually want to check the ingredients of their favourite burger? Or are they looking for a job? What should be the first things that a visitor sees on the site? How confident would you feel about making an assumption in that case? The answer is that you shouldn't – you should always go to the people you want to reach in order to get the answer about what they are looking for – and so that is where research comes in.

UX research

Traditionally, markets and customers were segmented on the basis of demographics. However, as discussed in Chapter 2, those approaches are no longer the ultimate answer to the question of who your customers are, as needs and behaviours make much better starting places for innovation. This points to one of the most important considerations in building digital products – ensuring that you never make assumptions. It is vital that a business takes every opportunity to fully understand its intended users and find out what they really want and how they behave. The best-practice approach of UX today involves using tools such as heat map software, user interviews and even ethnographic models of observation. Truly, the best experiences are created when a designer has been able to put themselves in someone else's shoes.

Tools used for UX research

Heatmap software
A tool that shows where users moved and hovered their mouse on your site, which gives an indication of the appeal of the elements of the page and the demand of the users.

Usability testing
Research that works directly with users, letting them test your UX. This gives you an opportunity to learn where there are challenges and areas for improvement.

Ethnographic models
Research similar to usability testing, but focused more on human interaction than technology. This helps to put you into the shoes of the user, understanding their social, cultural and psychological reasons for taking certain actions. This is more about understanding the *why* than the *what.*

Eyeball tracking
Often used in usability testing to monitor exactly where a user is looking whilst they interact with the page(s) they are testing.

Multivariant or split A/B testing
A testing method easily implemented on to a website to enable multiple versions of a page to run simultaneously and determine a best performer.

Web analytics
Commonly used across all websites to provide detailed data on visitor behaviours.

UX research and observation will often be distilled into personas, composite archetypes representing the different users and their needs, which can provide a more human guide to the creation of digital products. For more information on personas see Chapter 1. As discussed in Chapter 11 when we look at personalization, asking users what they want or think is not as helpful as you might imagine, which explains why ethnography is becoming popular. Users tend not to know their own minds as well as they think they do. To borrow car manufacturer Henry Ford's famous quote: 'If I had asked people what they wanted they would have said a faster horse.'

Ethnography

Ethnography is the study of people and cultures. It observes society from the perspective of the subject, therefore giving a unique view that comes from the individuals themselves. It has increasingly been used in research over recent years. Using ethnography for user experience research gives us more of an understanding of, not just behaviours, but the underlying needs and motivations of individuals. This can be achieved through participant observation, interviews, diary studies and scrapbooks. Each gives deep understanding of what an individual is doing and why. This allows us to get one step ahead of the data and be proactive in building an experience that users will want, rather than reacting to data that simply highlights what users do not like.

The two faces of UX

There are two distinct areas of activity falling under the broad banner of UX and they can be separated as follows:

- Tactical or technical UX: this is where the core principles of good interaction design are applied and where considerations such as conversion optimization will come to the fore. Good interaction design is ensuring that every interaction is well thought through to serve the user in the simplest and most effective way possible. Conversion optimization focuses on ensuring that users find their way to the end of the goal without dropping out of the conversion funnel.

- Strategic or human UX: this is where we get into the realm of insight and brand. The role of UX at this elevation is to uncover the needs of people and to design an experience that meets those needs in a way that is congruent with the brand.

Tactical or technical UX – making the internet better one click at a time

Conversion is the primary metric for a business operating an e-commerce website.

The conversion rate – the ratio at which people who visit a site buy something – is probably one of the most studied marketing metrics available. Indeed, conversion rate optimization (CRO) is a core focus of many businesses and an area that has significant crossover with UX. Data is analysed to assess every on-page element and typically a UX designer will be involved to construct differing permutations of the page that can be tested. This method of multivariant or split A/B testing is now routine in e-commerce and high-traffic environments in order to establish what page elements really influence conversion. Split A/B testing simply tests version one against version two in order to determine a winner. Multivariant testing uses the same principle but with more variants and deeper results.

That conversion rate can have a significant impact on a company is self-evident but the scale of the impact can sometimes surprise.

CASE STUDY   UK supermarket chain – signposting for conversion

Background

In the UK, a leading supermarket chain (name withheld), established in the market for many decades, had moved into offering financial services products through a white-label agreement. However, they were not seeing the conversion levels they had hoped for. Incorporating a range of financial services products on to their website, which was understandably focused on groceries, was a challenge and conversion was suffering in the purchase funnel.

Strategy and results

To overcome this, the supermarket commissioned some UX research both in the form of analysis by a UX company and through one-to-one consumer studies. This led to a range of issues being highlighted with the journeys: the navigation was not clear to many users, there was not enough help when trying to fill in difficult form fields and errors were not signposted clearly. As a result of these factors, users who would happily have bought the product were simply giving up. By making changes to ensure that the signposting was clear and specific, and ensuring simplicity throughout the funnel, the supermarket managed to increase conversion by 40 per cent, which led to a significant increase in sales and revenues. This was achieved through one specific principle – specificity.

Key lessons

- Your forms must be specific: most of us have used forms online or other interactions where something does not quite work as we expect and we get an error message. It is often not entirely clear what has gone wrong. We are told that we have made an error but everything had looked correct.

- Users become infuriated with these kinds of issues as they want to complete the actions, such as making a purchase, but are unable to understand what they have done wrong.

- Useful tips to remember are that if you need the phone number in a specific format, be clear what that format is. If the error is in one field, highlight that field to the user so that they do not have to go back through them all.

- Understanding this can be the difference between a successful conversion funnel and significant drop-off.

Strategic or human UX – bringing brands to life through experience design

We have already examined how important research is to the experience design process, because meaningful insights about human needs are the most potent stimuli in the design process. The context of the end users or customers is one of the aspects that designers must account for. Another is brand, because it can influence the end solution. As companies become more digitally evolved, their brands must develop to become a meaningful, tangible expression of the company, which can be lived through every channel and form of interaction with consumers. Digital content makes brand manifestation a new way to look at and think about the art and science of branding. How does this brand manifest digitally? What does it do? Or say? What are its interactions like and how does it come to life?

Your brand, from a UX experience, has many opportunities to stand out. The experiences that you give your users can create a direct emotional connection to your brand – or quite the opposite. There are a number of tactical approaches that can be taken here and some examples are listed below. You should consider which of these, or any other routes, are appropriate for your brand:

- Creating a fun place to hang out: if your goal is to develop your brand or support a major campaign you may want to create a site or micro-site that is purely for your consumers to enjoy themselves; somewhere to play games or watch videos. This can give a fantastic benefit to your brand's emotional connection.

- Creating a no-nonsense, solution-based experience: if your users are simply looking to buy, register or complete another goal, then getting to the point will ensure that your brand delivers what your users want. Making this type of site too similar to the point above would create frustration, not fun.

- Creating a deep, content-heavy site to absorb: if your brand is about thought leadership then perhaps you should not try to aggressively convert customers or distract them from your content. Providing deep and broad content will give them a real sense that you are experts and this will in turn affect your brand.

- Creating a place for people to chat, discuss and debate: you may exist to encourage debate on your forum or network. Pushing conversion, cynical fun or content at people who are not looking for it would damage your brand. Enabling great connectivity between people and tools to encourage engagement and sharing would be very beneficial.

- Creating an exclusive, members-only destination: if your brand is more premium then none of the above may be relevant. Perhaps you should focus on demonstrating to users that they are getting something special, and packaging your experience as something that demonstrates the premium service the user is getting.

There are many other models that all affect your brand in different ways and considering these is important when developing your UX.

Accepting that brands can be truly tangible in digital allows companies to say more to the world than an ad campaign ever could by modelling positive brand behaviour. Ultimately the brand of a business is its personality and this has been true for many years before the Digital Revolution. With consumers now able to interact with brands on a daily basis and hold two-way conversations it is vital that the brands are consistent and contemporary with their behaviour or real damage can be done. These two-way conversations can take place on social media, through chat software or simply through e-mail and this level of direct, real-time access needs to be well managed. We looked at customer service and direct interaction in Chapter 8 and will revisit it in Chapter 12.

Digital transformation

Digital transformation is probably the biggest topic of conversation in the digital arena today. If a company is not already doing it, it is almost certainly planning it. Google shows exponential growth in searches for 'digital transformation' as a set of keywords since 2011 (Figure 9.1) and many of the larger management consultancies have moved into this space, but this does not shed much light on exactly what it is.

FIGURE 9.1   Growth of 'digital transformation'

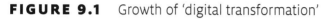

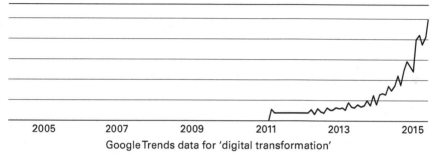

| 2005 | 2007 | 2009 | 2011 | 2013 | 2015 |

Google Trends data for 'digital transformation'

SOURCE: Google Trends

What it does tell us is that digital transformation is increasingly important. The difficulty in defining it is that most experts have their own subtly different definition. This urgent drive towards digital transformation evokes memories of the social media frenzy of the late 2000s and early 2010s and the website frenzy of the late 1990s. Everyone wanted a new website, many people were not sure why and most didn't know how to create one. Of course that wasn't the first of these periods of urgency in the digital age and it won't be the last. The same buzz happened in the early days of the internet when every company wanted a website but many didn't know why, and again with apps. In some ways, digital transformation can be looked at in the same way as any of these – a confusing mishmash of themes, trends, buzzwords and 'next big things'. Many organizations embarking on digital transformation are spending significant amounts on technology; yet while these solutions are clearly enablers, they should not be thought of as transformative in their own right.

Digital transformation is not just a technology journey but, more importantly, a mindset. It consists of these hallmark traits:

- A relentless, all-consuming focus on the end consumer and their needs, including actively co-creating solutions with those customers.

- An organization that does its best to go out of its way to pursue that customer focus (ie historical, cultural and structural standards).

- A can do, collaborative and flexible attitude to the customer and the work of serving customers (ie never accepting no for an answer).

- Agile and adaptable ways of working (ie sprints rule – see below).

- A focus on value creation and breakthroughs, rather than the incrementalism of efficiencies (though this is not to say that efficiency is not important).

- A greater focus on getting to outcomes, rather than process, quickly (ie the company is more interested in the customer and their needs than in itself).

- People and their ingenuity are prized.

- Technology is a smart enabler of the above hallmarks, rather than the adoption of technology being an end in itself.

The fundamental customer centricity of digital transformation means a commitment to best-practice UX design. It is vital to keep this focus in mind when thinking of digital transformation. It is in stark contrast to other technology and process developments such as cost reduction and efficiency improvements. Being efficient, effective and wise with regard to cost are, of course, still important business considerations, but these should now be part of the journey towards creating excellent customer experience rather than the goal in itself.

Design thinking

Underpinning customer-centric experience or design is the transformative power of design thinking. Workshops with Post-its, Sharpies and whiteboards have become de rigueur in digital circles and brainstorming, and they remain a technique that delivers results. These workshops can be challenging, however, and make some people uncomfortable or even self-conscious. Indeed the very nature of taking a group of people out of their comfort zone is intrinsically disarming. Tim Brown, the mercurial chief executive officer (CEO) of IDEO, said: 'Insofar as it is open-ended, open-minded, and iterative a process fed by design thinking will feel chaotic to those experiencing it for the first time.' He goes on to say, however, that 'over the life of a project, it invariably comes to make sense and achieves results that differ markedly from the linear, milestone-based processes that define traditional business practices' (Brown, 2009). There is much more to design thinking than running workshops, although they are tangible artefacts that often spring to mind when thinking of this discipline. In 2005 the British Design Council released the double-diamond approach as a way to neatly encapsulate the differing phases of divergent and convergent thinking necessary for design thinking (Figure 9.2).

FIGURE 9.2 The double-diamond approach

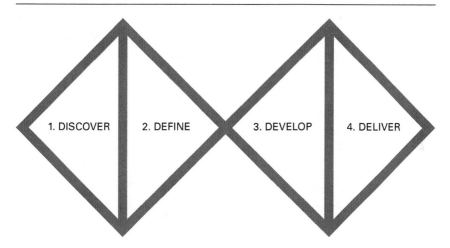

The double diamond was borne to represent the strategic design processes used at companies as diverse as Lego, Alessi, Microsoft and Virgin Atlantic Airways and is formed of four broad phases: discover, define, develop, deliver. Many designers have tweaked the process to their own needs, as is often the case with developed models, but the outline still gives shape to the core components. These are research, agreeing objectives or the problem to be solved, ideation and iteration of possible solutions, and then delivery of a finished product:

1 *Discover*: this is crucial to understand your users, challenges and therefore the design principles you need to work with.

2 *Define*: from the discovery phase we then need to build out what the problems that need to be solved are and the opportunities that are open to us.

3 *Develop*: this then needs to be developed, through the use of ideation, into a set of design principles to solve these problems

4 *Deliver*: finally, these solutions need to be put in place in order to complete the design process.

The power of co-creation

A piece of research entitled 'Closing the Delivery Gap' from Bain & Company in 2005 stated that 80 per cent of companies believe they provide superior services, while only 8 per cent of their customers agreed with them (Bain & Company, 2005). While this gap may have narrowed in the decade since that research was done (due to more detailed data and more direct relationships with customers, amongst other factors), we all have examples of poor customer experience both personally and professionally that would suggest that the 80 per cent figure is nothing more than aspirational. Regardless, the power of co-creation is that it starts with customers. Company executives have no choice but to hear the reality of what they currently offer, direct from the customers themselves. More importantly, the research, the workshopping and the prototyping that design thinking advocates should do hand-in-hand with the customer – the act of co-creating, co-designing a new service or product with the very people who will be buying it or consuming it – is, by its very nature, transformative for most companies. That cultural change remains challenging, and ultimately depends not on technology but on mindset, which, as we have examined, is the consistent theme surrounding digital transformation.

This approach to co-creation has been successfully adopted by Dell and Starbucks, who have both created digital platforms where customers (and prospective customers) can submit ideas around innovation they want to see. The platforms also give the companies an opportunity to provide feedback on what is feasible or not, and the reasons why. The remarkable thing about the Dell platform 'Ideastorm', which was launched after the company suffered a customer service issue, is the sheer volume of ideas, comments and interactions it has garnered. There is clearly an appetite among people to influence the design of the products and services they use every day. The Starbucks site 'My Starbucks Idea' has also seen huge numbers of people getting involved. Crucially, the company reports back on the ideas it has implemented in order to show that customer suggestions do in fact make a difference.

The business case and bottom line

Before embarking on a transformation journey the strategic drivers need to be understood, because the road ahead can be long, difficult and potentially costly. This means that a business case laying out how those drivers will be addressed is essential and fundamental for getting the necessary senior management's buy-in for the change journey – not to mention the investment, as we will discuss in Chapter 15. One of the other difficulties faced in embarking on transformation is generation differences. Boards are often made up of older, more experienced professionals who do not see the day-to-day impact of digital on their business, nor the role it will play in the future. They are also less likely to be impacted by new trends in their personal lives. These are, of course, generalist statements and not true of every board or decision maker. Mary Meeker, of venture capital firm KPCB, delivers an in-depth report every year about internet trends and their accompanying behaviour shifts. In her 2015 report she detailed US statistics that, in 2015, millennials became the dominant generation in the workforce, ahead of baby boomers and Generation X.

This is significant because millennials have grown up with the internet and will not have experienced a workplace without digital technologies. Their expectations and behaviours will therefore be quite different in many regards. According to Meeker, millennials expect different things from their work lives, and fully embracing technology is not considered a perk, but a hygiene factor. This means that robust cases for digital transformation must consider three areas – the customers, the employees and the business itself. Entering into a transformational process on the premise that 'our customers are online' is unlikely to be a sufficiently robust starting point (Meeker, 2015).

A transformation must be exactly that – a transformation. There is a danger that companies will spend large sums trying to fit existing business models into a digital delivery. This is not a transformation but an evolution and will not, in most cases, deliver the desired result. For those companies who are prepared to accept digital into the core of their DNA and undergo a transformation, there are potentially big rewards to reap. Data from the UK Design Council's report entitled 'Designing Demand' in 2007 revealed that every £1 invested in design returns £20 in increased turnover, £4 in increased profits and £5 in increased exports (UK Design Council, 2007). The US Design Management Institute reported that '2014 results show that over the last 10 years, design-led companies have maintained significant stock market advantage, outperforming the S&P by an extraordinary 219 per cent' (US Design Management Institute, 2015).

Evidently the effort and investment is worthwhile for the companies prepared to act. At the other end of the spectrum will be organizations that essentially try to preserve the core of what they have always done, perhaps trying to find ways to make it more palatable for end consumers. What this means is that, as well as the brand, the actual business model of any company must be reviewed as it goes through the process of digital transformation. Take car manufacturers, for example – not only are they competing with other car makers but now also with new digitally enabled services such as Zipcar and Uber, which are challenging the core ownership model for cars. It is not correct to infer from this that every company with an established business model needs a complete overhaul. However, it is important that companies embody a core element of digitally native behaviour where possible and relevant.

Escaping the legacy of the past

As we discussed in Chapter 3, many of the companies currently considering embarking on digital transformation will point to legacy systems as one of the key hurdles to be overcome. One of the ways to accelerate digital transformation is through the application of middleware – software to bypass older, problematic software.

CASE STUDY   British Friendly

Background

Pancentric Digital, a British service design agency, worked with niche insurance company British Friendly to help them begin their journey of digital transformation. British Friendly were looking to develop a more customer-centric business. Their business had been running on a patchwork of legacy systems that broadly corresponded to the different silos around which the operation of the business had traditionally been arranged. This created a challenge for the business strategy as they were very restricted about what they could deliver. For example, their legacy systems did not have an API, and when the system providers were asked to quote for developing an API, the costs were going to be too high to fit within the available budget.

Strategy

To prevent the project being derailed or delayed, Pancentric developed a layer of 'middleware' that interfaced with the legacy back end and allowed the front end of the website to be delivered in line with a new customer journey, thereby enabling the business to begin its customer-centric approach.

Results

The application of middleware has allowed British Friendly to revolutionize its digital presence and start leaning into a meaningful process of customer-centric transformation. They can renew their back-end stack, whilst still progressing in a digital transformation.

Key lessons

- Transformation can be a challenge.
- The key point for your strategy here is to ensure you explore all avenues.
- Budgets and legacy systems are common constraints within the area of digital transformation, but by seeking out experts and creating innovative solutions you can overcome most of these issues.

Summary

In this chapter we examined the importance of context when looking at creating experiences for consumers. We examined roles and responsibilities and considered numerous UX research techniques. We also considered the influence of ethnography and the differences between tactical and strategic UX. We then examined digital transformation and how this has grown in recent years. Looking at design thinking and true alignment to the business we can understand how to ensure that our business is fit for the digital challenges we face now and in the future.

Chapter checklist

- User experience ☐
- Digital transformation ☐

Further reading

- *On ethnography*:

  Hammersley, M and Atkinson, P (2007) *Ethnography: Principles in practice*, Routledge

  Murchison, J (2010) *Ethnography Essentials*, John Wiley & Sons

- *On digital transformation*:

  Baker, M (2014) *Digital Transformation*, CreateSpace. This looks at many case studies, risks and possibilities of digital transformation, and provides perspectives on how to transform your business to enable your digital strategy to succeed.

References

Bain and Company (2005) [accessed 1 November 2015] Closing the Delivery Gap [Online] http://bain.com/bainweb/pdfs/cms/hotTopics/closingdeliverygap.pdf

Brown, T (2009) *Change...By Design*, Harper Business

Ernst & Young (2011) [accessed 1 November 2015] The Digitisation of Everything [Online] www.ey.com/.../The_digitisation_of_everything.../EY_Digitisation_of_e...

Forrester (2014) [accessed 1 November 2015] The Future of Business is Digital, *Fenwick and Gill*, 03/10 [Online] https://www.forrester.com/The+Future+Of+Business+Is+Digital/fulltext/-/E-RES115520

Godin, S (2005) *The Purple Cow: Transform your business by being remarkable*, Penguin

Meeker, M (2015) 2015 Internet Trends Report, *KPCB* [Online] http://www.kpcb.com/blog/2015-internet-trends

UK Design Council (2007) [accessed 1 November 2015] Designing Demand [Online] https://www.designcouncil.org.uk/sites/default/files/asset/document/Designing%20Demand_Executive_Sumary_Final.pdf

US Design Management Institute (2015) [accessed 1 November 2015] Design-Driven Companies Outperform S&P by 228% Over Ten Years [Online] http://www.dmi.org/blogpost/1093220/182956/Design-Driven-Companies-Outperform-S-P-by-228-Over-Ten-Years--The-DMI-Design-Value-Index

CRM and retention

10

What we will cover in this chapter

This chapter looks at the digital methods that can be used to retain customers through effective customer relationship marketing (CRM) and marketing retention strategies. The key areas covered in this chapter are:

- Defining CRM and retention
- Contact strategy
- Cross-selling and up-selling
- Predictive analytics
- CRM systems
- Social CRM (SCRM)
- Loyalty

Chapter goals

By the end of this chapter you should understand the core features of customer relationship management (CRM) and retention programmes and how contact strategies play a part in shaping them. You should have an appreciation of cross-selling and up-selling techniques and an understanding of how predictive models play a part in retention decision making. You should also appreciate how CRM systems play a part in the process and how social CRM differs from standard CRM. Finally, you will have an understanding of loyalty programmes.

Defining CRM and retention

It is a well-known adage that it is cheaper to keep a customer than to acquire one, and so for many businesses, retention is key to profitability and growth. Whether your business has a membership, renewal-based or single sale model you will still most often be looking for your customers to stay loyal to your brand and keep purchasing from you as often as possible. This is where CRM and retention strategies come in. CRM is about developing a relationship with your customers so that they want to stay. Retention is about changing the mindset of customers who want to leave. CRM is therefore a proactive strategy (we are working to control a positive situation and therefore stop it from becoming negative) whereas retention is a reactive strategy (we are reacting to the negative situation that has arisen). Neither retention nor CRM are new or unique to digital but they are often overlooked when digital strategies are being developed, as digital is often seen as your acquisition channels and your website experience. This is not the case and there is a great deal of depth to digital CRM and retention.

CRM is often mistakenly thought of as the system used to manage your customer contact details and perhaps the scheduling of interactions with them. Whilst these systems are CRM systems, they are not the definition of CRM itself, which is the far broader essence of developing truly value-adding relationships with your customers. There are several factors that are vital to success in CRM and retention. Below is a guide to how these are covered in this book. You should use the following to inform your understanding and implementation of CRM:

1 Personalization: it is vital when developing a relationship with a customer that you demonstrate an understanding of who they are and what they are looking for from you. We tackle this in greater detail in Chapter 11.

2 Segmentation and profiling are important to ensure that communications are not sent out in bulk. Spam e-mails from reputable companies are less common than they used to be as strategies have developed, but they certainly have not disappeared altogether and will not for many years. We looked at segmentation and profiles in Chapter 1.

3 Content: to create a compelling CRM strategy you need to have something compelling to discuss with your customers on a regular basis. This content needs to resonate with each customer and give them some form of added value. To do this effectively you need a content strategy, which we will look at in Chapter 13.

4 Insight: we cannot hope to understand how to build a compelling CRM strategy or how to retain customers if we don't understand them. Insight and research are vital to understanding the needs, aspirations, beliefs and other factors that cannot be obtained purely through the data itself. We looked at this in Chapter 2.

Finally, another factor that plays a large part in customer satisfaction and retention rates:

5 Customer service: this has changed significantly in the last 10 years with the direct access to organizations that customers now have through social media. We look at this separately in Chapter 12.

Principles

The goal of an effective CRM strategy is to ensure that your customers feel they are getting value for money and have a positive relationship with your brand. As a result they would have to think very hard before going elsewhere. This does not only result in increased retention rates but can also allow you to raise your prices without affecting existing retention rates as customers recognize the value in staying with your brand.

The core principles of CRM all relate to creating brilliant relationships with your customers and they can be broken down as follows:

- *Frequency*: this is a difficult principle to get right. How often do you contact your customers? Each customer may have a different opinion of this. Ultimately this comes down to what you have to say to them: if there is no value in what you are saying then you should not communicate with them. Never contact a customer just to meet a schedule you have built if you have nothing tangible to say. For example, monthly newsletters will be fine if you have news to provide. Daily cross-selling e-mails are highly unlikely to be popular for most companies.

- *Timeliness*: are you talking to the customer at the right time? How do you know when this right time is? Understanding the customer and their behaviours will help you to deliver messages they want when they want them and will also mean increases in sales. Understanding your analytics and consumer mindset through data is vital to getting this right.

- *Accuracy*: is your data accurate? This means that you need to keep your data cleansed, ensure it is being correctly used in your communications and also check that data from time to time through appends. A fantastic CRM strategy can be ruined if the communications are being sent to the wrong individuals, or if, for example, John Smith is being referred to in the salutation as Mr S John.

- *Relevancy*: does your message truly resonate with the customer? If your customer is interested in fishing, for example, does your CRM programme talk to them about fishing products or do they simply receive the same e-mails as everyone else, which also include jet skiing and dance music?

- *Personalization*: if your customer has shown an interest in certain areas or displays certain behaviours then are you responding to that? Does the customer only open e-mails in the evening? Do they only ever click on the first item? Do they only like to hear from a specific sales person?

- *Value*: are you offering true value? What is the customer getting from your communications that they cannot get elsewhere? Are you delivering your company's unique selling proposition (USP) or brand values through your communications?

Whilst demand for value is a constant and the above principles apply to all CRM programmes, there are some differences in CRM depending on your business model. Below we look at some of the differences between B2B and B2C CRM:

- *Scale*: B2C companies are more likely to need to develop large and often complex CRM programmes with advanced systems to ensure that they are able to manage a large number of customers, potentially across a number of programmes. B2B companies tend to have smaller databases and fewer, but higher value, sales.

- *Frequency*: B2C customer touchpoints are often single, short touches whereas B2B relationships are often developed over a very long period of time.

- *Interaction*: B2B relationships tend to be primarily one-on-one and so personalities can play a major part, whereas B2C customers have a relationship with your brand rather than an individual and so your brand is your personality.

- *Goals*: B2B CRM is often about increasing and automating sales, whereas B2C is more regularly about decreasing churn and increasing up-sell.

Contact strategy

One of the principles we looked at above is frequency: the number of times you contact your customer in any given period. This can be a very difficult area to get right and will almost certainly evolve over time. You may also run several CRM and retention programmes together and alongside a number of other marketing and customer-led communications, and so the frequency of communications can be quite significant and getting this balance right is crucial.

We mentioned spam above and, whilst this is less common than it used to be, it is still easy to be perceived by customers, if you are not careful, as sending spam. Whereas spam used to be perceived as e-mails coming to you from companies that had obtained your e-mail address without your permission, it is now much more broadly recognized as any unwanted e-mail. This means in practical terms that should a customer actively sign up to your e-mail newsletters but then find them irrelevant or too frequent they may begin to perceive it as spam. In the purest definition of the word this would not be spam, but it is the perception that matters as that is what the customer makes their decision on.

There are three forms of marketing communications that most businesses follow: single campaigns, repeat campaigns and contact strategy, as set out below.

Single campaigns

These consist of the business running a campaign before moving on to a completely separate campaign. This is, in most industries, no longer a sensible marketing strategy. Each communication begins from a standing start and has no relationship with the previous communication, therefore it offers very little consistency to the communications and fails to tell a compelling story. This method will offer a spike in response and potentially sales but will offer very little if any ongoing activity and no halo effect on other activity (Figure 10.1). If we were to compare this to a movie it would be a one-off release and is not something that would form part of a CRM strategy.

FIGURE 10.1   Single-campaign response curve

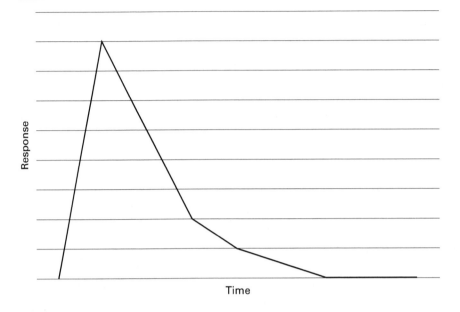

Halo effect

The halo effect is a term coined by Edward Thorndike who originally used it to refer to people. The term now more broadly refers to any form of bias based on positive feelings from elsewhere. This is often seen when reviewing above-the-line advertising, as consumers are more likely to respond to a communication from a brand that they recognize through advertising they have previously seen. If a consumer recognizes a brand, campaign or proposition they are more likely to respond to it and this plays a part in the success of contact strategies.

From a digital perspective, if you were to search for banks in the UK you would see paid search adverts and organic listings for a range of companies. These might include Barclays, Virgin, HSBC and many other leading financial brands. You are aware of these because you have seen their advertisements on television, in the press and elsewhere. You may also see advertisements for brands you have never heard of that have equally good, or even better offers on the services you are shopping for. Who do you click on? Well the fact is that a significant percentage of users will click on the brands they have seen in other adverts – and this is the halo effect. A digital marketer can take advantage of this through above-the-line advertising such as display or social media advertising, or simply through integrating creative with the offline above-the-line marketing.

Repeat campaigns

This is where a company repeats the same campaign(s) regularly over a period of time to encourage further sales (Figure 10.2). This ensures that the message begins to be seen by those who may have originally ignored it. It becomes more recognizable over time. It does, however, also become tired very quickly and so can become an irritant for some ('If I didn't interact with it the first time why do you keep showing it to me?'). It is also not going to convert anyone who has already converted and so the results will tail off over the period. If we were to compare this to a movie it would be releasing the same movie repeatedly over a period of time, perhaps with some remastering or added effects.

FIGURE 10.2   Repeat-campaign response curve

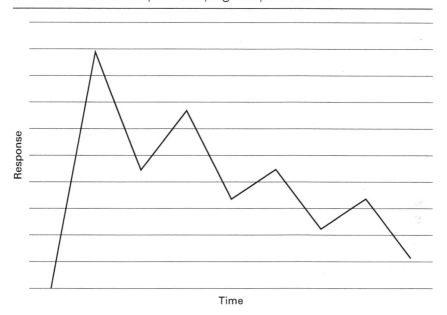

Contact strategy

Through developing a contact strategy your business can develop a meaningful programme of communications that take the customer on a journey and offer real value (Figure 10.3). This means that the consumer will get new and real value from every communication and may even begin to look forward to receiving the next communication. This is not just about sales or keeping customers but is about a journey. If we were to compare this to a movie it would be a strong series of movies that have been released over many years to continuing popularity such as *Jurassic Park* or *Star Wars*.

FIGURE 10.3 Contact-strategy response curve

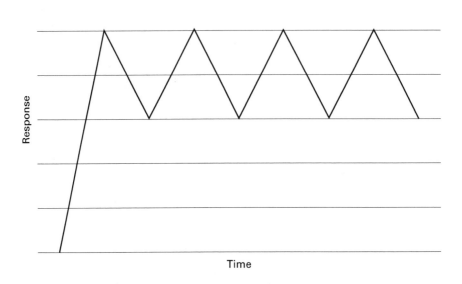

CASE STUDY Cineworld: contact strategy

Background

A good example of a strong contact strategy is the work that Response One did for Cineworld. Cineworld is a major cinema chain in the UK with over 4 million registered customers – a fantastic database opportunity. Their e-mail marketing programme needed a review in order to maximize engagement and increase bookings.

Strategy

In order to achieve this, Response One created a single customer view (which we have discussed in Chapter 11) by merging visit and e-mail data. This was then segmented into groups around factors such as visit frequency and average spend, and from this they developed a six-stage life-cycle e-mail programme. This programme meant contacting the customer at certain stages of their journey to encourage loyalty and actions.

This approach is common in any good contact strategy and allows you to look at the different customer life-cycle stages and what the appropriate actions should be, such as increasing awareness, improving sales, advocacy and cross-selling, win-back or refer a friend (known as member get member, or MGM).

Results

The result of Response One's work with Cineworld was £350,000 of incremental revenue in the first eight months (Response One, 2015).

Key lesson

This is a good example of how producing a well-thought-through contact strategy can have significant gains.

Types of messaging

There are many forms that messages within your contact strategy can take and these should be appropriate to your proposition, business, industry and consumer. Given below are some example of types of communications that can form a contact strategy:

Warm-up

Warm-up e-mails can be anything from an introduction to a series of compelling content such as 'How To' guides to a preview of an upcoming product or series. These e-mails, similarly to teaser campaigns, can give the customer a sense of anticipation and this will in turn heighten their appetite for your next communication, which strengthens your overall contact strategy. A communication that is expected is far more likely to be opened, read and interacted with than one that is unexpected.

Example

'Your series of guides on how to get the most from your new drum kit will be starting next week. Get a sneak peak of lesson one by clicking here.'

Follow-up

The follow-up communication is effectively the opposite of the warm-up. These can be very common in B2B contact strategies. Where the customer has received a phone call or e-mail on a specific subject, following it up after a short period of time can be crucial to closing a sale or capturing the purchase moment. The crucial detail here is the timing. If your initial contact has sparked an interest for the customer but they need to do their own independent research or review their finances, for example, then contacting them too early can be a significant irritation. Contacting them too late, however, may result in a missed opportunity as their online activity can be seen and acted upon by a competitor.

Example

'Thank you Jane for popping in to see us last week about getting a new laptop. If you need more information to help you decide we have these great guides and a help centre to answer your questions. If you need to chat to anyone you can call us any time on XXX XXXX XXX.'

Surprise and delight

This form of communication is value in its purest form. The purpose of a surprise and delight message is to do exactly as it says. There is no sales message here, no data capture and no directly commercial element. A voucher for money off your products would not be strong enough as they would still need to purchase your products to get this offer. A surprise and delight message is something that gives some value to your customer that they will love at no expense to them. You may, for example, offer your customers a gift on their birthday, just for being customers. This is one of the rare opportunities when something that appears too good to be true is actually true. It does of course create a good feeling about your customer service and brand that increases retention rates. It may also increase word-of-mouth advertising and result in positive discussions in public forums and even PR – so the advantages are clear.

Example

'Happy birthday Michael. You think that just because we're a company we don't care? Of course we do. We know you love buying your food with us so to prove how much we love having you as a customer here's a bottle of wine to enjoy with your dinner. Have a great day!'

Reward

This is similar to surprise and delight in that you are rewarding your customers, but this time it is clear that you are rewarding them for a specific behaviour. This may be a gift or some valuable information that is hard to find, and it would be in exchange for buying a product or reaching a certain milestone as a customer.

Example

'Hi Juan Carlos. We just wanted to say thank you for taking the time to complete our survey last month. These results really help us to improve our service, so next time you come to see us you can use this token to get 50 per cent off whatever you buy up to £100. We look forward to seeing you again soon.'

Win-back

This is actually an acquisition message rather than CRM as the customer has left and you are trying to win them back. It does, however, have a blurred line with CRM as you have data on this individual and so can talk to them in a tailored fashion. You have knowledge of their behaviours and can therefore engage them in a contact strategy to bring them back to the business.

Example

'Dear Maggie. We're very sorry to see you go. It wasn't you it was us. We messed up and we're really sorry. You might not be able to forget our mistakes but we hope you can forgive us. If you're willing to give us another chance one day then we hope this voucher for 25 per cent off will help.'

There are many more forms of communication and it is a valuable exercise to think about the different forms of communication that can fill your contact strategy.

Cross-selling and up-selling

Cross-selling and up-selling are two common forms of maximizing revenue from your customers and they continue to play an important part in many business strategies.

Cross-selling is where you encourage your customers to purchase another one of your products. If, for example, you are a retailer and a customer has recently bought a winter coat, perhaps you could encourage them to buy some matching gloves or a scarf that complements the look. This shows an understanding of the underlying need of the customer and presents an opportunity for revenue.

Up-selling is the method of encouraging a customer to upgrade their product to the next level. This may, for example, be a customer who has recently purchased a 'Bronze Level' cover from your motor breakdown company and you notice that they have historically had numerous issues with their car at home, which is only covered on the 'Silver Level' cover. Explaining this to the customer and trying to up-sell this product is both of value to the customer and to the company and so is a relevant up-sell opportunity.

Amazon

Amazon is a fantastic example of cross-selling. Amazon's now signature feature is 'Customers who bought A also bought B'. This recommendation is entirely tailored to the customer, works in real time and offers significant cross-sell opportunity. Over the years this simple method has expanded to 'Customers who search for C also bought D' and other similar methods. These are then presented to you when shopping, after purchasing, in e-mails and even on live tiles of apps. This gives the customer a true sense that Amazon knows them and can suggest items to customers that they themselves did not realize they wanted or even knew existed.

This method is one of many reasons that Amazon has become the global phenomenon that it has, and it is a model now imitated by many major digital retailers. It does, however, have its drawbacks if not executed correctly. Should the suggestion algorithm not be perfect then the suggestions can actually present a message that this is a machine that does not know me at all. Or, should customers change their behaviours temporarily due to an event in their life, they may suddenly be recommended a number of irrelevant products.

Amazon, however, have made a great success of this and continue to innovate and focus on the customer – two great methods of delivering success.

Cross-selling and up-selling, including the Amazon method, are ultimately reliant on what is known as collaborative filtering, which is a method of predictive analytics. With CRM and retention strategies, predictive analytics can be very powerful. We look at these below.

Predictive analytics

One of the vital areas of information for CRM and retention strategies is predictive analytics. Whilst retention is a reactive process, being able to predict behaviours and therefore anticipate customers leaving is very power-ful. Also being able to understand customer behaviour and therefore make advance decisions is equally effective. In this section we look at two predictive analytics models that are relevant to retention strategies: propensity models and collaborative filtering.

Propensity models

Propensity models are probably the most commonly known form of predictive analytics as they are commonly used in businesses to predict future customer behaviour based on known information. Propensity modelling can be used for many purposes, including predicting engagement and conversion, but we are most interested here in its use for retention.

By understanding which customers leave and then the behaviours they commonly exhibit before they leave we are able to see a potential issue before it happens. We can then introduce a specific contact strategy to softly warm this person back to our product or brand and therefore decrease churn and increase retention.

One specific form of this for retention purposes is 'next best action'. This is where a propensity model is used to assess the next conversation to have with the consumer. It is used in numerous scenarios such as up-selling, converting and saving customers. If a customer is looking to leave then your website (or customer service representative) may have a series of choices that can be made about how to save them. They could be offered a discount or even free products or services. The propensity model is designed to try the next action necessary to save this profile or individual – not jumping straight to the expensive option, which may be unnecessary.

Collaborative filtering

As mentioned above, many businesses now use recommendations to encourage customers to purchase other products from them – something that was pioneered by Amazon. This method is called collaborative filtering. The reason for this name is simple. Recommendations are being made by using filtered data from many users, or a collaboration of users.

By using the data of many people's behaviours we can effectively segment behaviours into many buckets and therefore many tailored recommendations from the outputs. As well as continuing to be used by Amazon it is also used by many other businesses in a wide range of industries, such as Netflix's movie recommendations based on social connectivity and Apple's genius recommendations.

CRM systems

There are many CRM systems on the market today and they continue to improve and become more sophisticated. Many, however, are not used to their full potential. In 2003, a report by the global IT research and advisory company Gartner estimated that 41.9 per cent of CRM software goes undeployed (Gartner, 2003) whilst the same company's 2013 report showed that over 20 billion US dollars are spent on CRM software worldwide (Gartner, 2014). The software itself remains an important part of the overall strategy, but implementing it and using it correctly are equally important. The features that you should expect from your CRM software are as follows, although the importance of each will depend on the priorities of your strategy:

- Customer support automation: the function that allows users to centralize, manage and automate customer support. This can include capturing e-mail and web interactions, sharing a knowledge base and self-service portals.
- Marketing automation: this includes creation and managing marketing campaigns in an automated fashion, therefore retaining consistency and reducing resource requirements.
- Reporting: a report on all of the activity that is managed through the CRM system, including marketing, sales and service.
- Sales force automation: primarily but not solely for the B2B user, this feature manages sales funnels, contract management, lead scoring, sales forecasting and much more.
- Contact centre support: some systems also combine CRM functionality with specific contact centre features such as interactive voice response (IVR) menus, missed call management and skill-based routing to enable the systems to be fully integrated with call-centre environments.

Other features such as workflow management, e-mail integration, data management and inventory management may also be useful for your specific needs and should be considered.

There are many systems available on the market today such as Salesforce. com, Microsoft Dynamics, Oracle, SAP, Zoho, SugarCRM, Sage and many more. These are not recommendations and you should conduct your own procurement exercise to fully understand your needs alongside the propositions of the potential suppliers available.

Social CRM (SCRM)

One area of CRM strategy that is more recent is social CRM (SCRM). This is the use of social media services and techniques to engage with your customers in a similar fashion to traditional CRM.

We look at these again later in the book but it is worth quickly highlighting the relevance they have to our CRM and retention efforts. There are two areas of social media that should be reviewed specifically in relation to this and they are: 1) social customer service; 2) sentiment analysis.

Social customer service

In Chapter 12 we look at the social media side of effective customer service and how to best manage customers through the channel. It should, however, be noted that social media is not a one-way form of communication. Customers are increasingly contacting organizations directly through their social media channels to ask questions and to complain. Ensuring that plans are in place to deal with these communications is vital – see Chapter 12 for how to accomplish this.

Sentiment analysis

This is the method of measuring feeling about our brand through monitoring conversations that are taking place across the social networks. By understanding these conversations we can understand or even pre-empt the behaviours of our customers and therefore improve retention and customer satisfaction. We can even take some of the comments and, with the customer's permission, feed them directly into our messaging to show that we are listening and taking action.

There is a risk, however, with SCRM as it can be very easy to make mistakes in this arena and, ultimately, damage your brand if not managed well. For example, Gartner made the eye-opening prediction that: 'By 2010, more than half of companies that have established an online community will fail to manage it as an agent of change, ultimately eroding customer value. Rushing into social computing initiatives without clearly defined benefits for both the company and the customer will be the biggest cause of failure' (Gartner, 2009).

Loyalty

Finally in this chapter we look at loyalty. Much of what we have discussed in this chapter is about encouraging loyalty, but loyalty itself is a specific area of CRM that needs to be looked at independently.

The ladder of loyalty

The ladder of loyalty is a model often referred to within marketing as it shows the five stages that a consumer steps through to become loyal to a brand (Figure 10.4). They are:

1 *Suspect*: no relationship with the brand; no reason to suggest they would or would not buy from you.

2 *Prospect*: shown some indication of interest such as visit, free subscription or enquiry.

3 *Customer*: has purchased from you and so has a basic relationship with your business.

4 *Client*: has developed a deeper relationship with you through repeat purchases but not necessarily a fan of your business.

5 *Advocate*: is showing signs of recommending you and is highly unlikely to stop shopping with you unless something drastic happens.

Other steps can be added to the ladder such as members, evangelists, shoppers. There are many interpretations that you can apply to your individual business, but the above list covers the core stages.

FIGURE 10.4   The ladder of loyalty

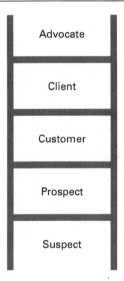

In order to guide the consumer up this ladder you will need to be successful in all areas of your strategy, from targeted acquisition and personalized content strategy through to social CRM and analytics.

Loyalty programmes

Loyalty programmes remain a strong method of forcing loyalty. Where advocacy and brand loyalty may sway a consumer towards choosing to visit one website over another from the search engine results, a loyalty programme can ensure that the consumer does not search at all but goes directly to the website. Loyalty can be a powerful thing: I myself spent many hours as a child being forced to travel around the roads of England, running desperately low on fuel, so that my father could find the right brand of petrol station to get his loyalty points from. There have been many highly successful loyalty programmes in the last 20 years such as Tesco, Nectar, Walgreen's, Canadian Tire, Flybuys, Boots, Payback and many more. These can be referred to as loyalty, reward, club, discount or points cards. Ultimately they all have the same purpose – to offer the consumer a high perceived value from regularly shopping at one brand and in turn to receive higher average sales and revenue per customer. The key here is the term 'perceived' value. This can be the ultimate decision as to whether a loyalty programme works or fails.

High-value loyalty

This type of programme offers items, services or discounts to the customer that are of a high value. This can lead to a significant increase in average sales per customer and retention rates but it can be costly to offer these rewards, especially as many of your customers would probably have shopped with your store anyway. That factor, combined with the cost of promoting and running the scheme, has in the past resulted in criticism for loyalty schemes.

High perceived-value loyalty

This type of programme is focused more on making the customer think that the items are of value whereas they may actually cost the company very little. This means that the cost of running the programme can be kept low and the customers will still show increased shopping behaviours. It can, however, result in criticism for not offering enough value to the customer. An example of this is buying a product in bulk and then adding it to your product for free or for a small increase in price. This could be a voucher or a service such as insurance.

The key to success is to ensure that the customer is offered some real value but not at the expense of the financial rewards of the scheme. This can take some significant adjustment of the programme over time and it is therefore wise to be as flexible with your loyalty scheme as possible at launch, and to build up the scheme slowly.

Summary

In this chapter we looked at what CRM and retention strategies are and how you can use them as part of your digital marketing strategy to deliver increased revenues and improved customer satisfaction. We looked at the benefits of a contact strategy and the principles therein, as well as methods of cross-selling and up-selling to maximize commercial opportunities from your sales funnels. Predictive analytics in terms of both propensity modelling and collaborative modelling have shown us how we can use data to make smart decisions and enable us to decrease churn and increase sales. We have looked briefly at some of the functions of an effective CRM system and how social CRM has been having an impact on customer behaviours in recent years. We explore this in Chapter 12. Finally we looked at loyalty programmes and the power they can have to encourage customers to return more often and spend more money.

Chapter checklist

- Defining CRM and retention ☐
- Contact strategy ☐
- Cross-selling and up-selling ☐
- Predictive analytics ☐
- CRM systems ☐
- Social CRM (SCRM) ☐
- Loyalty ☐

Further reading

- *On subscription marketing*:

  Janzer, A (2015) *Subscription Marketing*, Cuesta Park Consulting.
  Anne also goes into great detail on providing and nurturing value, as well as how to put your strategies into action.

References

Gartner (2003) [accessed 1 November 2015] 42 Percent of CRM Software Goes Unused', 28/02 [Online] https://www.gartner.com/doc/387369/gartner-survey--percent-crm

Gartner (2009) [accessed 1 November 2015] Gartner Says Companies Need to Pursue Four Steps to Harness Social Computing in CRM, 19/02 [Online] http://www.gartner.com/newsroom/id/889712

Gartner (2014) [accessed 1 November 2015] Gartner Says Customer Relationship Management Software Market Grew 13.7 Percent in 2013, 06/05 [Online] http://www.gartner.com/newsroom/id/2730317

Response One (2015) [accessed 1 November 2015] New Email Programme Drives an Amazing £350,000 of Incremental Cinema Bookings [Online] responseone. co.uk/our-work/case-studies/Cineworld-cinemas/

True personalization

11

What we will cover in this chapter

This chapter covers personalization, the options available to digital marketers and some of the challenges involved. The key areas covered in this chapter are:

- What is personalization?
- Defining true personalization
- User-defined personalization
- Behavioural personalization
- Tactical personalization
- Single customer view

Chapter goals

By the end of this chapter you should have an understanding of the benefits and types of personalization. You should understand the concept of the single customer view and the differences between personalization and segmentation.

What is personalization?

In Chapter 10 we looked at CRM and retention marketing from a digital perspective. A successful CRM or retention programme has always relied on delivering highly relevant messages at the right time. This is increasingly becoming a consumer's expectation of marketing as a whole but especially on the digital channels, from UX to advertising and e-mail, and so personalization is therefore growing in importance every day. Thankfully, technology has developed to a level where the possibilities are broader than ever.

Taking a personal approach has always been the best way to get your message across. Whether you are communicating with your customers or just chatting to your friends, no matter who the audience, putting your message into terms that are relevant for them will make your message stronger and clearer. It has long been a key factor in highly successful marketing campaigns, and direct marketing saw a significant growth in the late 20th century as a result of this type of communication becoming more and more accessible. The growth of digital has increasingly allowed us to do more, and we are now at an exciting stage where the realms of possibility are immense and the questions are more *why* and *when* than *how*. Indeed, at the time of writing, many surveys of marketers in recent months have shown that improved personalization is the number one goal for them in the coming 12 months; for example a survey by Evergage in June 2015 found that 91 per cent of marketers use or intend to use personalization within the next year (Evergage, 2015).

Defining true personalization

So what do we mean by true personalization? Well, there are many ways to ensure that your message is tailored to the individual and we have been using many of these for decades. Including the individual's name in the salutation 'Dear Mr Doe' or 'Hi John' is probably the most common. There is also the practice of pulling a fact about your customer from the database and inserting it into the communication such as 'Because we know you love *skiing*, we'd like to tell you about this great alpine vacation offer.' These are all great methods but they do not go quite deep enough to be really tailored.

Segmentation can be used, as discussed in Chapter 1, and this certainly helps to ensure that your message remains relevant whilst keeping down the logistics and costs of fulfilment. This is not personalization, however. Treating people exactly the same as other people due to a few common factors is never going to fully resonate with everyone. Take the incisive television commercial from eHarmony in the UK (2015). The commercial references the fact that the two individuals on screen are the same age and both like long walks on the beach – and that for some websites that is enough to make them a match. We see that one of the individuals is a young man and the other is a camel. This is a good (and fairly funny) way of bringing to life the fact that segmentation is not the answer if you really want your customers to get a truly personalized service.

There are two key methods of personalization that get us to the goal. In simple terms, you can let the individual tell you want they want (user-defined personalization) or you learn what they want (behavioural personalization). Let's look at these in more detail.

User-defined personalization

This method simply allows the individual to tell us what they want. The danger with many segmentation and even personalization models is that the decisions about what someone wants are made based on trends, assumptions and other indications, which may not be representative of that individual. The user-defined model ensures that this risk disappears. This method relies on the individual being prepared to provide you with data that allows you to tailor your communications to them. This may include their demographics, interests, routines and much more. This can be done through any channel such as an online form, phone call or even by post. This method would seem on the surface to be fairly black and white. A consumer tells us what they want and we give it to them. Surely you cannot get more personalized than that? Well, actually you can and there are a number of challenges with this method.

First, you need to collect this information. If someone is unwilling to provide you with this then your entire personalization model collapses. This results in some of your customers receiving personalised comms and some receiving generic comms. This may result in you needing to run two separate comms programmes – one for the personalized approach and one generic for everyone else. You will then need to ensure that this thinking is built into all of your marketing decisions, which is slightly messy and can lead to mistakes. This includes duplicating and complicating such complex areas as your content strategy, your contact strategy and your key website landing pages as well as separating data and reporting, which can be incredibly complex.

Second, you rely on the data being accurate. If, for example, you force all of your customers to give you this data then there is a strong chance, as with any mandatory field online, that a percentage of individuals will provide fake data as they do not want to give you what you are looking for. Birth dates, interests, occupations, even gender could be incorrect. This can then become hugely embarrassing and even brand damaging when you send a ladies beauty voucher out to a 78-year-old man with a message that reads 'Happy 40th Birthday Janice'.

Third, you are also assuming that people know themselves. Anyone with children will know that the answer you get from someone's mouth, no matter how genuine they think it is, is not always representative of the true picture. We all have our aspirations and beliefs in who we are and who we want to be. Pride sometimes overtakes reality and memory is not always reliable. There are reasons why someone may give you a genuine answer, but not necessarily a correct one. Adam may, for example, have been a keen cyclist many years ago with a plan to get back into it, so he still considers cycling to be one of his main hobbies. It has been over 10 years since he last sat on a bike but time has flown and it doesn't seem that long to him. Adam fills out a research form at his local supermarket and lists cycling as a hobby. The supermarket then starts to send Adam local cycle-route maps and vouchers for cycling products, which go unused. One of their other rewards programmes is around food, however, which Adam genuinely would have used had he known.

There are many studies on human psychology that make fascinating reading to illustrate this point. Notably, the Dunning-Kruger effect in which an individual believes themselves to be far better at a skill than is actually the truth (I think we all know someone like this).

So the user-defined personalization model does have some strong advantages, but you will need to be sure of the completeness and accuracy of your data.

Behavioural personalization

This is the area of personalization that marketers started getting excited about in 2015. We are at a stage now where we can learn from the behaviours of our customers and serve them with the relevant messages at the right time. This is the ultimate goal of direct marketing and something that is now very much a possibility.

Big data is another of the buzzwords in digital marketing today and also one of the biggest challenges for many organizations. Data is one of the largest assets a company can have, alongside its people, and the sheer volume of data obtainable from web analytics, purchase funnels, research, call-centre operations, finance and many other areas creates a complex web of possibilities. We look at big data in more detail in Chapter 14 but it is worth noting that organizing and maintaining the quality of your data is vital to success in personalization and your wider marketing strategy.

Behavioural personalization takes indications of an individual's behaviour from signals received through various data collection points such as visiting a website, opening an e-mail, engaging with some content or even visiting specific areas of a store. This data can then be fed into a model that can make decisions in real time. The possibilities for this are truly endless. Do you offer a great deal to a customer who has come to your site several times and added items to the shopping basket but never bought? Do you personalize every e-mail journey so that the content is only relevant to an individual and only sent at the time they like to open their e-mails? Do you message your customers directly to their phone once they reach an area of your store because you know they have interacted with that area of your website?

This opportunity means that consumers can start to receive only the marketing information that is relevant to them. Spam becomes a thing of the past and marketing effectiveness levels soar. Surely this is the future and it is understandable why so many marketers are excited about it. However, behavioural personalization does come with challenges. First, using the data correctly is vital to success. It is likely that the data will be correct (unless there has been a tagging error or similar) but how you use that data is important and so having a strategy for this is the key to success. It is often the way that, when presented with new technology and a large list of options, we as marketers can be guilty of getting a little over-excited and doing things because we can, rather than because we should. The one thing to always keep in mind in marketing is to think of the customer first. Is what you are doing actually going to benefit them? If so, then you probably have a sensible strategy as long as you can make it work for your business.

Not only do you need a strategy but you also need to be able to interpret the data and make the right decisions from what you see. In order to do this, you will need to make certain assumptions and it is these assumptions and interpretations that can render high-quality data worthless. Where the user-defined personalization model excels is that we know the data is correct from the consumer's point of view as they have given it to us. With the behavioural model we are trusting our view of this data. Imagine, for example, that we see a user, Miss Kennedy, repeatedly visit our site and add cycling gear to the basket but then decide not to buy. What do we know from this? Is Miss Kennedy a keen cyclist who is undecided about the products or our brand? Is Miss Kennedy thinking about getting into cycling but is not sure? Is Miss Kennedy considering buying cycling gear as a present for friends or family? Is Miss Kennedy experiencing technical difficulties or a user experience issue when trying to buy? The answer could be any of these, or a thousand others – it might even be Miss Kennedy's 14-year-old son who is using her user ID. Without the individual supplying us with data we have to be careful what assumptions we make.

Finally, privacy is an ongoing challenge in this area. The amount of data being collected now is simply enormous and the ethics of what we should know about people, even in anonymized form, is constantly being questioned. Many brands have been damaged by trying to own too much of our data in recent years and this has resulted in a number of public exposures and scandals for such high-profile businesses as Sony and Facebook. One such example is Disney, who back in May 2011 allowed their Playdom business to enable children to post their full names and locations online. This is a violation of the Children's Online Privacy Protection Act (COPPA) and as a result they were fined £3 million (Marsan, 2012). Consumers are becoming increasingly savvy about giving away their data, and regulation continues to restrict the ability for organizations to obtain and use this data. Ofcom's 'Adults Media Use and Attitudes Report 2014' found that 42 per cent of internet users are 'happy to provide personal information online to companies as long as they get what they want in return'. It is possible, however, that businesses may have to purchase this data from us in the future – after all, it is an asset.

The future of behavioural personalization is very strong and it offers the best result for both organizations and consumers, but there is still a difficult path ahead before this becomes comfortable.

It's not either/or

One thing to remember with the models above is that you do not necessarily have to choose. Both models have their merits and there are times and places for both. Behavioural personalization is the more modern approach, but that does not make it better for any given scenario. For example, you may want to ask your customers to tell you which e-mail programmes they want to be a part of, and what content they are interested in so that you don't need to serve them some irrelevant content for three months whilst you work this out (by which time they may have become frustrated and unsubscribed). You may wish, however, for their experience on your website to adapt to their behaviours.

Bad personalization: Facebook mood experiment

I have included this as a bad example of personalization. Not because the mechanism failed but because the experiment was poorly received by many as being deceptive and it therefore cost Facebook a degree of trust that it may never regain from those users who left the network. A poll on the *Guardian* newspaper's website in the UK suggested that 84 per cent of respondents had lost trust in Facebook with 6 per cent considering closing their page (Fishwick, 2014).

The experiment manipulated the feeds that users saw in order to try to control their moods – and then reviewed their posts to see if their mood had indeed been affected. This concept caused anger as people generally felt that a corporation had no right to conduct psychological experiments on people for their own benefit and without permission from the participants. This was an effective delivery of the personalization strategy but a poorly thought through experiment for the user.

Tactical personalization

Not all personalization has to include data collection and be part of a complex strategy. Sometimes a level of personalization can simply offer a user something unique and enticing. For example, if you allow your customer to alter the design of your product or change the background image of the app they are using then are you really going to gain a great deal of insight about them? No, but you are offering a level of value that the customer may appreciate.

Single customer view

A single customer view is a full and complete picture of your customer that is created by combining all data from across your organization into one holistic view. It is challenging but can be incredibly rewarding.

There is a need to increasingly move away from treating different areas of the customer journey separately and this is worth considering when building your personalization strategy. Working in silos is something that has caused many businesses to fail and this is never more true than with customer experience. If you understand your customer with a single customer view (SCV) then you must personalize your experience at every touchpoint wherever possible. This includes your website, e-mail programme, call-centre operations and even social media customer services. Many businesses have been moving towards developing an SCV over recent years and never has it been more urgent than now. The reason for this is because social media and review sites make it abundantly clear when an organization is bad at this. If you are perceived as delivering poor or inconsistent customer service then your business will suffer. For example, Salesforce.com reports that 92 per cent of companies reported a decline in customer satisfaction as a result of inconsistent service (Fagan, 2013). Aside from the visible ratings you will find that your customers will also vote with their feet and leave. Also, those who are receiving a more personalized service are likely to stay with your business and may even become advocates.

Summary

In this chapter we have looked at what personalization is and how modern techniques allow businesses to go far beyond segmentation and simplified personalization techniques. We looked at user-defined and behavioural personalization and how the two techniques differ, but also how they are not mutually exclusive. Finally we considered the single customer view and its increasing importance in delivering a consistent message to your customers.

Chapter checklist

- What is personalization?   ☐
- Defining true personalization   ☐
- User-defined personalization   ☐
- Behavioural personalization   ☐
- Tactical personalization   ☐
- Single customer view   ☐

Further reading

- *On the Dunning-Kruger effect*:

  McRaney, D (2012) *You Are Not So Smart: Why your memory is mostly fiction, why you have too many friends on Facebook and 46 other ways you're deluding yourself*, Oneworld Publications.

References

Evergage (2015) [accessed 1 November 2015] New Evergage Survey Finds 91% of Marketers Currently Use or Intend to use Personalization Within the Next Year, [Online] http://www.evergage.com/blog/press/new-evergage-survey-finds-91-of-marketers-currently-use-or-intend-to-use-personalization-within-the-next-year

Fagan, L (2013) [accessed 1 November 2015] Customer Service Stats: 55% of Consumers Would Pay More for a Better Service Experience, 24/10, *Sales Force* [Online] https://www.salesforce.com/blog/2013/10/customer-service-stats-55-of-consumers-would-pay-more-for-a-better-service-experience.html

Fishwick, C (2014) [accessed 1 November 2015] Facebook's Secret Mood Experiment: Have You Lost Trust in the Social Network?, 30/06 *The Guardian* [Online] http://www.theguardian.com/technology/poll/2014/jun/30/facebook-secret-mood-experiment-social-network

Marsan, C D (2012) [accessed 1 November 2015] 15 Worst Internet Privacy Scandals of All Time, 26/01 *Network World* [Online] http://www.networkworld.com/article/2185187/security/15-worst-internet-privacy-scandals-of-all-time.html

Customer service

12

What we will cover in this chapter

This chapter looks at customer service through the lens of digital. This has been a growing challenge and opportunity in recent years. The key areas covered in this chapter are:

- Customer service principles
- Service channels
- Social customer service
- Measurement

Chapter goals

By the end of this chapter you should understand best-practice customer service principles and channels. You should have an appreciation of social customer service and how to measure effective customer service. You should understand specific digital challenges and opportunities in serving your customers as part of your strategy.

Before we get into the detail of this chapter it is vital to understand how customer service and marketing interact so as to appreciate why we need to cover this here. Many years ago marketing was purely about growing your company whilst customer service was about solving customer issues. The increased focus on customer satisfaction and the increasing power of the consumer in the 21st century has led to much more of a service element to marketing. Also, the launch of social media has led to a need to directly interact with consumers in two-way conversations whilst pushing marketing content out on the same channel.

All of this means that the content strategy you have must fit with your service goals and your customer service principles must support the messaging from your content. Your website must also fit with your service goals. For example, will you be including online chat functionality or simply promoting your call-centre telephone number? Do you need a secure messaging function within your customer logged-in experience? All of these questions change your UX.

We can quickly see that customer service and marketing now overlap a great deal and so understanding how to build this into your digital marketing strategy is important.

Customer service principles

One of the key messages of this book is that digital is an integrated part of your strategy and must not be a separate silo within your business. That principle does not apply anywhere more than with customer service. Whether your customers are coming to you with questions or with complaints they will expect to be treated well and served quickly by experts – at this stage more than any other.

Within your digital strategy you have opportunities to talk directly with customers through social media, which is now an expectation of many consumers. You are able to provide real-time online help and information and all without the need for the consumer to go through a phone system. This is no longer an add-on to a customer service strategy, but is an essential part of it.

In order to understand how to achieve this within the digital arena we first need to understand how to achieve the best possible customer service levels and to do this we will review the key service principles (Figure 12.1).

Understand your customer

We have discussed throughout the book how important it is to understand the consumer and your customers. This primarily involves research, insight and analytics, which together give you a broad mix of data and direct feedback to shape your strategy. Part of this data must be understanding the views and opinions of your customers. This can be broken down into two core areas: trends and individual customers.

FIGURE 12.1   Customer service principles

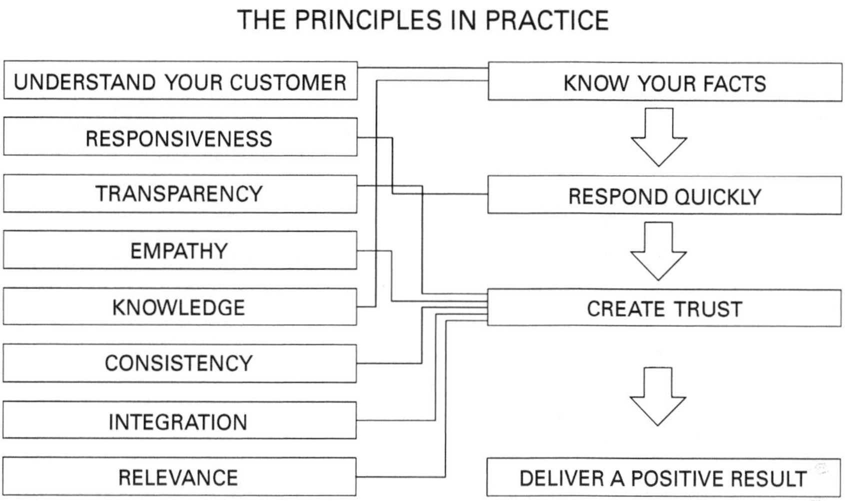

THE PRINCIPLES IN PRACTICE

Trends

Trends give us a broad view of the common issues that customers experience and can also show us where we have been doing a great job. Analysing your data to understand how customers are behaving at key touchpoints and what feedback is being received via your call centre, service e-mail or other communication method is crucial to understanding the trends. Only by finding the common factors that your customers are struggling with will you be able to prioritize the work and truly understand how to help them.

Trends can come from your data, for example you may find that customers from Germany are struggling to pay their annual fee online as they are dropping out of the funnel at a very high rate on the payment screen. This could be due to a technical error on the German version of your website or it could be that German consumers do not use credit cards as widely as your UK customers and so you need to offer another payment method. Seeing this trend can enable you to tackle it and improve your customer satisfaction levels.

Trends can also arise directly from your customers' feedback. This may be through any of the open communication channels such as e-mail or social media. Looking for the common themes here can be harder than through data analytics, but by understanding what the trending areas of complaint are you can focus your efforts towards those.

Individual customers

Whilst trend analysis is important, it is also vitally important to demonstrate an understanding of each customer individually and this is increasingly becoming an expectation rather than simply a desire of customers. We looked at personalization in Chapter 11 and that principle remains relevant here.

Ensuring your systems allow you to know your customer is a challenge that large businesses have always faced, as knowing each individual customer personally is impossible when operating at scale. There are many software solutions that store all conversations and interactions in one place with features such as complaint monitoring, known issue management, knowledge base and social media integration. These features can be very powerful when used in conjunction with a customer database.

Ultimately, understanding your customer is the most important stage in delivering excellent customer service.

Responsiveness

One area of frustration for customers that has increased significantly in the digital age is the time taken for organizations to respond. Consumers are less patient than they used to be and have higher expectations when it comes to response. No longer do we need to follow the lengthy process of sending a letter, ie:

- write a letter;
- take it to a nearby postbox;
- assume that it arrives within the following few days;
- hope it is effectively sorted by the company's mail team and arrives in someone's in-tray;
- wait for them to write back;
- sit at home checking the post for a reply every morning.

And yet this was the scenario only perhaps 20 years ago. We know that we can receive instant responses from our friends, some businesses and even directly from celebrities on social media. We know that e-mails arrive almost instantly and that websites can respond in real time. So why would it be reasonable to accept a business taking 48 or even 24 hours to acknowledge or respond to your message? You need to be prepared to structure your business to enable fast response and therefore meet the demands of your customers.

There are a number of ways that we can at least acknowledge a message straight away and be proactive in responding to our customers. A quick response with an appropriate and, where possible, personalized message can make the difference between dealing with a simple complaint quickly and it escalating into a serious issue.

For example: 'Thank you Eliza for your message. Below is a copy of what you sent us for our records and we will get back to you within two hours. If you have any questions in the meantime please call us on XXX XXXX XXX.'

Even if Eliza is not happy with the two-hour time frame at least she knows what the time frame is and her expectations have been set. She can now choose to wait up to two hours or call the company directly. This can reduce complaints.

Transparency

Another area that has continued to face increasing scrutiny in the 21st century is transparency or, put another way, openness. In the 20th century it was largely accepted that organizations conducted their business in the way that was necessary to provide their services and products to the consumer. However, a number of scandals in the early 21st century including hacking, data leaks, corruption and the global recession of 2008 have led consumers to become more savvy. Also the increase of challenger start-ups that lead with consumer-centric messaging and peer-to-peer businesses has also given the consumer more power and a desire to drive the behaviours they want to see from organizations.

Transparency is something that ethical businesses will be looking to operate with wherever appropriate and possible, but it should always be a core principle of customer service. Hiding anything from a customer is likely to be discovered now more than ever and so an open and honest approach is always a sensible path to follow. Consumers are more cynical than ever and a great deal of information on businesses such as turnover and management teams is available online. When something goes wrong it is often quickly publicized and can even go viral.

Toyota

Toyota in the United States, in 2010, took what was generally considered too long to respond to a crisis regarding a vehicle defect. By the time their head of sales for the United States publicly responded they had already recalled 2.3 million vehicles and their president had issued a 75-second apology. The recall cost Toyota $21 billion in market value. The slow response may have cost them much more through a loss of trust in the brand.

Transparency has never been more important.

Empathy

The tone of voice used in marketing communications is an essential part of delivering on the principle of empathy. A tone of voice is the way in which you write, speak and generally communicate. This could be formal, business language or casual, conversational language for example. This should be driven from your brand and must be consistent across your organization. You should not speak very differently to your customers than you do to your prospects, although there may be some slightly different changes in language and approach. To explain this, given below is an example of how tone may differ.

Company customer service tone of voice

- A friendly, conversational tone: 'We're sorry you didn't love your experience. We're going to return your money right away.'

- A formal tone: 'Apologies that your experience was sub-standard. Your account will be refunded within the next 24 hours.'

Your tone of voice, similar to your strategy, must begin with your values. It is the voice of your brand and so must be completely integrated with your visuals, messaging and other brand elements. Your tone comes through such important elements as vocabulary, humour and storytelling. It can be more powerful than many people would imagine. Your tone of voice can build trust and demonstrate understanding. It can be a key factor in creating advocacy, as some consumers will feel that you speak like one of their friends – and how you say things resonates with them.

There are also some key areas to consider with your tone of voice, including:

- Are colloquialisms or use of slang appropriate for your brand? These may make your brand a little more funky but may also leave some consumers feeling you are too casual to be respected.

- Is it appropriate to use jargon to demonstrate expertise and therefore create trust or will it alienate and confuse? If too much jargon will confuse then will too little be patronizing?

- Profanity is too much for most brands but can be used in some circumstances. Tread very carefully here but it should still be considered.

Decide how correct you want your language to be. For example, if you are writing in English are you willing to split an infinitive? Are you willing to start a sentence with 'And' or 'However'. These techniques break English language rules but can be powerful in marketing copy.

An example of a business with a tone of voice that is widely liked is the drinks company Innocent. Their tone is simple and conversational and it feels, to their target audience, to be friendly and relatable. It is also positive and aspirational, which helps to create a nice feeling around the products, ultimately aimed at people who are likely to want a healthy, ethical, happy life.

Empathy itself is vital as a customer who does not feel that you understand them (even if you do) will become frustrated. The line here is in showing that you understand the customer and can empathize with their position but ensuring that you do not go so far as to agree with any views that may show your business to have been negligent or not to have operated according to the customer's best interest. There may be extreme cases where this is true, but admitting this in a customer service environment can lead to escalation of an otherwise relatively minor issue.

Knowledge

This area is very different from knowing your customer. Knowledge in this sense is related to knowing your business and so looking inwards rather than out. Another frustration that customers can have when speaking to your agents or using your website for help is that the knowledge isn't there. Needing help with a product or service can be frustrating and speaking to someone at the company, either on the phone or digitally, can exacerbate the issue if they do not know more than you do. Therefore ensuring your online information is up to date and correct is vital as is ensuring that all staff are experts in the field they are responding to.

Consistency

We have all experienced issues where we phone a company and speak to a department that gives us an answer and then redirects us to another department that gives us a completely different answer; perhaps even the same person in the same department giving us different answers on different days. This can seem like being stuck in an endless loop and be extremely frustrating. It is important that your service approach, language, training, documentation, service levels, systems and all other factors are aligned into one consistent approach no matter what the channel. Taking a channel agnostic approach is essential as it ensures that you put the customer and the process before the channel and not vice versa. In order to achieve this you will need to review your business's brand guidelines alongside any service principles you may have in place. Where there are none it is important to build a set of processes and procedures that create consistency across your service touchpoints. You will need to set your tone of voice, your processes for handling certain types of calls, your systems used for decision making and record keeping.

Integration

Integrating your customer service with your broader business is crucial. This also includes integrating your digital service with your broader service. It can be tempting to buy some new customer support software and integrate it into one area of your business to show everyone else what is possible. Whilst this can be a good technique for creating competition and therefore raising the game of other departments, it can create a disconnect for customers as they receive very different levels of service in very different areas of your business, which again can cause frustration. Integrating into your existing systems is of course also a practical process in terms of cost and efficiency savings. Dependent on the age and complexity of your systems you may find that integrating can cost millions of dollars and so building in sections may be unavoidable. It may also take several years to complete this type of project.

Relevance (eg channel)

Finally, relevance is important. Forcing a customer to talk to you via a specific channel, because you have just launched that channel and want to prove that it works, is not a sensible strategy. Pushing customers through a process that they do not want to follow, in order to hit certain targets, can also be counter-intuitive. Ensuring that your customers have a choice of channels to use and can therefore contact you through the method that they wish will be far more productive and create better and faster resolutions. It is worth adding a note here that, although the above principle is true, it can create significant cost savings to have a purely digital customer service process and remove or significantly reduce call-centre service if this is appropriate for your customers. This model is fairly common today and, whilst it can cause frustration for some customers, it can be an entirely valid strategy if implemented correctly.

Service channels

There are many channels available for digital customer service but some are often overlooked. Not all channels are appropriate to all organizations. For example, an e-commerce site may offer a live chat facility to enable people to get quick answers but this would not be appropriate for a B2B manufacturing business where customers have dedicated relationship managers. This comes back to the relevance principle mentioned above.

Online content

There is a great deal that organizations can do to proactively solve customer service demands simply by answering common questions and providing information openly. As we mentioned above, by understanding our customers we can deliver what we know they want without the need for those customers to get in contact with us. This information can come in a number of forms but must at all times be fresh. This means that providing product specifications, guides, 'how to' videos and much more can be useful, but if these are not updated regularly then they become a customer issue rather than resolution.

There is also far less value in online documentation if customers do not know it is there. You should ensure that customers are made aware of your 'help zone' when they become customers and you could consider promoting it to customers on a regular basis or including it within your newsletter. If you keep the content really fresh, with monthly guides on how to use your products or services, then customers may proactively seek out your content. This all reduces e-mails, calls and chat requests, which keeps your customers satisfied and keeps your resource requirements low.

Live chat

Live chat, sometimes known as web chat, allows your customers to use an online chat window to talk directly to your customer service representatives. This is text based and should not be confused with video chat. This method, whilst digital, still has a traditional offline service approach in that you need agents to hold the conversation and these agents need to have good product knowledge, access to a customer service system and to follow all of the principles we mentioned above.

There are some distinct advantages and disadvantages to live chat versus the traditional call-centre approach and, whilst they are not mutually exclusive, this is a useful lens to use when assessing the channel:

- *Advantages to live chat*:
  - Not always on: it can be switched off or changed into a contact form when you do not have the capacity to be able to handle the volume.
  - Copy and paste: you can send direct links to helpful areas of the site rather than having to talk the customer through how to navigate to somewhere.
  - Knowledge: as well as accessing a knowledge base, an agent has the ability to ask their colleagues without having to put the customer on hold.
  - Language: the issue of regional accents disappears through text-based communication. This can remove what can be an issue for some customers.
  - Multitasking: agents are sometimes able to help multiple customers at once without each customer knowing, which can be far more efficient.
- *Disadvantages to live chat*:
  - Appropriate: it may not be appropriate for your audience. Almost all people are comfortable using a phone but some are still not comfortable using digital technology.

- Patience: if you do not respond quickly the customer is likely to have less patience than if you do not answer the phone quickly.

- Mobile: whilst calling someone from a mobile is very simple, live chat does not always function well from a user experience perspective . This is primarily because much of the software has not yet been optimized to as broad a range of devices as is necessary. Whilst this is likely to change in the future, it remains a current issue.

Based on the above list of advantages it can be seen why live chat can be a very powerful tool if used with an appropriate audience.

Forums

Forums have been around for many years and remain an important part of the internet. As we continue to drive towards creating digital communities the forums remain a powerful tool for sharing information and helping others. They can also be an incredibly powerful tool for reducing contacts from customers by proactively solving problems. Some consumers can have as much, if not more, knowledge of your products or services than your customer service representatives. At the very least they can offer a different perspective – that of the practical use by a peer. Your representative, no matter how talented, can never offer a truly independent opinion in the customer's mind. Forums have one common feature that is simultaneously the major advantage and the major disadvantage. This is that there is little input needed from your organization. You may steer the categories and some of the subjects but you will not be originating the content that is posted. This means that there is no need to produce the content or manage it on an ongoing basis. This clearly creates a significant efficiency saving and ensures that you have helped your customers to find the answers they need with very little direct effort. This sounds too good to be true.

As with most things that sound too good to be true – it is. The other side of this feature is that anything can be posted to your message board. This could include profanities, spam, details of any serious issues that you would rather keep between yourself and the one customer in question, and even illegal content. This is where moderation needs to play a role. Moderating a forum can be an intensive use of resource, dependent on the size and type of content. They therefore need to be moderated effectively. Below are some good principles for moderating a forum to ensure that your brand and broader content and experience are not affected by these issues.

Transparency

As with the customer service principle we mentioned above, this is important. You must not delete content simply because you don't like it or you disagree with it. Keeping the forum open and honest is vital to its success. You should, however, engage with the user and try to take the issue offline to be solved.

Rules

Develop a set of rules for your forum that are clearly promoted to ensure everyone who signs up has read and accepted them. This is not a way of guaranteeing the correct use of the forum but is a way of removing the content that does not follow the rules, without causing any complaints. First, however, it is important to try to get the user to remove the post themselves before you take further action; this will help to maintain a personal approach.

Stay involved

Take part in discussions and try to help and guide wherever possible. Do not get into disagreements in the forum but try to add value and steer conversations away from negative views towards positive outcomes.

Frequently asked questions

These are very well established and exist on many if not most customer-facing sites. Frequently asked questions (FAQs) again stem from understanding your customer. This could literally be the output of your data on the questions that customers frequently ask, it could simply be the questions you expect customers to ask – or anywhere in between. FAQs should be ordered in a manner that is easy for a customer to use to find the question that they are looking for and must be easy to find on the site, as with any other help content. This is where many FAQs fall down. A long list of questions in no logical order creates an irritant for customers who may already be frustrated. Ordering them alphabetically or in logical categories is a sensible approach here.

These are important for your digital marketing strategy for a number of reasons, but perhaps the most important of these is that including answers to common questions can remove concerns a consumer may have – and that will usually result in an increase in conversion rates. Trying to proactively remove the negative is an important consideration for almost all businesses as we all have goals, whether they are e-commerce or simply engagement.

E-mail

E-mail customer service has been used for many years now and remains a common method of communication for many. It allows customers to take their time to build their argument and attach relevant information. It also reduces the need for a conversation, which many customers will find difficult due to the potentially confrontational nature of a complaint. From an organization's perspective it allows you to assess the information provided and return a response within a prescribed time frame, which can be helpful. It also maintains a written history of the conversation. It can be argued that many digital channels offer these same features but, though that is true, e-mail is the channel that has been established for much longer than most digital service channels and so is the one that almost all customers will feel most comfortable with if their need is not urgent. What is important within e-mail, however, is managing response time frames and this can be done effectively through automated messaging.

Similar to the old post method we mentioned at the beginning of this chapter, once an e-mail is sent, the sender has no way of knowing what will happen next. It is vital therefore that when the customer sends you an e-mail, either directly or through submitting an online form, they receive a response that sets their expectations. These e-mails should state the time frame of response and also what the customer submitted and any details such as the date and time. This e-mail should be personalized and where possible should include details about who will be making contact with them, so as to set up a personal relationship. Having some set replies for specific areas ready to send out can be hugely advantageous in ensuring consistency and saving time. These are sometimes referred to as 'canned replies'. These can simply be copied and pasted into the e-mails to answer the relevant queries. It is vital, however, that these are read through and checked to ensure they still seem personal and contextual before being sent. We discussed tone of voice above and, again, that is highly relevant here. Ensuring that your e-mails are friendly, positive and simple (without being patronizing) is vital. You can, and should where relevant, also include links to key documents and relevant locations on your site that the customer can visit to solve their issue.

Finally, ensure you are always moving towards, demonstrating and speaking of an end resolution so that, with each e-mail in the chain, the customer feels that progress is being made.

Callbacks

Callbacks remain a common form of customer service for those customers who are not looking for an immediate response. They can, therefore, be frustrating for those customers who need help quickly but are presented with no other options. Callbacks have the advantage of enabling customer service departments to manage the call levels entirely as they wish but clearly take this control away from the customer. Best practice is to include a time frame for when this call will occur and this should be precise. If it is possible for your organization to manage your call times to within half an hour then this would be a good aim for businesses where customers are looking for a quick response. Where the response can be slower, ie a matter of days, then simply suggesting time frames such as morning, afternoon or evening are normally acceptable and allow for simpler management within the service centre.

Co-browsing

In simple terms co-browsing is two or more people accessing the same web pages at the same time and this duplication of experience allows a customer service agent to understand a customer's needs better. This can be especially helpful in helping a user to complete an action such as a purchase and it offers a more personal experience than a simple phone call or live chat. It is often used when a conversation is proving difficult without being able to see where the user is struggling. It can therefore deliver stronger results than other channels alone.

According to Kate Leggett in 2011, 'Live-assist communication channels (phone, chat, co-browse) have much higher satisfaction ratings than asynchronous electronic channels (e-mail, web self-service). Satisfaction ratings are: phone (74 per cent), chat (69 per cent), co-browse (78 per cent), e-mail (54 per cent), and web self-service (47 per cent)' (Leggett, 2011).

This is a very powerful tool and, when combined with a click-to-call function, can offer real insight into the customer's unique situation and can be especially helpful in technical support and other areas where your products or forms may be complicated. It is essential, however, that this technology is integrated with your service centre's existing technology and this can be one of the biggest challenges.

There is another opportunity with co-browsing – the ability to up-sell, but which would, however, be inappropriate in the majority of service situations. Whilst helping to guide a user through a process you have the opportunity to talk to them about the decisions they make and this may help them to realize that they should be purchasing something that they had disregarded when browsing alone. This should not be a primary goal of co-browsing but it can be an advantage.

Social customer service

One area of digital customer service that continues to undergo a major transformation is that of social customer service. One of the major differences between social customer service and other channels is that it is often initiated and continued in a very public channel. Responses are demanded quickly, as in other channels, and the principles above all still apply.

One of the key challenges is around the process of social media within your organization. Social is often managed by either the PR or marketing team (which may be one and the same) who are unlikely to have the skill set or capacity to handle the customer service elements. Therefore, should there be a dedicated customer service Twitter handle, for example? Customers cannot be guaranteed to use this handle so in practical terms this is difficult to manage. Should marketing therefore pass on the messages to customer service? Well, this seems in fact like a resource drain on a marketing department. As social media increasingly becomes a two-way communication for organizations rather than a 'push' message channel, ownership is moving away from marketing. Once companies reach maturity with social media they will be using the channel as an integrated part of their customer service process, which would include use within the contact centre.

Another challenge is amplification. When a complaint is made on social media it has the opportunity to be picked up by friends and other followers. It may go viral and can then even become newsworthy. This can be brand damaging or, alternatively, it can be an opportunity. An excellent example of how to turn this challenge into an opportunity was when, in 2014, United Airlines lost Rory McIlroy's golf clubs immediately prior to a tournament.

Rory McIlroy's golf clubs

After the US Open in June 2014, Rory McIlroy flew out of Newark and headed for Dublin, Ireland. When he arrived he discovered that his clubs had not arrived with him. As he was flying there to play in the Irish Open his clubs were fairly important. As a result, Rory took to Twitter with the following tweet:

@McIlroyRory: 'Hey @united landed in Dublin yesterday morning from Newark and still no golf clubs... Sort of need them this week... Can someone help!?'

This received 3,700 retweets and 3,200 favourites. It could have been very bad news for United Airlines. Receiving that level of exposure of a mistake with a much-loved celebrity could have been brand damaging. United, however, followed all of the good customer service principles we listed above and responded quickly and delivered a result fast. In less than two hours United responded with this:

@united: '@McIlroyRory We have good news. Your clubs will be in tomorrow and we will deliver them to the tournament for you. ^JH'

This then received 160 retweets and 116 favourites. Clearly that is not to the extent of Rory's tweet, which perhaps is to be expected, but it then became newsworthy and was highlighted by many websites as a great example of how to get social customer service right. United, through understanding their customer, having empathy and responding quickly turned around a negative situation into a positive.

We have looked above at how responsiveness is vital as a customer service principle and this is very true within social customer service – people expect and even demand a response within minutes rather than hours or days. There are now more and more businesses doing this well and the barriers to exit continue to shrink in many markets, so responsiveness is crucial.

Social media can, however, result in more resolutions per hour for an agent than calls and therefore lowers cost per interaction, which is a vital metric within a customer service environment.

We also looked in Chapter 8 at social listening and one area to use that to our advantage is for customer service. By simply tracking your brand name on Twitter for example (with or without the @) and including common misspellings, as you would when determining an SEO keyword strategy, you can monitor and respond to mentions across the social landscape whether they be negative or positive. The latter point is an important one to remember. Acknowledging positive comments can be just as powerful as responding to negative ones.

Measurement

In Chapter 14 we explore how to measure effectively your digital marketing but we will look here at specific measurements for customer service, as they are unique.

Content engagement

One of the channels we mentioned above was online content and we need a measurement for how this is performing. This can differ dependent on how your content is managed, organized and consumed, but the constant is engagement. This could be the number of times your video is viewed or watched all the way to the end. It could be visits to a page, shares of a piece of helpful content or guide downloads. You may have 'like' buttons on your blog or forum or comment posts. All of these interactions can give us a view as to engagement with the content you are serving to your customers and therefore how useful it is proving in helping customers with issues or concerns. You will need to consider what the relevant measures are for your content – these should play a part on your customer service dashboard but are often overlooked. This should be measured through your web and social analytics platforms.

Hold time and abandonment

This applies not just to call centres but also to any live interaction with an agent and so live chat is a good example here. As we mentioned above, a significant percentage of customers will expect you to respond immediately and so understanding that demand and how your business is meeting it is crucial to measuring success. This should be measured through your phone systems.

Response time

This measure is primarily in relation to channels such as social media and e-mail. With social media you should be looking to respond within a number of minutes that is appropriate to your market. For e-mail this could be hours or days. This should be reviewed on a regular basis for response times; documentation should be kept electronically to enable future improvements.

First-contact resolution

This is another measure that is common in both offline and digital channels and refers to the quality of your response. The above 'response time' measures how fast you are but fast, poor responses are not helpful so we need a quality measure. The measure is therefore what percentage of resolutions are provided at the first contact. For example, if I contact a business that has a secure login area because I have lost my password, will you provide me with a reset or reminder straight away or will you need to pass me to someone else, or perhaps even forget to send me the e-mail?

Net promoter score (NPS)

There are many methods of gaining customer feedback and one measure that also enables you to have a quick view of how you perform as an organization is net promoter score (NPS). NPS is a concept developed by Reichheld in his 2003 *Harvard Business Review* article 'The one number you need to grow'. The article has certainly had mixed reviews but has been widely used by many organizations as a guide to general customer sentiment. This measure works by simply asking customers to score your organization out of 10 in response to the question 'How likely are you to recommend X' where X is what you are looking to measure. People who score 9 or 10 are considered promoters, 7 or 8 are passives and all others (6 and below) are detractors (Figure 12.2). By averaging out the score you can understand whether your business is primarily delivering satisfactory outcomes for customers or not.

FIGURE 12.2   Net promoter score

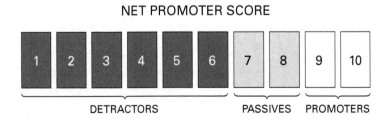

NET PROMOTER SCORE

| 1 | 2 | 3 | 4 | 5 | 6 | 7 | 8 | 9 | 10 |

DETRACTORS   PASSIVES   PROMOTERS

This can then be applied to specific areas of your business such as your customer service. Customers can be asked to score the service they have received out of 10 and an NPS score can be determined as a result. Some believe that NPS can give a result that is below that of other satisfaction surveys and can therefore paint an inaccurate picture; and the different interpretations of scoring in different cultures affects global results. There are also no details behind the score so understanding the motivations for the scoring would require further research. Whilst there are challenges such as this it is fair to say that NPS will give a sensible guide as to the satisfaction of customers of many businesses. Other measures such as customer lifetime value (see Chapter 1) and retention or churn (see Chapter 10) should also be considered.

Summary

The key to digital customer service is to retain the many decades of learning about best-practices customer service from the more established channels and to integrate digital into your existing processes. In this chapter we explored what these principles are and how we can apply them to digital servicing. This includes the challenges of social customer service and measuring success in customer service. It is vital that when building your digital strategy you consider some of the technical implementation and integration challenges around some of the channels listed above. It is therefore also essential to ensure that you implement only the channels that are most appropriate to your customers – and you can only achieve that by truly understanding them.

Chapter checklist

- Customer service principles ☐
- Service channels ☐
- Social customer service ☐
- Measurement ☐

Further reading

- *On customer service strategies*:

  Heppell, M (2015) *Five Star Service: How to deliver exceptional customer service*, Pearson

  Stevens, D (2010) *Brilliant Customer Service*, Prentice Hall

References

Leggett, K (2011) [accessed 1 November 2015] Forrester Technographics Data Points to Increased Communication Channel Usage with Inconsistent Satisfaction Ratings, 29/08, *Forrester* [Online] http://blogs.forrester.com/kate_leggett/11-08-29-forrester_technographics_data_points_to_increased_communication_channel_usage_with_inconsistent_satis

Reichheld, F F (2003) The one number you need to grow, *Harvard Business Review* (December)

Content strategy

13

What we will cover in this chapter

This chapter covers content strategy and how to develop engaging content that fits with your digital strategy. The key areas covered in this chapter are:

- What is content marketing?
- What is content?
- What content types should you use?
- Why content marketing?
- People and process for creating content
- Distribution
- Measuring the value of content
- International content

Chapter goals

By the end of this chapter you should understand how to build an effective content strategy and create engaging content for your customers. You should appreciate how to measure the value of content and how to distribute it effectively. You should understand how to use different types of content and how content works in an international business.

Content marketing has been, at the time of writing, one of the hottest topics in digital marketing for at least two years now. That is pretty impressive for a discipline that is hardly new – I would suggest it is at least 100 years old. After all, the *Michelin Guide* ticks a lot of the 'content marketing' boxes (useful, shareable content produced by a corporate) and they have been running since 1900. So content marketing is in fact not the hottest *new* thing in digital marketing – it is the hottest *old* thing in marketing. So lesson one, and perhaps the most important of all the lessons in this chapter, is to remember that it is nothing new. There is no reason to reinvent the wheel: what made good content 100 years ago still makes good content today. The difference is in the execution and delivery.

I have collaborated on this chapter with Glen Conybeare of the digital agency Stickyeyes who are experts in search and content marketing. I met Glen at an event we were both speaking at and our presentations synced nicely together on content strategy, so what follows is our combined view of this well-established yet fresh and exciting area of digital marketing.

What is content marketing?

Well, for a start it is very broad: as we will see later, 'content' can take many forms. There are already hundreds of definitions for content marketing, in fact Google has 53 million results for the search term 'definition of content marketing' and I see no reason to add to that figure. So rather than an encyclopaedia definition let's look at how an established content marketer would assess whether content is 'great' or not. Great content needs to be all of the following:

- credible;
- shareable;
- useful or fun;
- interesting;
- relevant;
- different;
- on brand.

The unfortunate truth is that quite a lot of content produced fails to hit many of the above and unless it does it is unlikely to fly. Given this, these pillars of great content warrant further consideration:

Credible

Audiences are fickle, they always have been (even Shakespeare complained about it) and always will be. One sure-fire way to turn an audience off is to present them with content that lacks credibility. In short, they have to believe it. This does not mean that they require a robust data set to be behind every statement made but it does mean that the statements made need to be substantiated enough to be believable. Take one of the many quizzes that appear on Facebook, for example, that purport to identify what type of person you are. A recent example was a quiz that 'estimated' your IQ by asking 10 questions. Of course 10 questions is not enough for anyone to truly believe the result was accurate but it was enough for the result to have enough credibility for the audience it was directed at (ie someone in 'fun' not 'work' mode). As part of your strategy you can create credibility through establishing the profile of the author as an expert (including a biography), through including facts and references from well-known sources or through ensuring that your content is authentic to your brand by only speaking on subjects that are relevant to your expertise.

Shareable

Great content only becomes great if lots of people consume it, or rather if a significant percentage of the target audience do. To achieve this, it needs to be shareable. If all the other content pillars are met then the content should be shareable by default, but the acid test for any content that you or your team produce should be this question: 'will my audience want to share this?' While some consumers will go to great efforts to share good content (note that copy, paste, insert = great effort in the digital age) it is also good practice to make it easy for consumers to share your content via quick links to the most relevant platforms for sharing (eg Facebook, LinkedIn, Google+). A great way to make content shareable that is relevant to many industries is offering tips and advice. If you can create 'how to' videos or useful guides that help consumers learn how to achieve something then you will find that this content can be very shareable.

Useful or fun

Content is useful or fun if it passes the 'so what?' test. Take the *Michelin Guide*, of its time a fairly unique publication that was highly useful. Fun speaks for itself, however what is and is not fun is heavily dependent on your target audience. I have friends who love an LOL cat; I hate LOL cats; my mum doesn't know what an LOL cat is. The 'how to' guides above are a good example of useful but what about fun? Can you create an engaging game or fun tool that helps users to achieve something? This route can help customers to find a result they are looking for whilst also enjoying the process, making it both useful and fun.

Interesting

There is some definite crossover between 'useful/fun' and interesting. However, it is still an important pillar. For example, it may be useful to know that you bought bread every time you went shopping this year but it is not particularly interesting. But how do we define whether something is interesting or not? After all, it is very subjective. A great measure is whether the content is interesting enough to be remarkable, ie it is worth making a remark about. This is a similar principle to one of the rules of good PR. Just because you find something interesting does not mean that your audience will – so, as with anything in marketing, consider it from the consumer's perspective.

Relevant

Relevancy is probably the most crucial content pillar. As we will cover in depth later in this chapter you cannot start to create content until you understand your audience. You need to know what makes them tick and ensure all the content you produce is relevant to them. For example, if you are a manufacturer of chairs then creating content around basketball is likely to be beyond what is relevant to your business. If you can create a link between chairs and basketball then you can create relevant content and tap into both, but if there is no link then your content will be irrelevant and not engaging.

Different

Great content needs to be different. It does not necessarily need to be unique; there is absolutely nothing wrong with taking a good idea and making it your own. There are hundreds of guides to the best bars in Barcelona but that should not stop you creating your own: just be sure to create one that differentiates itself from the rest. Of course it is more difficult to cut through in a crowded market, so the closer to unique you can get, the better. The best check for the 'different' pillar is to ask two questions, 'has this been done before?' and if so, 'is my idea unique enough to cut through with my audience?'

On brand

It is very easy to get carried away with content. I have witnessed some brainstorming sessions both at agency and client side that have resulted in some amazing content ideas but the end result is zero progress. Why? The group forgot about the brand. Companies spend millions crafting their brand and, whether written down or not, there are generally a number of dos and a lot of don'ts. In addition, think about your audience again. Consumers of content expect to see a link between the content and the brand. So if Ferrari produces an interactive guide to Formula 1 their consumers would see the connection. However, a top 10 list of cars that dogs prefer would probably not.

What is content?

This may seem like a stupid question, but in fact many types of content are often overlooked.

So what is content? In a nutshell, content is anything that can help engage the end users of your product or service. It can be consumed both on and off your website and in any medium that is capable of delivering a message (so it is much wider reaching than just the written word).

Some of the most common content types are listed below (this is not meant to be an exhaustive list but hopefully demonstrates the many guises that content can take):

- website articles;
- news;
- case studies;
- white papers;
- blogs;
- video;
- mobile apps;
- mobile content;
- testimonials;
- e-books;
- infographics;
- images;
- online presentations;
- annual reports;
- research papers;
- podcasts.

What content types should you use?

There are no hard and fast rules as to what types of content you should use. However, there are some general rules of engagement when it comes to selecting the content type, or types, to use:

- *Target audience.* Who exactly do you want to consume the content? It goes without saying that this is dependent on your brand and products but there is also more detail you should consider. For example, your target audience for this specific content may be a subset of your overall audience. If you sell 10 products and one of them is most suitable for older consumers then testimonials and white papers might make great sense, as an older audience will more often look for trust and proof points. How to define your target audience is covered in detail later in the chapter.

- *Buying cycle.* At what stage of the buying cycle are the audience you want to connect with? Again there are no hard rules here, but give it consideration. If you are mainly trying to target consumers who are at the 'decision stage' (the moment of decision) then detailed product information on-site and analyst reports/white papers might make sense. During the 'consideration stage' (still shopping around) case studies and testimonials could be the best choice.

- *Think plural.* If you have a great content idea that ticks all the content marketing pillars then don't necessarily limit yourself to one content type. An infographic can make a great presentation and vice versa. If you have points that you are making within a slide show that you will share online then can these points become an infographic... and can that infographic fuel a white paper... and can that white paper be shortened into an article... and can that article be further shortened into a blog post... and so on.

- *Don't just take the easy street.* Publishing content on your website is easy and certainly makes sense. Indeed your website should be your home for content (see the section on search engine optimization in Chapter 5) but, unless you have a household name, the unfortunate truth for many businesses is that only a fraction of your target audience will be visiting your site. Analysis from the Content Marketing Institute suggests that the least effective content type is publishing on your own site.

FIGURE 13.1 Effectiveness of content marketing tactics

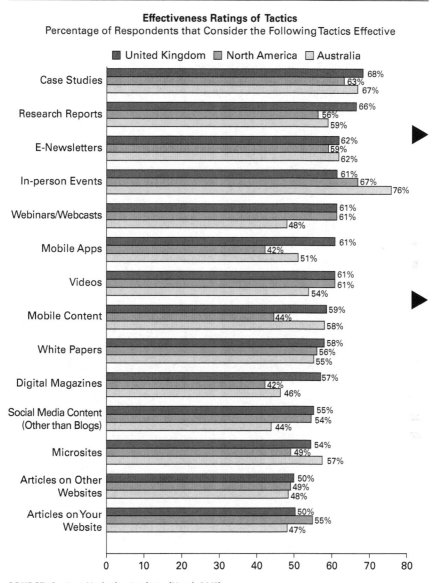

Effectiveness Ratings of Tactics
Percentage of Respondents that Consider the Following Tactics Effective

■ United Kingdom ■ North America □ Australia

Tactic	UK	NA	AUS
Case Studies	68%	63%	67%
Research Reports	66%	56%	59%
E-Newsletters	62%	59%	62%
In-person Events	61%	67%	76%
Webinars/Webcasts	61%	61%	48%
Mobile Apps	61%	42%	51%
Videos	61%	61%	54%
Mobile Content	59%	44%	58%
White Papers	58%	56%	55%
Digital Magazines	57%	42%	46%
Social Media Content (Other than Blogs)	55%	54%	44%
Microsites	54%	49%	57%
Articles on Other Websites	50%	49%	48%
Articles on Your Website	50%	55%	47%

SOURCE: Content Marketing Institute (March 2013)

Why content marketing?

So we now know what content marketing is, and we know it is an extremely popular discipline at the moment. But why is this? What is all the fuss about?

While there are likely many contributing factors to the meteoric rise in popularity of content marketing I would suggest two primary factors that are driving the groundswell: 1) changing consumer behaviour; 2) Google.

Changing consumer behaviour

The process for selecting which good/service to buy has not changed much from a high-level point of view. It still starts with awareness and ends with evaluation/decision and the key elements remain unchanged. In short, we tend to like to do some research and know what others think.

What has changed is how we go about doing this. The internet has been around for longer than most think (it went public in 1989) but it arguably only started to realize real commercial potential at the turn of the 21st century. If we consider some of the basic elements of the buying cycle (Table 13.1) we can see how the internet has had a dramatic effect on consumer behaviour.

TABLE 13.1 Buying cycle

Steps in the Buying Cycle	Pre-2000	Post-2000
Awareness	In-store, TV/radio commercials	The multitude of additional advertising formats online from pre-rolls to advertorials
Research the product/ service	Magazines, brokers	Manufacturer sites, retailers' sites, blogs, YouTube videos, comparison sites
Peer reviews	Word of mouth (small network)	Numerous online review sites and systems (wide network)
Final decision	Done in isolation or with one or two trusted peers/ family members	

The real tipping point was when big brands realized that consumers were turning to the internet in ever increasing numbers to research (and buy) products/services. Consider the following stats for the United States and the UK:

United States

When researching products to buy 62 per cent of millennials (18–29-year-olds) use Facebook (G/O Digital, 2014).

FIGURE 13.2 Preferred method for researching and purchasing products (according to US digital buyers, March 2014)

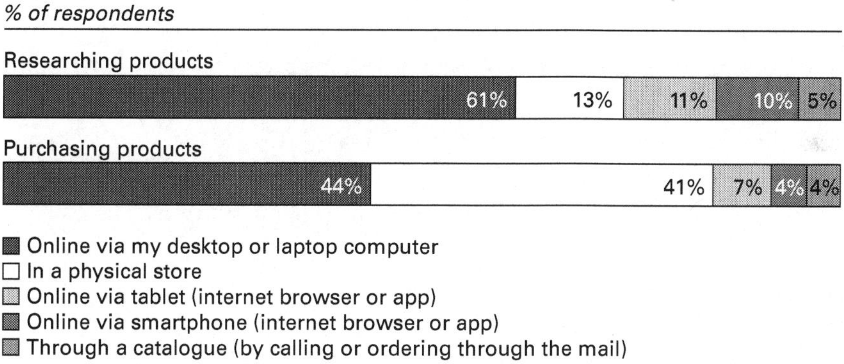

% of respondents

Researching products

| 61% | 13% | 11% | 10% | 5% |

Purchasing products

| 44% | 41% | 7% | 4% | 4% |

- ■ Online via my desktop or laptop computer
- □ In a physical store
- ▨ Online via tablet (internet browser or app)
- ■ Online via smartphone (internet browser or app)
- ■ Through a catalogue (by calling or ordering through the mail)

Note: n=5,849
Source: UPS, comScore Inc. and the e-tailing group 'Pulse of the Online Shopper', 11 June 2014

SOURCE: www.eMarketer.com

UK

The Nielsen Global Survey of Ecommerce found that 56 per cent of Britons researched their purchases online before buying in a shop, while 43 per cent check out products in a shop before buying online (Nielsen, 2014).

This shift in consumer behaviour has led to both brands and retailers scrambling to 'own' the best content. The brand/retailer that provides the right content, in the right place, is more likely to win the sale (or in the case of non-transactional sites, the audience).

Google

The role that content plays in SEO has been discussed at length since the dawn of Google. Whilst content was always a notable ranking factor, Google's relationship with content in the early days was questionable at best. In

Google's eyes, it wasn't the quality of the content that was important, just that you had it. Indeed it was not that long ago that keyword-stuffed content was the 'best' content in Google's eyes. In other words, we had SEO technicians writing content and leaving professional content writers out in the cold.

Over time, we have seen Google placing a greater reliance on content factors in determining a site's credentials to rank. We have gone from simply keyword-heavy, electronically-spun paragraphs to a situation where quality, context, relevancy, format, social shares, bounce rates and time on page are all considerable factors. As an example of how extensive this has become, Stickyeyes monitors around 150 known 'ranking factors' using their proprietary software, Roadmap. This effectively tries to 'decode' the Google algorithm by identifying correlations between ranking factors and ranking positions. What Roadmap demonstrates is a clear correlation between good content and strong rankings. As of October 2014, there was a 97 per cent correlation between an increased 'time on site' and Google ranking positions. Overall, sites ranking in the number one position had an average time on site in excess of 263 seconds (Figure 13.3).

FIGURE 13.3 Time spent on site

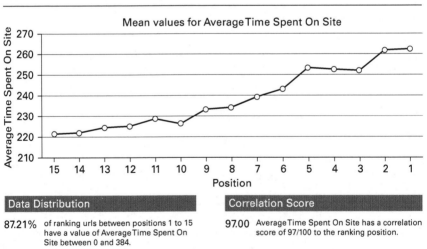

SOURCE: Stickyeyes

We see a similar correlation with bounce rate. In this instance, the sites with the lowest bounce rates attract the strongest rankings. Both average time on site and bounce rate are strong indicators that the content on a site is compelling and engaging enough to encourage users to seek more, or to navigate deeper into a site.

FIGURE 13.4   Bounce rate

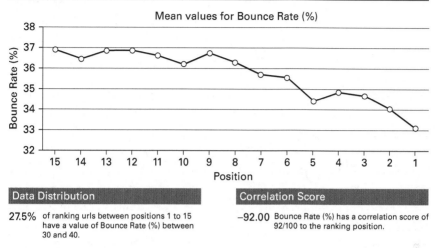

Data Distribution

27.5% of ranking urls between positions 1 to 15 have a value of Bounce Rate (%) between 30 and 40.

Correlation Score

−92.00 Bounce Rate (%) has a correlation score of 92/100 to the ranking position.

SOURCE: Stickyeyes

These correlations are a growing trend, signalling that Google is very much focused on rewarding content above many other known ranking factors. This is good news for the content experts. Only a few years ago journalists and copywriters seemed to have a bleak future, the print industry continued to decline and the new digital world seemed to have less need for them. We have now turned full circle and in most decent digital marketing agencies, especially those with an SEO focus, you will find as many content experts as developers.

People and process for creating content

So content is important. Consumers increasingly demand it and the most dominant search engine in the majority of markets favours quality content. In this section we cover what people and processes you need to create content.

People

Conceptually, content is not that difficult to grasp. There is a lot of common sense involved. Unfortunately, many brands still struggle, and continue to get content marketing wrong, because they have wrongly determined who is responsible for content marketing within the business.

It starts at the top. Many brands and organizations continue to operate in silos. They have PR sitting on the upper floors, the SEO teams halfway up the building and, as ever, IT down in the basement. When an organization has different teams working individually, often to different performance metrics, it becomes incredibly difficult to develop a culture that allows content to thrive.

Content marketing is a form of marketing that touches every department, not just a handful of creatives and copywriters. It needs strategists and analysts to understand the market, branding teams to understand the customer psyche, marketers to create the idea, copywriters to produce the content, search marketers to understand the impact on SEO, PR to identify earned media opportunities and IT to make sure that it all works together. And that is just for a purely digital campaign. Content marketing only works when the walls between teams are broken down and silos are removed, allowing teams to collaborate freely and work to a single, customer-centric goal. That is a culture that has to come from the chief marketing officer (CMO), or even the CEO. And it is this person who is ultimately responsible for content marketing in a brand. Without a clear focus and a culture that encourages collaboration, making content marketing work becomes infinitely more difficult.

CASE STUDY   Adidas

Background

A great example of a brand that has got content marketing right is Adidas.

Strategy

In March 2014 the Adidas Group, which encompasses both the Adidas and Reebok brands, announced that it had year-long plans to create 'digital newsrooms' for its brands. The move was part of a long-term strategy to capitalize on hot trends and build on 'moments of celebration and acknowledgement'. Adidas states on its website that it wants to own the stories that global superstars create and capitalize on the action in real time. It also states that it wants to be seen as pivotal to the success of players and remain in the focus of sports fans watching in a range of locations around the world.

Key lessons

So what makes their approach different? The key factors of the digital newsroom concept that you can learn from as a marketer are:

- People: lots of them. Adidas has invested heavily in a skilled team from both online and offline backgrounds.

- A wealth of content: Adidas sucks up as much sporting and related content as possible. The majority has nothing exciting about it, the key is finding the needles in the haystack. And as Nike and Puma have similar set-ups there is also a race to find those needles first.

- Speed: in the newsroom set-up speed does not mean quick, it means immediate. To be truly effective a content team needs to be 'switched on' for the events that its audience cares about, be ready to act and have the resource to spring into action when the biggest stories break.

- Trust: marketers regularly come up against hurdles that prevent them from producing fast, groundbreaking content. From slow sign-off procedures and legal compliance, through to overzealous brand protection and a lack of resource, many creative content teams find themselves stifled, unable to publish content until it is too late. To be immediate the reins need to be loosened, or perhaps even cut. This does not mean that you can let your creative team go wild and publish what they want, it does mean you need to define the boundaries very clearly.

While the newsroom concept will be a step too far for many organizations, the key principles can and should be adopted by any company that is taking content marketing seriously. Recent stats from the United States suggest that most companies still need to work out exactly what they are doing with their content marketing from an organizational structure point of view.

Processes

Once you have the organizational structure and people in place it is time to create a plan and set of clearly defined processes. Most companies don't have this in place; according to the Content Marketing Institute only 27 per cent of content marketers have a documented strategy (Content Marketing Institute, 2015).

FIGURE 13.5   B2C content marketing

45% of US B2C content marketers have a dedicated content marketing group. [Source: *Content Marketing Institute*, October 2014]

Percentage of B2C Marketers Who Have a Dedicated Content Marketing Group

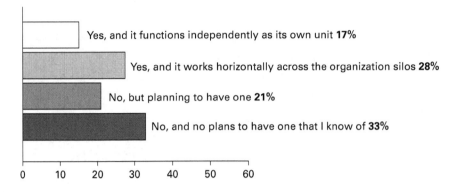

Yes, and it functions independently as its own unit **17%**

Yes, and it works horizontally across the organization silos **28%**

No, but planning to have one **21%**

No, and no plans to have one that I know of **33%**

FIGURE 13.6   B2C content marketing

27% of US B2C content marketers have a documented strategy. [Source: *Content Marketing Institute*, October 2014]

Percentage of B2C Marketers Who Have a Content Marketing Strategy

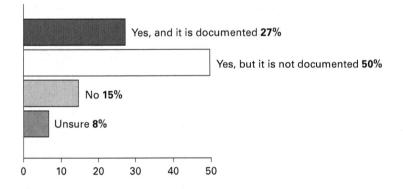

Yes, and it is documented **27%**

Yes, but it is not documented **50%**

No **15%**

Unsure **8%**

The key stages to create content are:

- objectives and strategy;
- data analysis and target groups;
- ideation;
- creation and planning.

Objectives and strategy

One of the biggest mistakes organizations make when starting down the content journey is to jump straight to creating content. This is typically for one of the following reasons:

- Someone in a position of authority is shouting, 'I want content and I want it now.'
- The content creator assumes that they know their brand/audience well enough so why not just get started.
- Jumping straight into creating content is easier (and potentially more fun).

As tempting as it might be to do this it is crucial to start with setting your objectives and strategy. Jay Baer summed this up very nicely: 'Content helps achieve business objectives, not content objectives' (Baer, 2012).

So objectives and strategies need to start with what your business wants to achieve. For example, if the focus is on retaining and growing existing customers then the content requirements will be very different to a focus on attracting new customers. Broadly speaking, content marketing strategies can be linked to the sales life cycle and therefore typical objectives are to:

- Create awareness: increase visibility of the product service.
- Change perception: change views on the product service (for example following a product recall).
- Create engagement: increase interactions with the brand and website.
- Drive transactions: increase leads and conversions.
- Increase retention: improved loyalty and customer satisfaction.

An alternative and perhaps simpler approach is to classify the objectives into brand engagement or demand generation:

- Brand engagement:
  - thought leadership;
  - improve brand perception;
  - increase loyalty;
  - create brand advocates.
- Demand generation:
  - increase traffic;
  - generate leads;
  - nurture leads.

Of course, brand engagement and demand generation are far from mutually exclusive. It stands to reason that creating lots of brand advocates is a sure-fire way to generate demand.

Finally, it is important to agree up front whether the content required is functional, engaging or both:

- *Functional content*: this is the content that sits on your site and performs a very functional role, typically to help you sell your products/services. A good example is product descriptions or user reviews. This content is often overlooked as it is not the 'sexy' content that gets presented at digital marketing award ceremonies. It is, however, the most crucial to get right as good functional content helps you to convert browsers into customers and also has a significant impact on natural search rankings.

- *Engaging content*: this is the content that is typically used to communicate information to your target audience in an interesting and engaging manner. The purpose of this content is to encourage people to talk about it digitally (across the web and social media) and naturally link to it. As well as enhancing your brand, this content can also help to improve your natural search performance as it garners links from authoritative sites. Typically this content sits off-site although it may well have its home on-site.

Having defined your high-level strategy and objectives the next step is to perform some detailed analysis to inform the brief.

Data/analysis and target groups

Having set the high-level strategy you then need to perform analysis to inform the content approach. The most important consideration by far is your target audience; however, there are also a number of other data points/tools that are worthy of consideration first:

- Brand guidelines: most sizeable companies have brand guidelines and good content marketers know them inside out. As well as providing creative cues and tone-of-voice guidance they should also give a good idea of the acceptable boundaries for the brand.

- Competitor analysis: what are your competitors doing? This market intelligence is crucial for a number of reasons. It will give you an idea of what content is being consumed, where it is being consumed and crucially what content already exists so that you do not simply replicate it.

- Customer interviews/focus groups/surveys: ask your customers what content they consume, where and why. Also ask what they would like. But ask with caution... one of the smartest marketers I ever met gave me some sage advice when he said, 'What people say they do and what they actually do can be very different.' So ask away but do not rely 100 per cent on this; make sure you test the hypothesis that your face-to-face research is telling you, by looking at real data.

- Analytics: utilize your own analytics to ascertain the most valuable content you already have.

- Keyword analysis: utilizing Google Keyword Optimizer, or other third-party tools such as Moz (Moz.com) you can get a good idea of what your customers are searching for. See Chapter 5, which discusses SEO, for more details on keyword analysis.

Target groups

Unfortunately many brand marketers still are under the illusion that customers love their brand. The unfortunate truth is that your customers do not care about you. They do not care about your products, your history, your service or that you even exist. They only care about themselves.

So why would those people care about your content? The reality is that no one craves branded content, so the only branded content that achieves any recognition whatsoever is the content that fills a need or that solves a problem. As a brand, you need to make yourself and your content relevant.

Overcoming this challenge requires a deep understanding of your target audiences, the challenges they face and how they interact with brands online. It comes down to three key questions:

1 What is your audience's problem?
   If your product or service does not solve a problem, it is extremely difficult to create content that is going to grab their attention. Do your audiences have a problem that they need to address, do they want to do something differently or do they simply want to be entertained? Whatever those challenges are, understand the pain points of your audiences and articulate how your product or service solves them.

2 Where are your audiences digitally active?
   Different audience groups are active in different places online. Younger audiences may be more active on social media and mobile devices, whilst older audiences may prefer to consume digital content

on specialist blogs or mainstream media sites using desktop PCs. Consider where your audiences are likely to be most digitally active, who they are most likely to be influenced by and where they are likely to consume content. Consumer analysis tools, such as Hitwise or GlobalWebIndex, are incredibly powerful at identifying where your target audiences spend their time online, giving your brand a clear indication on how you should shape and distribute your content.

3 How do they like to be communicated with?
Knowing where your audience is, is one thing; knowing how to communicate with them is quite another. Different audiences consume content in different ways and different formats. Some prefer long-form written copy, other audiences may prefer infographics or video content. Again, Hitwise and GlobalWebIndex are extremely useful sources for this insight, informing the format that is likely to be most effective for your content.

Pulling it all together

Ideation

Having defined the strategy and objectives, performed the research and gained a detailed understanding of the target groups it is time to move to ideation. Of course this can, and often is, done by one person but if you want to create a number of great content ideas quickly then it is preferable to use a group. Anyone, within reason, can contribute to an ideation session. The only prerequisite is they must be privy to all the previous research. Indeed an ideal session starts with an overview of objectives, research performed and the target audience. While it is perfectly reasonable to simply sit a group of people in a room and see what emerges, a more structured approach is recommended. Brainstorming is one method but, as it is commonly used and understood, I will suggest an alternative and lesser known approach – brainwriting.

Brainwriting was developed by Bernd Rohrbach in 1968 and allows a small group (six participants and a moderator) to create 108 ideas in just 30 minutes. The approach is as follows:

- Ensure all participants are fully briefed on the goals of the session and any background research.

- Create a 'problem statement'. For example, 'We want to drive awareness of our new product.'

- The 'problem statement' is written on top of worksheets (a grid where the heading of the columns are Idea 1, Idea 2 and Idea 3) handed out to all participants.

- Each participant is then given five minutes to complete the first row with three ideas on how to solve the problem.

- The sheets are then passed to the right and the process is repeated, with each participant being free to gain inspiration from the new ideas presented.

- The process ends after six rounds and the worksheet should be filled with 108 ideas.

The ideas are then quickly screened to remove any duplicates and then the group decide on the best ideas to develop further.

Creation and planning

Having decided on the broad content theme(s) you want to create it is time to plan out the creation. Whether the content is to be created in-house or by an agency, a detailed brief is required. The good news is that all the hard work of the previous steps gives you the essence of a great brief.

However, given that content marketers are going to be juggling multiple content projects at any one time, it is advisable to implement a content calendar to keep track of all the briefs. A simple Excel sheet will do, the core elements being:

- publish date;
- location/media;
- author;
- designer;
- audience/target persona;
- title;
- synopsis;
- assets required;
- dependencies.

In addition to the content calendar the content owner should also have a content editing checklist to ensure that the end deliverable meets the brief.

Distribution

So creating content is not easy and, once done, it is all too easy to consider the box ticked. Content created, job done. However, without a rock-solid distribution plan (and effort) all the hard work will go to waste. As a rule of thumb you should allocate 30–50 per cent of your budgeted time to distribution.

No matter how good the content is, creating traction in a crowded market is a key stage in delivering success. This is typically achieved using a mix of three channels: owned, earned and paid (Figure 13.7).

FIGURE 13.7   Three channels: owned, earned and paid

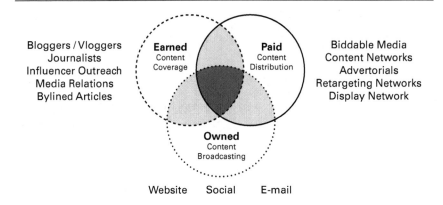

Bloggers / Vloggers
Journalists
Influencer Outreach
Media Relations
Bylined Articles

Earned
Content Coverage

Paid
Content Distribution

Biddable Media
Content Networks
Advertorials
Retargeting Networks
Display Network

Owned
Content Broadcasting

Website   Social   E-mail

Owned

These are the channels that are fully controlled and owned by you. They can drive early groundswell and engagement with any content-led campaigns. The obvious owned channel is your website, but also give consideration to your social channels and how the content you have created can be leveraged on these channels (although note that social channels now invariably need paid placements to kick start). It is also easy to forget about your e-mail database, bearing in mind that the content message might need to be tweaked for existing versus potential customers.

There are a number of tools to help with owned media; two in particular that are worthy of mention are:

- Buffer: this helps businesses to analyse when their target audience are most active on social, and schedules new content releases accordingly.

- Advocate: many companies forget about one of their biggest assets for owned media distribution – their employees. Advocate helps to encourage social sharing by employees of corporate content by providing a tool that demonstrates how their shares are making a difference.

Earned

These are channels that you cannot buy exposure on, but you can earn it by providing value to the user. This requires a concerted effort to sell your content to journalists, bloggers and website owners. If you have done your audience research and followed a structured approach to content strategy and ideation you should find that your content resonates. While earned media exposure can be performed in-house it is common for brands to turn to specialists for this service who have both the contacts and tools (such as Gorkana Media Database) at hand to make the task easier.

Paid

These are the channels that typically involve some form of media or partner spend in return for exposure for your campaigns. They are also often the most overlooked, as digital marketers tend to wrongly associate paid channels as acquisition-only channels. While they are highly effective for driving traffic for e-commerce they can also help to generate groundswell for content. Examples of paid media uses include:

- a paid search advert on Google to promote a new white paper;

- use of Outbrain or Taboola (both content distribution platforms that tend to serve content on major publisher websites) to push out a fun/ novel piece of content;

- Facebook advertising to a targeted demographic of early adopters;

- LinkedIn advertising to promote a webinar;

- display adverts to launch a new app.

It is worth noting at this point that social sits in both the owned and paid sections. The unfortunate truth is that in order to genuinely leverage social you need to pay to reach people – including your own fans. That does not mean you should avoid non-paid posts; rather, if you really want to engage people via social you will need to consider paid placements as well.

Measuring the value of content

Given that content can have many guises and the objectives can be quite different there is no one standard measurement approach or tool set. Below is a list of common metrics used; which ones you utilize will depend on the content being measured and the objectives for that content.

Volume and reach metrics

These metrics look at the volume of touchpoints with an audience as well as the quantity of campaign/channel-driven goals. Examples include:

- Social reach and followers: is your social reach/followers increasing?
- Impressions: how many impressions did your content receive?
- Media coverage gained: what coverage was gained? What is the reach of the publications that have published the content?
- Social mentions: how many times has your content been mentioned on social channels?
- Links back to your site obtained: time-poor consumers of content will of course be more inclined to visit your site if a link is provided in the content. In addition, links from quality sites also bring SEO benefits.

Engagement and consumption metrics

These metrics look at the quality of customer interaction and discussion, as well as how campaign or channel content is consumed. Examples include:

- Content interaction: how many page views/downloads has the content generated? What are the bounce rates for the content? (Bounce rate is the percentage of users who visit a page and then immediately leave.)
- Social triggers: retweets, shares and posts.
- Social engagement: this is where content is actively promoted by the consumer and, more than just a like or a share, there is real engagement. For example, adding comments to a post. Linked to this, and a more sophisticated measure, is amplification. Amplification measures the real value of the social sharing by considering the audience of the person sharing a piece of content. For example, a share by Katy Perry, who has over 60 million followers on Twitter, is likely to be more valuable than a share by this book's author (depending on the context!).

Acquisition and value metrics

These metrics look at traffic acquisition as well as the full range of sales and revenue metrics:

- How many conversions/leads have been generated?
- What is the attributable sales volume and revenue?
- What is the cost per lead/action/sale?

Depending on your content objectives, a combination of the above metrics should provide the analysis you need to ascertain what content is working and what is not.

Measuring failure

This is an important consideration for content marketing. When it comes to making engaging content you should expect, and indeed celebrate, failure. That is not to say that if you produce 100 pieces of content you think are engaging and they all fail you should be happy, but it is important to recognize that not everything you produce will work. In fact if everything is working you might ask whether you are pushing the boundaries enough.

The key to success is to have your measurement in place. Understanding the features of each piece of content and how you have distributed it will help you to understand the reasons for failure when it happens. For example, the subject of your content, the author, which social channels were used, on what day and time and whether it was imagery, copy or video will all be factors in success or failure, so being able to analyse these is important to being able to refine your content strategy over time.

CASE STUDY   Hertz Europe

Background

Hertz is a well-known global car rental company. However, in recent years the brand had come under pressure from low-cost operators, particularly in the holiday rentals market.

Strategy

To counter this competitive pressure, Hertz commissioned a detailed analysis of the European vehicle hire market to identify where they could steal a march on their competitors in six European territories. This analysis revealed a gap in both functional and engaging content compared to the competition. The lack of content was hurting the brand both in terms of SEO performance for non-brand terms, especially location-based and in terms of conversion. The challenge was deploying a huge quantity of functional content in an incredibly short space of time, as well as developing creative content concepts to support rankings growth for both local and core keyword terms.

Their solution was a major deployment of both functional and creative content. Whilst Hertz's organic rankings were relatively strong on generic keyword terms, by virtue of the strength of the brand, there were a number of key opportunities to drive improvements for localized keyword search terms. These city- or region-specific keyword terms had significantly lower volumes, but would drive considerably better conversion rates due to the intent of the searcher. For example, a person searching for 'Car hire Malaga' is certainly showing purchase intent.

The result was the creation of over 11,000 pages of localized content across the six international domains covering every town, city and region served by Hertz. Of course this was a mammoth task; however, Hertz followed a logical and audience-centric approach, which made the production process relatively seamless. Crucially, the focus was on added-value content; a side result was SEO benefit.

This functional content was supported by creative, engaging content campaigns that aimed to inspire people to explore a Hertz location. From encouraging leading journalists to try new experiences with a Hertz van, and sharing great walking destinations outside of Edinburgh, through to ghost hunting in St Pancras and finding vintage fashion in Islington, north London, the creative content would reach new audiences and enhance Hertz's online reach.

Results

Outstanding revenue growth across six European markets. The localized content strategy delivered outstanding returns on investment for Hertz, with both booking and revenue growth exceeding all expectations. The creative content helped Hertz to secure excellent levels of coverage, and high-quality referrals, from leading publications across Europe. This included the *Telegraph*, *TNT Magazine*, *Scottish Daily Record* and the *Herald* in the UK, as well as *Le Parisien*, *Grazia*, *GQ* and the Huffington Post across Europe. The localized content strategy resulted in significant rankings uplift for city- and region-specific search terms. These pages, which contained useful information regarding the destination in question for the end user, supported revenue growth in all six of the core European markets. This ranged from growth of 11.06 per cent year on year (YoY) in the UK, up to 121.13 per cent YoY revenue growth in the Italian market.

Key lessons

- Hertz's adoption of a content-led strategy helped to drive significant improvements in all markets through solid research, broad and relevant content that was well distributed.

- The key content goals, discussed above, were all met and this is ultimately why their strategy was so successful.

International content

While the processes remain the same, regardless of the market, there are some key considerations for international content marketing that need to form part of your content briefs:

- Are the personas different? Your segments and personas may be similar in another culture but with small differences or they may be completely different.
- Are the platforms different? For example, the dominant search engine in Russia is Yandex and in China is Baidu. The dominant micro-blogging site in China is Sina Weibo, not Twitter.
- Cultural differences? This is particularly the case when it comes to using humour. What is considered funny in one country might be highly offensive in another. We looked at cultural differences in Chapter 2.
- Legal implications? For example, in China the content can be censored on Baidu to keep in line with the country's laws. Privacy laws differ in countries and regions, as do laws around the freedom of speech and the right to be forgotten. Ensure that you understand the relevant laws and how they apply to your strategy.
- Seasonal events? Thanksgiving, Chinese New Year and Bonfire Night, for example, are all very significant celebrations in their home countries but much less so elsewhere. On the other hand, events such as St Patrick's Day and Christmas are often celebrated in countries that have no specific tie to the celebration but that still enjoy taking part.

- Localization: while it may be tempting simply to get your great content translated, you may well lose the intended audience if you do. Having your content written and reviewed by local native speakers will ensure that it is both culturally and linguistically accurate.

Audit checklist

> *A three-step content audit checklist is available to download at:*
> **www.koganpage.com/DigitalMarketingStrategy**
>
> Conducting a content audit is one of the most critical aspects of content marketing, but it is also one of the most difficult. This guide will take you through the three major stages of a content audit, highlighting what to look for and how to find the insight that you need to make the best possible decisions. This online resource will help you to develop your content strategy.

Summary

Content has many forms and is much more than just the written word. It can be both functional (descriptive content) and engaging (designed to provoke interest or a reaction) and its meteoric rise is largely down to changing consumer behaviour and Google's emphasis on ranking sites that provide great content. In order to resonate with the intended audience it is important to consider the content pillars. Content should be:

- credible;
- shareable;
- useful or fun;
- interesting;
- relevant;
- different;
- on brand.

Creating great content is not easy. First and foremost it requires the right people and the right organizational structure; without this the content produced is unlikely to be the best it can be or reach its potential. Content production starts with setting high-level objectives and strategy. Having defined this it is important to analyse the data you have, review competitive output and, crucially, define your target audience using personas. Ideation can then begin and brainwriting is a great way to create over 100 ideas in under 30 minutes. Content creation is, however, only half of the challenge. Content becomes successful when it is distributed well. In order to maximize coverage it is important to consider all channels:

- Owned: the channels you own – for example, your website, your social channels (to a degree), your e-mail database.
- Earned: the coverage that money cannot buy; often editorial in nature and closely linked to traditional PR.
- Paid: bought coverage has a role to play, in particular to help initially seed content on publisher sites or socially.

In order to measure content effectively we need to consider three key elements:

- volume and reach;
- engagement and consumption;
- acquisition and value.

Finally, creating content for international markets requires a very local approach; a simple translation will likely do more harm than good.

Chapter checklist

- What is content marketing? ☐
- What is content? ☐
- What content types should you use? ☐
- Why content marketing? ☐
- People and process for creating content ☐
- Distribution ☐
- Measuring the value of content ☐
- International content ☐

Further reading

- *On content strategy:*
  Casey, M (2015) *The Content Strategy Toolkit*, New Riders. This includes the research phase, creation of your strategy, gaining buy-in and delivery of your strategy.

References

Baer, J (2012) [accessed 1 November 2015] A Field Guide to the Four Types of Content Marketing Metrics [Online] http://www.convinceandconvert.com/content-marketing/a-field-guide-to-the-4-types-of-content-marketing-metrics/

Content Marketing Institute (2015) [accessed 1 November 2015] Annual Research: Content Marketing Budgets, Benchmarks and Trends [Online] http://contentmarketinginstitute.com/research/

G/O Digital (2014) [accessed 1 November 2015] Facebook Advertising: The Social Commerce Lifeline [Online] http://www.godigitalmarketing.com/wp-content/uploads/2014/08/Facebook-Advertising-The-Social-Commerce-Lifeline-for-Small-Businesses-FINAL.pdf

Nielsen (2014) [accessed 1 November 2015] The Nielsen Global Survey of Ecommerce [Online] http://ir.nielsen.com/files/doc_financials/Nielsen-Global-E-commerce-Report-August-2014.pdf

Analytics and reporting

14

What we will cover in this chapter

This chapter covers how to build effective measures for digital marketing success, the tools needed to track your achievements and how to communicate them consistently as part of the story of your digital strategy. The key areas covered in this chapter are:

- The data landscape
- The reliability of data-based decisions
- What are analytics?
- Tools and technology
- Attribution modelling
- Reporting

Chapter goals

By the end of this chapter you should understand the importance of analytics and key techniques in developing your reporting structure. You should understand attribution modelling and have an appreciation of data-based decision reliability. You will understand tag- and server-based analytics as well as social and web analytics.

The data landscape

The final part of developing your strategy is also quite possibly the most important. Delivering a strategy that is not effectively measured can create confusion or a lack of transparency that is impossible to come back from. In other words, if your strategy is set in motion but you cannot prove that it is delivering any results then it can quickly receive negative feedback from your internal stakeholders and can even be cancelled by your decision makers. If your goals cannot be demonstrably met, how will you or, perhaps more importantly, your stakeholders ever know if your strategy has been a success or how to adapt it going forwards? Everything before this point becomes utterly meaningless without ensuring that your analysis is implemented correctly and is future proofed as much as possible.

Digital marketers are fortunate (and some may say also unfortunate) to have endless tools and data at their disposal to enable full transparency. The challenges here are, therefore, not the limits of technology or visibility, but in the strategic implementation and reporting of the data that is outputted. Understanding how best to use this data and how to fit the pieces of disparate information together to form solid insights is an art form as much as a science.

'Big data' is a phrase that has been heavily used in digital marketing over recent years. This is a great way to express exactly what we are looking at here. Big data simply refers to data sets so large and complex that they are difficult to process using standard tools and techniques. It therefore also refers to being able to make smart decisions through interpretation of the full data set rather than the separate parts. The term big data was coined by NASA in 1997 when describing a problem they had with visualization. It began to be used in a wider sense from 2008 by computer scientists and has been used in digital marketing since around 2010.

Big data

'Data sets whose size is beyond the ability of typical database software tools to capture, store, manage and analyse.' (McKinsey, 2011)

We have already examined research and insight in Chapter 2 as key areas of data that will inform your strategy and will continue to influence it over time. These remain key measures of success but are unlikely to make it on to your reporting dashboards and so we will not look at those again now.

The reliability of data-based decisions

There is a great deal of data available to us and, as mentioned above, this can be a real asset to our decision making. It can, however, be dangerous if used incorrectly. There are two primary challenges that we need to be aware of: the human factor and data alignment.

The human factor

Data is in itself worthless. A simple set of information achieves nothing without some action being taken on it. Whether that action be through direct human interaction or through a human-created algorithm or formula there is some human interaction necessary to turn the data into something actionable. This creates an opportunity for error. The human interaction is even deeper when we consider that human interaction is also necessary to set up the collection of the data in the first place. Not only could our interpretation of the data be wrong but the data itself may be wrong. For example, if we look at the implementation of a fairly standard and simple-to-use analytics tool such as Google Analytics we see four main stages where humans play a key role:

- Someone working at Google designs the product.
- Someone installs Google Analytics on their website.
- Someone sets up the preferences and reports within Google Analytics.
- Someone uses those reports to make decisions.

So the product may be perfect but the set-up may be wrong. The set-up may be fully functional but the interpretation of the reports may be wrong. Or the set-up and interpretation may be correct but there may be a glitch in the program.

Data alignment

Very few businesses rely on one data set to make decisions. It is rarely possible for one organization to look at their financial data, sales, staff numbers, marketing spend, fixed costs, investments and a great number of other data sets together in one system. This is not a technology issue but much more one of confidentiality and convenience. Managing your paid search activity in the same system that you pay your creative agency and manage your staff salaries does not make a great deal of sense. Therefore there is a very strong chance that your systems will not always agree. Even when using two very similar systems, sometimes ones produced by the same company, you will find discrepancies in the numbers. This can occur due to the definition of a term.

If for example we take a 'hit', how might you define that? Immediately there are two commonly used options: 1) an element of your page is loaded (eg an image); 2) someone arrives on your page.

Technically option 1 is the correct answer – a hit is when a file is downloaded – but many people still use the term 'hit' to refer to a visit. If no files other than the web page itself are downloaded when someone visits then a visit or page view is the same as a hit. There are many discrepancies between data sets that will cause your data not to match – and being aware of this is crucial.

What does this mean for my digital strategy?

This demonstrates that it is essential to understand what you are trying to measure so as when any issues arise with the data you can immediately understand which definition or option is the correct one to use. In the above example you may use the actual definition of 'hits' to evaluate server requirements, whereas you would be far more interested in page views and unique visits for your website traffic analytics.

What are analytics?

In Chapter 2 we looked at defining key performance indicators (KPIs). We are now looking at how we measure and report on those KPIs and the key method of this is through analytics. We have mentioned them throughout the book and we will now examine them in more detail. In simple terms analytics are reporting tools that allow the user to view key statistics on the performance of their site. These statistics have expanded significantly since 2005 and now include some advanced data sets such as real time, demographics, social media, attribution, multichannel and cross-device data. There are two forms of analytics that are server based, where the web server log files are read and tag based, where tagging code is added to the pages of the site to allow data to be collected. It is worth taking a quick look at the differences of each now.

Server-based analytics

This was the beginning of analytics and so arrived before tag-based services. Server-based analytics collects data from the log files that are kept on the server and therefore show a picture of the activity on the site. Challenges have arisen with this method since its arrival in the early 1990s. First, it only measures hits, which as we mentioned above do not show a true picture of visitors. This was addressed when page views and visits were added. Search engine spiders or robots (the methods used by search engines to crawl the internet and index websites) and other challenges such as caches then made it more difficult for server-based analytics to detect humans. This means that you may not see cached visits and may see some spider visits.

Tag-based analytics

These arrived in the mid-1990s and those of us old enough will remember seeing bright-green visit counters on the bottom of many pages. You can still find them dotted around the corners of the internet. Most of these had disappeared by 2000, or so it seemed. Instead of the graphic disappearing completely it had been replaced by a small invisible pixel, which when sent to the analytics software was able to log information about the activity on the page and behaviour of the user. This method continues to evolve and the pixel itself has been replaced by code (although some people still refer to this code as the pixel), but it is now the more commonly used form of web analytics as it is able to overcome some of the challenges that server-based analytics has faced. It does not, however, offer some of the solutions that server-based analytics can.

Server-based versus tag-based analytics

The advantages of server-based analytics are primarily in its integration and SEO solutions. This method uses the server logs that are already created by the company and so nothing new need be built; this also means that the company owns and retains the data at all times, which is a key consideration when buying data services from a supplier. Also, because the server-based method includes search engine spider data it can provide better SEO information than the tag-based solutions. This is because you have access to the real spider data itself rather than having limited data pulled into your tag-based software. Google Analytics, for example, is well known to have decreased its SEO analytics within its tag-based solution.

Tag-based analytics is by far the more preferable method when looking for rich user interaction data. This method enables logging of specific actions on elements within the page and gathering of advanced user data such as browser. Tag-based analytics also has the advantage of being able to count cached pages, which account for around one-third of all visits.

The most popular analytics tool has historically been Google Analytics (a tag-based solution) and it remains the leader today, primarily due to its freemium model and solid performance. There are some restrictions around what the free Google product can offer but the standard offering is robust enough for most organizations. There are still several other key players in the market and we will mention those below, as Google certainly does not have a monopoly here.

A useful case study here is Nissan's use of Google Analytics.

CASE STUDY   Nissan

Background

Nissan Motor Company runs a large number of websites around the world, aimed at guiding their customers in their vehicle purchase decisions. Nissan offers the visitors to their site a variety of resources to help them choose, including product specifications, downloadable promotional materials and test-drive booking services. These websites are therefore not merely e-commerce sites. Nissan wanted to achieve more than just tracking simple goals and had the ambition to understand their visitors' preferences around the cars on offer, for instance what car models and colours were the most popular.

Strategy

Nissan implemented Google Analytics software and used the e-commerce functionality in an innovative way to capture this information and gain this understanding. When a prospective customer books a test drive or requests a brochure, they are prompted to complete a form, which as well as asking for contact information also inquires about their preferences for the vehicle they are interested in. The simple addition of an e-commerce tag, added to the 'thank you' page that appears after form completion, enabled this information to be captured.

Results

Nissan were then able to analyse the data and understand which vehicles were regularly generating interest and therefore tailor their marketing strategies appropriately in each market.

Key lessons

- The key for your strategy is to understand that gathering detailed data can inform commercial decision making and the shape of your digital strategy.
- Using analytics tags in innovative ways to gain this data can be hugely valuable.

Tools and technology

There are many tools available to track your digital data and these can be broken down into several areas. We look at five of the most common of these here:

- web analytics;
- social analytics;
- SEO analytics;
- user experience;
- tag management.

Web analytics

What is it?

Web analytics is the tool that we are usually referring to when discussing analytics. It is the tool that collects and reports on all of the key data on the performance of our website. There are many tools available with very strong offerings and it is important to consider your needs when selecting which tool to move forward with.

The standard data you should expect to get from your web analytics tool includes the following:

- Page views, visits, unique visitors, bounce rate, session duration.
- New versus returning visitors: users who have visited before or not.
- Language and location: helpful for geographical purposes.
- Demographics: data on the user's high-level information such as age.
- Device type, make and model: technical data on your device hardware.
- Browser, resolution and operating system: technical data on your device software.
- Traffic source: which pages people came from.

- Keyword analysis: a review of the keywords used to reach your site.
- Goal conversion: the percentage of times that a business-defined goal is met.
- E-commerce tracking: data on user behaviour in your online shop.
- Funnel conversion: the percentage of shoppers who make it from the start to the end of your purchase journey.

Major players

Throughout this section we examine a few of the options for each service. It should be noted that none of these are recommendations and the lists are not exhaustive, so it is important that you research your options thoroughly to find the best option for your digital marketing strategy. There are a great number of solutions available for whatever your web analytics needs might be. These include offerings from Google, Adobe, Webtrends, Kissmetrics, GoSquared and ComScore, amongst many more. Each has its own advantages and we will take a quick look below to give a sample of the market:

- Google's standard freemium offering of Google Analytics (often known as GA) has now moved on to its more advanced product known as Universal Analytics. This tool offers all of the key metrics you would expect above plus a great deal more. Google also offers its paid product, known as Premium Analytics, which offers a great deal more customization and scale. Google Analytics is the most widely used web analytics tool on the market.
- Adobe Analytics, previously known as Site Catalyst, is an advanced web analytics tool with a very broad set of data that is used by many leading e-commerce brands and is part of the Adobe Marketing Cloud, which offers a great deal of strength when integrating a number of tools together.
- Webtrends is another established major player that offers a good overview of the key metrics you would want to measure.
- Kissmetrics is less well known than some of the major players but has a strong offering when monitoring funnel paths and conversions, and for that reason it may be worth reviewing their offering for e-commerce sites.
- GoSquared is a tool that has a strong real-time offering. Real time is itself not unique to GoSquared but reviews of their offering remain very strong in this field.

How it fits into your strategy

Web analytics is vital to any digital strategy. This tool is the stalwart of your strategy, whatever your strategy may be. If you are focused on high-volume e-commerce then using real-time analytics, visitor demographics and conversion funnels are all crucial so that you can react quickly, personalize your experience for optimal conversion and monitor your sales process closely. If you are spending a great deal on digital advertising then understanding your conversion paths, attribution and traffic sources is vital to be able to improve your UX, understand which digital channels are contributing to conversion and which directly provide the traffic. If you have a content-based site then understanding what content is popular, who is reading what and on what device is essential. All of this requires web analytics. Without web analytics you are blind to the activity on your site – and without this data you cannot make the decisions you need to in order to make your strategy successful.

Social analytics

What is it?

Social analytics refers to the tools used to monitor the effectiveness of social media. Social media itself, as we have already examined, is a relatively young channel and so the tools used continue to evolve. There are, however, some very clear metrics that should be monitored to determine the effectiveness of your social strategy.

There are two distinct areas of social media that can be measured and they are content and promotion. Your business may operate in one or both of these. Using social media to share engaging content is a goal of many businesses and one that can and should be monitored closely to learn how to improve future content plans. Using social to advertise your products and services to highly targeted and engaged audiences is also an increasingly common way of using the channel but one that involves very different metrics.

In order to understand how your content is resonating with your audience you need to have visibility of how users are engaging with this content, what topics are the most popular and to whom, when users engage and on what device. All of these questions are vital if you are to understand how to deliver content that will interest your customers and prospects. Your users may prefer lengthy articles or short videos, they may only consume your content at night or almost entirely on mobile devices. Your users may choose to share only very specific content types or maybe only your true brand advocates share your content. It is vital to understand this level of detail. Once you understand this level of detail you can make key decisions such as which content to produce and how often. This will influence how you manage resource internally and how you publish content. If your users read on their mobile devices and convert on tablets then optimizing your site for content on mobile is essential; ensuring you have a good video solution is vital if your users would benefit from video to make their decisions.

When using social media as a channel for promotion the metrics may be very different. If you are looking to improve your social footprint then you may be looking at more of the 'vanity' metrics, ie those that do not really indicate the success of an organization on social media but do look impressive to the casual viewer. These include followers and social rank. If you are looking to use social as an acquisition tool then you would also want to include clicks, visits and conversions.

Finally, you may want to measure broader metrics that are beyond your control, by which I am referring to the conversations that happen without your input. This is where social listening tools become a key part of your analytics portfolio – understanding what conversations are happening around your brand or products, your share of voice, the influence of those discussing it and the sentiment of users towards the specific conversations or your brand generally.

Some of the key metrics you should be considering here are as follows:

- Reach: the total users mentioning your brand plus their followers.
- Engagement: the people taking an action on your content.
- Average engagement rate: the average rate of people who took action versus people who saw your content.
- Impressions: the number of times your content has been seen.
- Visits: the total number of times people have been to your site/page.
- Unique visitors: the total number of individuals who have been to your site/page.
- Bounce rate: people arriving and then leaving without visiting another page.
- Click-through rate: the percentage of people who see your content and click through to the end location.
- Conversion rate: the percentage of people who buy versus those who arrived on your site or began a purchase journey.

- Sales: total number of sales (you could also split this into the separate sales channels, eg social, website, phone as a result of the activity).

- Response rate: the percentage of people who have in some way responded to your content.

- Mentions: the number of times that your brand has been mentioned.

- Followers: the number of followers you have on any or all networks.

- Buzz: combination of a number of factors that suggest how popular you are right now.

- Share of voice: the number of conversations about you versus your competition.

- Sentiment: reviewing the types of message about you for positive and negative sentiment.

Major players

As mentioned above, the social metrics arena is constantly changing and evolving and so new powerful tools are added to the list of options almost every day. Some, however, have become established as strong players in the field so it is worth touching on these briefly:

- Facebook Insights is the native Facebook analytics tool for tracking activity on your page. If social media reporting is not a key requirement for your digital strategy or budgets, do not stretch to paying for a tool when you can get a great deal of information from the default Facebook analytics. The tool includes audience demographics, engagement rates, likes, reach, check-ins and also gives an indication of who is talking about your page. For paid campaigns you are also able to monitor the core metrics of each campaign individually. These metrics will go a long way to providing the data you need to measure success on Facebook.

- Twitter Analytics is a simple but effective native tool for measuring success on Twitter. You receive data on each of your tweets including impressions, engagements, link clicks, retweets, favourites and replies. You also receive an average engagement rate, which is helpful for monitoring ongoing content quality. As with Facebook you can monitor your ad campaigns easily through the dashboard, including demographics, conversions, spend and more. Twitter therefore provides a tool that will be useful for a company with a light-touch social media strategy.

- Brandwatch is a social media monitoring company that is widely used globally for social listening. The tool offers its own proprietary technology and supports 43 languages. Data available includes historical, meta, location, influence and sentiment. The interface is simple to use and can be customized. Overall, Brandwatch is a strong option for social listening.

- Radian 6 is part of the Salesforce marketing cloud and is a strong tool for monitoring and managing social posts from both influencers and detractors. As with Brandwatch, there is a wide range of data and strong support. Radian 6 also helps you to discover purchase signals and, using this kind of tool, you can learn to proactively get involved in conversations even when your brand is not the preferred option. It also integrates with the wider Salesforce marketing cloud products and so is worth considering if, for example, you use Exact Target for your e-mails or Salesforce as a CRM system.

- Hootsuite is often thought of as a tool for managing multiple networks together and it has certainly been widely used for that purpose for many years now. It is sometimes overlooked for its analytics offering, however, and so is worth a mention here. Hootsuite Analytics measures brand growth, sentiment analysis, social demographics, content engagement and identifies influencers. This has all been made possible by Hootsuite's acquisition of uberVU in 2014.

There are many more social tools offering a range of analytics and you should conduct thorough research on these to ensure they are providing you with the data you need to measure success.

How it fits into your strategy

The first point to realize here is that social analytics is important whether or not you are running social media advertising or a content plan. Even if it is not appropriate for your business to include social media within the channel mix there is still a strong chance that your brand will be mentioned or discussed there. This is of course significantly more likely if you are a B2C brand than B2B. If you are running a content strategy, as we discussed in Chapter 13, you will need to measure this via social analytics tools. If you are running advertising on social platforms then again you will need to have your measures of success defined and monitored.

Many businesses also measure the 'vanity' metrics mentioned above. These include followers and social rank. You should be cautious when using these metrics for decision making or as measures of success. Followers can be tracked without using any analytics tools, whereas social rank would be tracked through tools such as Klout. The caution lies in the fact that these metrics do not indicate that your content is engaging, that people are converting from your content, that you are reaching the right audience or that you have genuine followers. There are many tools and methods to grow your followers quickly but this is counter-intuitive unless done organically. Purchasing followers who have no real interest in your brand or content is akin to buying links for SEO and should be avoided. It may look impressive to the casual viewer to have 50,000 followers but if only 200 of those are genuine followers then you are disguising the true metrics and making decision making difficult for the sake of vanity.

SEO analytics

What is it?

SEO analytics is the method of tracking the signals that dictate your overall organic search performance. Without using specific tools for this purpose, you will be blind to your achievements or risks within this space. This is an area that is often overlooked or misunderstood due to the rather secretive nature of the channel. Search engines have long hidden their methods from public view and have even removed SEO metrics from analytics tools altogether. For example, Google Analytics gradually increased the percentage of 'not provided' keyword results in its organic search metrics to the point where almost nothing could be gained from looking at this data. There is more detail on this in Chapter 5. Also, simply searching Google for your site may return a ranking but this is just one ranking for one term on one day and is subject to significant change. That result may also be affected by your previous behaviour through a cookie.

Specific SEO tools are therefore needed and these can report on SEO signals. When combined these give a powerful view of your overall SEO performance and the areas to focus on to improve performance.

SEO metrics that can be monitored include:

- inbound links (or backlinks) and link quality;
- search visibility;
- crawl errors;
- site speed;
- broken links;

- rank tracking;
- competitor backlinks;
- brand monitoring.

Major players

All organizations should investigate these major players as they offer important data sets for decision making:

- The Searchmetrics suite is one of the leading tools in SEO analytics and measures content depth and relevance. As content has continued to grow in importance, tools that can measure the impact and return on investment (ROI) of your content have become highly valuable. The suite looks beyond your content to assess competitors' content and therefore provide insight as to how to create stronger content and landing pages to attract converting customers.

- Moz has long been a major player in the SEO arena and the Pro subscription offers a range of tools that will cover almost every metric you could need. These tools include metrics such as keyword rankings, search visibility, link metrics, competitor analysis and brand mentions as well as useful insights such as on-page keyword analysis, keyword difficulty and site audit. You can also install the Mozbar for metrics in real time on every search.

- CognitiveSEO offers backlink analysis, content audits and rank tracking and so provides link quality metrics, social media share, gained and lost links and keyword performance changes. The tools are widely used in the industry and are also a useful part of the process should you be unfortunate enough to suffer a Google penalty, as they have the functionality to find bad links and even submit disavow files directly to Google.

- Majestic is another of the well-established companies often used in link analysis and therefore the removal of any penalties. Majestic has a range of tools, including Site Explorer, which gives in-depth information on a specific site; Search Explorer, which gives search results for a specific keyword; and Keyword Checker, which shows how many times a keyword or phrase appears in their extensive index. They offer many more tools besides these and so can deliver a great deal of insight.

- Google Webmaster Tools (WMT) is a tool that is for simple SEO submission and monitoring. Through WMT you can submit your

XML site map and robots.txt files to give Google a clear view of your site from your perspective. You can monitor site speed and directly monitor any issues that Google finds with your site. It is not a complex tool but is an essential part of your SEO analytics.

How it fits into your strategy

SEO, for the vast majority of businesses, is a key channel within your strategy. If you have a website then you usually, but not always, want your site to perform well in the search results. As mentioned above, SEO can be misunderstood by all but the experienced digital marketer, and so SEO analytics tools are vital to helping you tell your story. Reporting on how the content that you produce, and design changes that you make, are affecting your performance are vital to gaining investment into the channel. Similarly to social media analytics – the other often misunderstood channel – you need to be wary of vanity metrics. The cry from the boardroom is often 'Make us number one on Google' but this is not necessarily the aim. Number one on what terms? For how long? And it may not even be possible if the wider business is not willing or able to create the content or link profile necessary to achieve this. Using the above metrics and tools will help to focus minds on the results of one of the most cost-effective channels for generating traffic to your site.

User experience (UX)

What is it?

UX tools include everything from ensuring that the user is having a pleasant experience to optimizing conversion, and more. The tools in this area are varied and can offer a great deal of insight on behaviours. Some of the outputs are less quantifiable than the other analytics tools as they will show only the behaviour not the cause or intent. For example, if you are viewing a heatmap of user behaviour and you see that your new homepage design has led to more users focusing on your secondary content, and fewer on your primary content, then you can decide that the change has had a negative effect and choose to revert the design to the previous version. You will not, however, know whether this was caused by the new content that you have released, the colours, layout or even macro factors such as what is in the news. You also will not know what the users intended when they arrived. Perhaps the new design performs better for different organic keywords and so you are now attracting a different user group to your site and they are more interested in the secondary content.

UX tools give you the opportunity to test different theories and optimize towards these to create the best possible outcome for the user and your goals.

Major players

- Optimizely is one of the most widely used A/B and multivariate testing tools available. The offering includes personalization, targeting and real-time analytics of your tests to deliver learnings that can be inputted into a continuous improvement of your website UX.

- Clickdensity is a heatmap tool that enables you to see clear areas of interest to the user by showing a visual representation of what elements are clicked on the most. This is easily and immediately understood by most audiences and so the outputs are easy to translate. This also, of course, shows where users are not clicking.

- Browsershots is a simple but effective tool that gives a snapshot of the compatibility of your website across a large number of browsers. This can help you to quickly identify potential issues.

How it fits into your strategy

UX analytics is vital to your strategy as it offers something that none of the other analytics tools can. Traditional analytics can provide a great deal of data for interpretation but UX analytics can display real user journeys, funnels and behaviours. This gives you a fresh perspective on the same data and enables you to gain rich insights into what users really think of your site and how they interact.

Tag management

What is it?

Tag management is a solution that is implemented by many larger organizations in order to make the implementation of other systems easier and to solve some issues that tags create. Tags are pieces of code that you put into your website code in order to fulfil certain tasks such as monitoring traffic or understanding visitor data. Tag management is therefore not a pure analytics tool itself but is worth looking at alongside the above tools, as it should be considered simultaneously.

When tags are called upon by the browser (or 'fired') they can cause a number of issues.

These include:

- Changes to a page could result in a tag no longer functioning correctly.

- Some older tags will fire one after the other rather than asynchronously (see Figure 14.1), which can slow down a site, especially if any of these tags have errors in them.

- Adding new tags to a site will normally involve IT resource, which can very often be difficult to get, especially at short notice.

Synchronous and asynchronous tagging are two different methods of tags firing. Synchronous tagging is where tags fire one after the other and this can result in site delays. Asynchronous tags fire simultaneously and as such are able to speed up site performance.

FIGURE 14.1   An example of asynchronous tagging

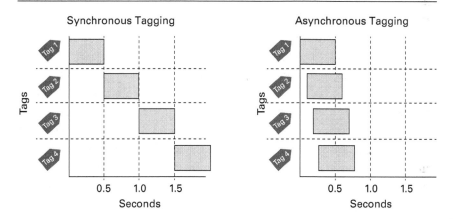

Tag management offers a solution to these problems by offering a simple interface where anyone, usually a marketing professional rather than IT professional, can manage the tags themselves. The tag management product hosts all the tags together and dynamically manages which tags need to fire and when. Marketers can then add, edit or remove tags as needed. This is a significant advantage and one that is becoming more in demand as the need for a greater range of tags increases.

Major players

Google and Adobe both offer tag management solutions and these are worth considering if you are using their other products. There are, however, many other companies offering excellent products such as Tealium, TagMan, BrightTag and many more.

How it fits into your strategy

As mentioned above, tag management is a solution that, as well as solving some issues that tags create, also puts the power to manage tags in the hands of the marketers. This frees up much-needed resource in the technology or IT department and gives the marketing department the ability to manage the digital strategy much more closely and respond to the demands of improved analytics, programmatic marketing and other tag-based solutions in a more agile fashion.

What to look for when selecting a partner

Integration is an important factor. We have already mentioned data discrepancies, above, and so ensuring that your choice of analytics tool will fit with your established systems is a key consideration and should be discussed with your potential and existing suppliers. As we have already looked at, privacy and data collection is a sensitive area and one that is highly regulated. You should be comfortable that your supplier is adhering to any relevant laws and regulations on this.

Future proofing is important. For example, if your chosen tool is free to use then does it have any restrictions around traffic volumes or any other metrics? If so, then would you expect to exceed these in the next three to five years? If the answer to this question is yes, then you must consider whether this is affordable and whether this is the most effective solution to implement. Changing technology in the future could be difficult and may result in a loss of data.

Is your chosen supplier a reliable one? Some companies have been providing their services for many years or are part of a long-established group that is highly unlikely to go out of business. However, as is the nature of the digital world, some of the most innovative new solutions are offered by young companies. Not seizing these opportunities may result in a loss of competitive advantage, but they do present a risk if the business is not successful in the long term, and protecting yourself for this is worth considering.

Performance can vary greatly and so ensuring that you have adequate service level agreements (SLAs) in place with the supplier is important. Should you expect a customer service agent to answer your call quickly, then this needs to be stated. You may also require the service to have downtime of no more than 0.1 per cent, and other considerations.

Data ownership is another important consideration. We mentioned above that an advantage of server-based analytics is that you own the data. Most analytics solutions now are tag based, which means you may not own what you consider to be your data (see tag-based analytics above). You should investigate this thoroughly and consider your position carefully.

Attribution modelling

Attribution modelling gives marketers the ability to see what effect different components of their campaigns have on their customers and therefore how valuable they are. This can be measured within a channel, which in the case of display might be used to make sure that an awareness campaign is being delivered to people who are mostly new customers. Cross-channel attribution, which is more commonly implemented by advertisers, looks at the interaction between people and their exposure and/or interactions with each element of the digital mix. This provides a picture of how each channel is playing its part and therefore how valuable or efficient each channel is compared to its peers.

Advertisers use attribution modelling to place a more accurate worth on any channel or activity. Having this information available also allows advertisers to know where to place budget more accurately (planning). There are two key variations of attribution – data-driven attribution and rule-based attribution. The differences are the methodology used to define how to credit is awarded to each channel for the part it plays in a sale (or other campaign goal) compared to the other channels involved. Rule-based attribution is the simpler version and while still very important does sometimes require a certain amount of trial and error to determine that best set of rules and variations of reporting needed to give a picture of campaign activity. Rules-based attribution is very similar to 'path to conversion' reporting. Rules-based attribution will vary slightly depending on the provider of the service, but generally there are several default reports that advertisers use to get an understanding. It is commonplace for a combination of these to be used at the same time. These reports look at placing credit for conversion in the following ways:

- The *linear* model might be used if your campaigns are designed to maintain contact with potential customers and keep the product fresh in the consumer's mind. This might be an especially useful way of measuring success for a product that has a prolonged research phase or for an advertiser with products in a very competitive space. The linear attribution model will place equal credit for all of the campaign elements. If a marketer is using attribution to look at the display activity, the scores will be placed on the sites or networks that the activity has been booked to run on, or it could represent different creative messages. If this was cross-channel, the segments would represent the different channels and/or key strategies within those channels.

- The *first interaction* model can help you to understand which campaigns create initial awareness for your brand or product. All the credit is given to the campaign component that is the first that is seen by any user. Therefore this is a useful report to run on a campaign that has awareness-objective elements tasked with finding new customers.

- The *position-based* model is far more useful in giving insight into how campaign elements can be used to adjust credit for different parts of the customer journey, such as early interactions that create awareness and late interactions that close sales. Where an advertiser is trying to raise awareness of a product but also sell units with a limited budget, this can be helpful in giving credit only to those partners on the media plan who make people aware and close the deal by creating sales.

- A *custom attribution model* potentially becomes very useful to a marketer who has used a combination of the pre-set models to understand their activity and has a framework that they can confidently apply to summarize the path that most of their users take on the way to becoming customers. This advertiser will typically run constant display activity (or multichannel digital activity). Their framework will account for how valuable any one element of activity is over its peers most of the time. The model can be used to provide a good sense-check of their ongoing marketing activity. With the development of a custom rule-based attribution model the nuances of any business's interactions with customers are better accounted for.

As may be apparent from comparing the common rule-based attribution models, a marketer will have to run these models in conjunction with each other and often run a set of the models for each element of the activity running, whether that be different sites that adverts are placed on or, more likely in the case of programmatic executions, the different strategies and campaign elements, eg awareness, action and retargeting strategies. This can prove quite lengthy and, although rule-based attribution represents a vitally important step forward in allowing advertisers to understand consumer behaviour in a multichannel world, it is still quite assumptive and therefore does not provide perfect measurement of how budget is deployed. On the other hand, data-driven attribution looks to solve that issue entirely. It is difficult to comment on exactly how data-driven models operate. The companies that provide this service collect all possible campaign and site data from an advertiser and use a mathematical model to analyse the importance of each touchpoint. The algorithms they use to do this are their proprietary-developed intellectual property and as such are closely guarded secrets. However, enough about their methods can be explained for a decision on which supplier to select.

Fundamentally, every user journey and touchpoint of paid (and non-paid) media are assessed against all other customer journeys and a set of algorithms determine how effective a contribution the different campaign and marketing components contribute – thus allowing advertisers and marketers to assess the performance of individual components and work out the best way to deploy future budgets.

The intensity of work required to set up an attribution modelling system, as well as the support and investment required to train staff to interpret the results, is resource intensive. As a result, data-driven attribution services are expensive to implement. As with all technologies, the price will fall as they become more commonplace, and the implementations become easier as the attribution companies and marketers become more experienced at doing them. Despite these limitations, data-driven attribution is still the very best at providing a complete picture of the value that marketing activities provide.

Ultimately, attribution modelling allows marketers a robust as possible way to avoid channel conflict. Savvy marketers have always looked at activity holistically but the available data often forces them, often inadvertently, to put their channels into conflict, looking at the pricing and values of channels individually and not at how they interact together and the effect that they have on each other.

Reporting

All of these analytics tools are incredibly powerful and give you the data you need to report on the success of your digital strategy, but ultimately they are worthless if not pulled together into a strong reporting format and process. In order to enlighten yourself and your stakeholders on the progress you are making, and to see the challenges that you face, a strong dashboard is necessary and this will need to be appropriate to your goals as well as your stakeholders' objectives, which may necessitate different versions. There are two primary areas to consider when building your reporting: the data and the presentation.

Data

The data you use, no matter from which source, must be tailored to the audience that will be consuming it. This means understanding the needs of your audience and also their knowledge of digital. The focus of your content providers will be on the engagement in their content and which themes are gaining the most interest. An important measure of this may be bounce rate, but if your content providers are not digital savvy then they may not understand what this metric means. Having this perspective is crucial to ensure that your reports resonate with the end user and enable you to tell your story to a receptive audience.

As well as tailoring your reports for your audience, you will also need to ensure that your strategy is represented. If you have implemented a digital marketing strategy that focuses heavily on organic search then this should feature in all reports. How is your content featuring in the organic rankings? How have your new designs improved site audit results? What SEO signals have been created by your social strategy? Ensure that you align the reports with your goals as well as those of your audience or your story will be incomplete. How often you produce and circulate these reports also needs consideration. Producing reports can take time, and automation should be considered where possible. Many of the above tools have options to deal with this. Also there will be meetings in your business that demand reports, but no reporting should be produced without robust data available. You should never compromise the quality of the report simply to meet a meeting timescale, or you can do serious harm to your story.

One key element to build into your reports is how you will measure success. For example, are you comparing against sales targets or historical achievements? When comparing against historical data there are a number of common comparisons but each of these has it disadvantages, which you must be aware of:

- *Year on year (YoY)*: comparison with last year's results can be useful in showing growth over time and also ensures that any seasonal differences are almost eliminated. It does not, however, give true visibility of changes in market conditions since 12 months ago, which in many industries can be vast.

- *Month on month (MoM)*: this can be useful for reporting against budgets and any growth or decline over the year. It does not, however, account for seasonal changes. In many industries, for example, January will always be stronger than December or vice versa, so this really tells us very little.

- *Week on week (WoW)*: this can show very dynamic and recent fluctuations in data, which can be useful in seeing where changes have had an impact but it also means that many other factors will be playing a part in the fluctuations, and so pulling the data apart into actionable insights can be difficult.

Finally, considering predictive analysis is important. Using the data to report historically is useful but using the data to predict what will be coming is far more powerful. Forecasting should be a key part of your reporting processes and you should be able to make recommendations to the business on what your stakeholders can be doing to capitalize on the trends you are seeing. Hindsight by itself offers little value.

Presentation

When producing your reports, presentation can be just as important as the data itself. Ensuring that your audience can immediately understand what they see, what it means to them and what actions they can take from it is vital to taking your stakeholders on the journey with you. In order to do this you should always keep the following principles (consider this a checklist) at the front of your mind:

- *Tell a story.* Every good story has a beginning, a middle and an end. Your report should be no different. Not just a collection of numbers but a narrative about why I should believe your message. These three stages can be defined in the following three simple questions: what are we trying to achieve? Did we achieve it? What do we do next? If your dashboard can do this then you will have a strong start.

- *So what?* This is a question you should be asking yourself all the time. We achieved 10 per cent conversion rate this January? So what? Last year we only achieved 9 per cent. So what? So we have increased by 1 per cent, a gain of over 10 per cent. So what? Market conditions were difficult so this increase actually represents a significant gain. You can go on for some time with this challenging question, but ultimately this means you will always have a strong output from your data. Commentary is important in a dashboard to show that you understand and are acting on the data you have, so ensure you ask the 'so what?' question at all times.

- *Keep it simple.* This is always a good principle in marketing. Never assume knowledge or that what is obvious to you is obvious to anyone else. Really challenge yourself to create something that everyone will understand. This does not mean you need to dumb down the content but that you need to communicate it clearly. Remember that you are deep in the knowledge whereas your audience may not understand the context. Keep the graphs simple, the data clear and the commentary sharp and to the point.

- *Graphics.* Using graphics to bring data to life is a very strong way of communicating your message, especially when dealing with time frames. Trends can be absorbed much faster and easier by the human brain with the use of graphics than through numbers or words.

- *Label it up.* Ensure you label everything clearly. It is easy to forget to add the axis to the chart or to label whether you are working in GBP or USD. Incorrect labelling can lead to incorrect assumptions, which can prove costly if not discovered before decisions are made.

- *Check, check and check again.* Finally, it is obvious – but always check your data. The number of reports produced with faulty data, incorrect labelling or unrealistic assumptions is astounding. It is easily done as reports often evolve over a period of time before being circulated so always check, check and check again. It is also often worth having an independent person to check, as fresh eyes can often spot the mistakes that you may miss.

Summary

In this chapter we examined how the data landscape has evolved, with big data becoming a more common challenge for businesses. We looked at how data needs to be managed and interpreted carefully due to the issues that can be presented through the human factor and through data alignment. We reviewed analytics and the key areas that these tools cover, as well as the metrics you should expect to review from each. We also looked at some potential suppliers, but there are many more available and so you should conduct your own research before making any decisions. Finally, we looked at reporting and how turning your data and analytics into meaningful dashboards is vital if you are to take your stakeholders on your journey with you. In the next and final chapter we look at how to present your strategy to your decision makers to ensure you gain the approval and support you need to deliver a world-class digital marketing strategy for your organization.

Chapter checklist

- The data landscape ☐
- The reliability of data-based decisions ☐
- What are analytics? ☐
- Tools and technology ☐
- Attribution modelling ☐
- Reporting ☐

Further reading

- *On web analytics*:
  Kaushik, A (2009) *Web Analytics 2.0*, Sybex. In his book Avanish covers web analytics in a great deal of depth and so this is a very useful read for anyone who will be using analytics in their strategy, which is most of us.

- *On a broader view of marketing metrics*:
  Davis, J A (2013) *Measuring Marketing: 110+ key metrics every marketer needs*, John Wiley. This is recommended if you want to gain a broad understanding of the key metrics for marketing as a whole, rather than specific digital marketing.

References

McKinsey (2011) [accessed 1 November 2015] Big Data: The Next Frontier for Innovation, Competition and Productivity [Online] http://www.mckinsey.com/insights/business_technology/big_data_the_next_frontier_for_innovation

Presenting your strategy

15

What we will cover in this chapter

No matter how thorough your approach to building your digital marketing strategy, no matter how effectively you plan to exploit each channel, it is all pointless if you cannot convince the decision makers in your organization to adopt it. This chapter focuses on:

- Decision making
- Budget
- Key channel benefits
- How channels interact
- Website
- Further considerations
- Structuring your proposal
- Advocacy

Chapter goals

By the end of this chapter you should understand the decision-making process and how to influence it. You should understand how to strengthen your argument and give yourself the best possible chance of convincing your decision makers to invest in your strategy. You should also understand how to use the 6S Framework™ to structure your proposal and therefore how to create your written plan.

Decision making

First, it is essential to identify the decision makers in the organization and understand the process by which they reach their decisions. This is essentially a process of internal marketing and, as with any marketing campaign, you need to understand your customers and their psychology.

This includes looking at the different personality types and decision-making processes represented in your organization, although this is not the place for in-depth psychological theory. I recommend further reading in this area to help your understanding, but for now we just look at some of the key areas that will help you to position your proposal effectively.

The decision-making process within each organization depends on the people involved and the culture of the organization. There may be one sole decision maker to win over or you may have to present your proposal to a group who will take a vote on whether to proceed or not. The process may involve consultation with stakeholders across the organization, or a straightforward pros-and-cons exercise by one individual.

Whatever the situation, you will need to understand this matrix of power. Figure 15.1 shows where these various models lie on the continuum from individual decision at one extreme to group consensus at the other.

FIGURE 15.1 Types of decision making

Individual	**Personal Preference**	This is simply the preference of the individual with no analysis or consultancy
	Pros and Cons	These simple methods help to frame the decision but ultimately result in one person's decision
	Flipism	A flip of a coin. The individual cannot decide but does not look for input, leaving it to 'fate'
	Participative Decision Making	Where one decision maker seeks input from a group to gain additional input
	Voting-Based Decision Making	Where a group score the various options and proceed based on the combined results
Consensus	**Consensus Decision Making**	A majority must approve the given course of action but the minority must also accept the decision

Whatever the decision-making model, it will inevitably be affected by the bias of the individual or individuals involved. We cannot help being influenced by our likes, our dislikes, our past experiences and so on. So if at all possible, try to establish whether your decision makers have any previous experiences or influencers that may affect their thinking. You will then be able to make your presentation more relevant and also identify in advance any potential objections, which will help you to overcome them.

Here are some examples of bias that might impact on the process of decision making, with some ideas on how you can address each – note, however, that this is not an exhaustive list:

- *Selective search for evidence*: people tend to seek out or pay attention to facts that support the decision they favour.
  Address this by: ensuring your proposal is well balanced.

- *Peer pressure*: some individuals will be influenced by stronger personalities.
  Address this by: gathering a strong network of advocates in advance, and making sure that every decision maker has the opportunity to put questions and offer comments.

- *Anchoring and adjustment*: the information you present first has a tendency to shape how people perceive the rest of the message, and to influence their decisions.
  Address this by: paying attention to the way in which your presentation/proposal tells a clear story. We discuss this in more detail below.

- *Recency*: most people tend to favour recent information over historic data in their decision making.
  Address this by: ensuring your proposal is well balanced and that it includes data that covers all the key factors.

- *Credibility*: if someone has a low opinion of the presenter, or conversely someone they value highly appears not to support the idea, they will be likely to view the proposal negatively.
  Address this by: getting support from others in place up front. Make sure the decision maker has a high opinion of you. Find out who it is they respect and get that person on your side, or consider having a credible advocate present on your behalf.

One well-known model that is particularly useful when analysing the psychology of decision making is the Myers-Briggs Type Indicator (MBTI), developed by Katharine Cook Briggs and her daughter Isabel Briggs Myers.

This family team developed a set of four cognitive-behavioural dichotomies, which are widely used to assess the personalities and attributes of employees. The four dichotomies or scales are:

- thinking and feeling (T/F);
- extroversion and introversion (E/I);
- sensing and intuition (S/N);
- judgement and perception (J/P).

The theory is that these will dictate whether an individual will make decisions on an analytical or an emotional basis: there is some debate over its predictive accuracy but it remains a useful perspective, and it is worth reading up on the model to help you frame your thinking on the decision-making style of your decision maker(s) and therefore the best way in which to present your case.

Another key factor will be the criteria used by boards in their standard decision-making process. These criteria will vary depending on the business but you should aim to cover these five areas in your proposal:

- *Logic*: how does this proposed investment fit with our agreed strategy?
- *Reward*: what is the size of the prize, and how quickly can we realize the benefits?
- *Risk*: if this doesn't work, what is the worst that can happen? Can we recover quickly?
- *Execution*: do we have the right resources – staff, skills, knowledge, time – to carry out this plan?
- *Competition*: if we DON'T do this, will we fall behind our competitors?

Budget

It is a harsh, immovable law of business that any decision ultimately comes down to budget, the effective use of scarce resources. You need to convince your decision makers that your strategy is a good use of their budget. How can you demonstrate to them that your proposal represents the best way to spend the company's money?

The amount of cash that companies are prepared to spend on digital marketing varies considerably, from almost nothing to multimillion-dollar budgets. Whatever your budget, you need to understand your business's

KPIs (discussed in Chapter 2) and the level of spend associated with each. You may be promoting a low-margin product, for example, with a very specific cost per acquisition but no documented budget, in which case your challenge is to maximize volume within that cost per acquisition (CPA) limit. If on the other hand the priority of the business is growth there may be a budget dedicated to achieving maximum growth in minimum time. Whatever the priorities of your business, they will be reflected in the core principles behind the allocation of the budget, and it is vital to ensure that you bring this out in your proposal. There are four key principles:

- *Channel optimization*: it is important to identify your best-performing channel and ensure your proposal maximizes that before you move on to others. If, for example, you have a PPC campaign that is achieving lots of enquiries at a highly effective CPA, then it makes sense to gain maximum volume from your account by optimizing keywords, ad copy, customer journey and so on before you open up another channel.

- *Website optimization*: all of your digital channels will be driving traffic to your site, so it is vital to optimize this end touchpoint, otherwise you are damaging the effectiveness of all your other channels. This may require some budget, depending on your technical and management set-up.

- *Maximizing the use of free channels*: effective, integrated social media and SEO strategies are essential in today's digital world and these can be a fantastic source of low-cost business.

- *Understand your business's budget cycle*: no matter how compelling your argument, if the budget is simply not available your proposal will fail. Make sure you are fully aware of any constraints around budget allocation, including timings, before you commit to an amount or schedule that could render your proposal worthless.

These principles will allow you to shape your budget allocation effectively.

Your organization's channel split will depend on all the factors above, together with your specific objectives and business model. For example, if your consumers are primarily discovering and purchasing from you on their mobile phones then you would increase the spend on the mobile channel.

Resource is another consideration. The management of digital marketing involves a number of skills that must be sourced either in-house or at an agency, such as content creation, technical build, copywriting, media buying, negotiation, SEO and more. While organizations can often achieve cost savings and greater control by keeping these in-house, agencies can usually offer a greater breadth and depth of expertise, and will often have stronger media-buying power. It is worth modelling different options as it can be beneficial to keep some of these skills in-house, particularly copywriting and creative. The details of resource allocation and agency management will be covered below.

Key channel benefits

We have looked in detail at some of the key digital channels (Chapters 5 to 8); here we are concerned with how to use those channel benefits most effectively when justifying digital marketing investment to decision makers.

No matter what mix you have chosen for your digital strategy, no matter how small the budget, multiple channels will almost certainly be involved, even if they are only SEO and social strategies. How can you utilize the specific benefits of each when pitching your proposal?

SEO

Search engine optimization is an art that is constantly developing. It is founded of course on developing a compelling website and digital marketing strategy that deliver high-quality content together with a great user experience. Whether your SEO budget is limited to simple website development or embraces a multichannel content strategy, its purpose is always to bring in as many potential customers as possible across a wide range of search terms for the best possible cost per visit.

Starting an SEO strategy can feel like pushing a boulder down a hill; it is slow to begin, but once it gains momentum it picks up pace quickly. It is harder to steer than other channels, such as PPC, and it takes longer to see results from the initial investment, but it is important to make the point that an effective SEO strategy will ultimately generate significant volume at a relatively low cost per visit (or cost per acquisition). Another key point to stress is that the more prominent your website is, the greater your visibility at the expense of your competitors, as there is limited space on that critical first page of search results.

Paid search

Unlike SEO, paid search offers a high level of control and flexibility. You can choose your keywords, generate as many adverts as you wish and place them in whichever position you like, whenever you choose, to be displayed to the target audience you define, and you can switch the campaign on or off in real time as you please. There is simply no comparable offline tool.

There are several ways to use this channel, which means you can customize your proposal depending on the priorities and preferences of your decision makers. You can stress that paid search allows you to test marketing messages and audience demographics and use the results of those tests to inform the rest of your marketing mix. For example, you can see when your audience is online and most receptive to your advertising.

You can also remind your decision makers that paid search can be targeted to fill the inevitable gaps in organic search results so that you can access 100 per cent of potential visitors. Don't forget too the simple truth that paid search can deliver high volumes of traffic at low cost, which is reason enough to include it in your digital marketing strategy.

Social

These days it is difficult to argue for a strategy that does not include a social strand. Facebook now has well over 1 billion users and at the start of 2015 over half the population of most developed countries had at least one active social media account (Kemp, 2015). No matter who your customers are, they are almost certainly using social media.

One of the key benefits of including social in your digital strategy is therefore clearly the volume of users, but equally important is the ability that the main platforms provide to target advertising by sophisticated demographic factors such as age, location and even interests. The insights they can provide on your audience can also be very valuable: Facebook, for example, shows you in detail not only who your visitors are but when they are online and how they compare to the average Facebook user. You can experiment with advertising with incredible flexibility, and monitor the results in real time, and of course all this information can be fed back into the wider marketing plan to increase its effectiveness.

Social also facilitates the holy grail of viral marketing: there are many videos on YouTube and posts and images on Facebook that have reached hundreds of thousands, even millions of users. Viral marketing is an art, and there is no definitive guide to creating a campaign guaranteed to go viral, but it is certainly true that if you want to go viral, social media is a key part of your distribution mix. If you succeed, viral marketing can create a level of brand awareness that would cost millions of dollars to achieve through other channels. It is important to be realistic in your forecasts – viral campaigns are notoriously unpredictable – you should make it clear that your chances of going viral are infinitely greater when you are using social channels effectively.

Display

Display advertising has a mixed reputation: on one hand it is a great way to get a brand in front of a wide audience but, on the other hand, the resulting click-through rate is typically quite low, which means it is often considered ineffective as a direct channel, and justifying its use to decision makers can therefore be difficult. It is vital to understand objectives clearly.

If you know that brand awareness is a key objective then it will be easy to argue for the use of display advertising. If, however, you need to justify it as a means of generating visits and sales, you will need to evidence attribution modelling and post-impression tracking: just because people do not click through from a display advertisement directly does not mean it hasn't played an important role in that person's journey to your site.

Increasingly, the web serves as the world's shop window. There are comparison sites for all manner of products and services, such as travel, accommodation, financial services, utilities, property, cars and many more. People use the internet to research before making a decision to buy, whether they finally make the purchase online or not, which means that if your brand is positioned prominently during your customers' online search, there is a greater probability that it will be at the front of their mind when they come to make the purchase itself. There is also the opportunity to remarket, to follow a customer with your message (which can include a specifically tailored price) wherever they go online – again, an option that is simply not available offline.

All of this means that when you are arguing the case for display marketing you need to look at the bigger picture, not just simple conversion metrics.

Affiliate

Affiliate marketing can be a time-consuming and complex exercise. You need to spend time validating, de-duplicating and quality checking your leads (or you need to spend money outsourcing this work to an agency). It will also take time and expertise to negotiate satisfactory terms with your affiliate network, and you need to make sure that the necessary costs in terms of time, money and skills acquisition are included in your proposal.

However, affiliate marketing when done well can deliver a high volume of good-quality leads from relevant sources such as websites or e-mail marketers operating in your market, at a CPA of your choosing, which is a rare opportunity. To optimize this channel you need to back up these leads with compelling propositions and a website that converts well, of course, and before you argue for this channel it is essential to consider whether you can offer attractive remuneration to affiliates, and to be sure your propositions are sufficiently competitive and your conversion rate sufficiently strong to make it worthwhile.

If this is the case, however, affiliate marketing really is an obvious choice as a sales message, as it brings in traffic that you simply will not be able to capture elsewhere. More to the point, if you do not partner with affiliates in your field, you leave them free to partner elsewhere and send their volume to your competitors instead.

E-mail

E-mail marketing costs very little and offers a number of options.

The most obvious place to start is a win-back campaign, targeting lapsed or cancelled customers from your own database – previous shoppers or those who have started the purchase funnel but not completed – who are by definition interested in what you have to offer and might be persuaded to come back and purchase if you have a sufficiently strong supporting proposition. This is usually a fairly easy strategy to sell to your decision makers.

Another option is a member-get-member (MGM) programme, rewarding your customers for recommending a friend, which can be an effective way to build your customer base quickly. The incentive is key and its cost needs to be built into your CPA calculations. The conversion rates for this channel are typically high because you benefit from 'borrowed trust', the confidence the purchaser has in the individual who is recommending you.

E-mail is also an excellent channel for cross-selling and up-selling messages to existing customers and can increase their customer lifetime value (CLTV) but it must not be overused, otherwise you run the risk of irritating or even losing a customer who tires of your relentless e-mail campaigns. If you avoid this error, however, regular e-mails support retention marketing, improving your chance of keeping or renewing a customer, further increasing CLTV.

When it comes to acquiring new customers by e-mail, you will need to access external sources of data and this is where it becomes vital to understand who your customers are and how they convert. Buying e-mail lists is a potentially fraught area, and it is essential to work with reputable suppliers, but if you get the right data at the right price then the CPA can be superb.

One last important consideration is that the delivery cost of the channel – in terms of both content creation and actually getting that content to the customer – is also very low. It is relatively easy to sell the idea of e-mail marketing to your decision makers, because you are presenting them with the opportunity to improve both acquisition volumes and customer lifetime value at very little cost.

Mobile

Globally, mobile as a channel is growing at a phenomenal rate (Figure 15.2). In the United States, mobile internet access overtook that from desktop or laptops in 2013 (Bosomworth, 2015) and mobile is the key driver behind the fast-growing rate of internet access in the developing world (GSMA, 2015). There is not the space here to explore the implications fully, but I recommend further reading on the growth of mobile and the opportunities it presents for businesses.

FIGURE 15.2   Global device sales 2008–15

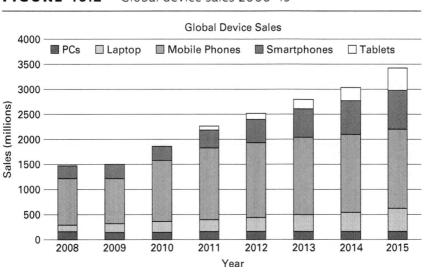

SOURCE: http://www.statista.com/statistics/220120/global-mobile-device-sales-forecast-by-device/

The most fundamental requirement for mobile marketing is to ensure that your customers can access your products on their mobile devices, which will probably mean a responsive website or mobile app. I am willing to bet that if you check your website's analytics, and assuming you can see historic patterns, you will see that the proportion of visitors accessing your site from a mobile device has increased in the last 12 months. You can assess the quality of your mobile experience by analysing whether these users are converting into sales. You will need to include in your proposal both the costs of improving your mobile experience and the benefits of doing so.

In addition to the simple prospect of more sales, there are a number of other factors to consider when you are making a pitch for mobile marketing investment. When your customer engages with your mobile site or app, they literally have your product in their hand. You go with them wherever they go, at all times. They do not need to remember your phone number or log on to their PC in order to buy your products or services, and that lack of friction is incredibly powerful. Mobile marketing also includes the possibility of SMS as a channel, which can open up dialogue with your customers. Text messages can, however, also be perceived as invasive, so their use needs to be considered carefully.

As with social media, mobile marketing opens up fantastic viral opportunities. That lack of friction means it is very easy for a consumer to forward a message instantly, thereby increasing the chance of your message spreading to more potential customers.

Perhaps the single most exciting point to note about mobile marketing is that while the opportunities it offers are already significant, it is growing at an exceptional speed.

How channels interact

Now that we have identified and analysed the benefits of each channel, let's look at how they interact with each other. A key word in digital marketing strategy is 'attribution', in other words how the results of your marketing activity should be attributed or allocated to each channel. For example, consider how a customer could potentially engage with your various marketing channels:

Alice has just finished watching *Game of Thrones* on TV and after the credits roll she sees your commercial for your new flight-friendly luggage range. She pulls out her mobile phone and searches for your offer on Google but cannot remember the brand and ends up visiting a competitor's site instead. The phone rings and she forgets about her search.

Two days later Alice is flicking through her e-mails on the bus when she notices a message from you. She doesn't click on your e-mail but she remembers the subject line. The next day she searches again for luggage on Google using her mobile phone, and this time clicks on your paid search advert and goes on to purchase the case.

To which channel would you attribute the purchase? The TV commercial made Alice aware of your offer and prompted her to search, but she did not actually complete the purchase as a result; in fact she did not even reach your site. The e-mail (which she did not even open) prompted her to go back and search again, perhaps with a clearer idea of your brand and offer, but ultimately it was the paid search advert that brought her to your website to complete the purchase. However, Alice had almost certainly seen that same paid ad before without taking action: so which element of the digital marketing mix is responsible for changing her mind and getting the sale?

Not surprisingly, many different models have been devised for attributing value to each channel and no single one can claim to be entirely correct. Here are the different models to consider along with their relative advantages:

● Single source: last interaction

FIGURE 15.3 Last interaction

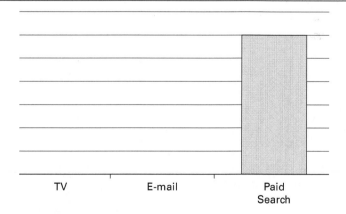

In this model the entire value of the conversion is attributed to the final interaction of the consumer with your marketing before the purchase itself, so in the example above this would be the paid search advertisement.

● Single source: first interaction

FIGURE 15.4   First interaction

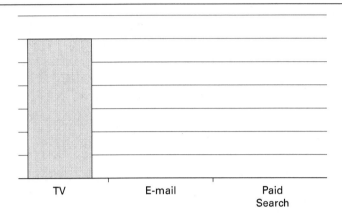

In this model the conversion is attributed to the customer's first interaction, on the basis that this is what created the others. In the example above this would be the TV advert (but note that it is much more difficult to identify the first interaction of a long sequence – the customer might not even be able to identify it themselves).

● Equal weight/linear

FIGURE 15.5   Equal weight/linear

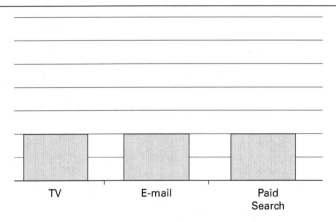

This model reflects the fact that no one interaction can be definitely identified as the single decision-making factor and simply gives equal weighting to all known interactions.

● First and last priority, or U-curve

FIGURE 15.6 First and last priority

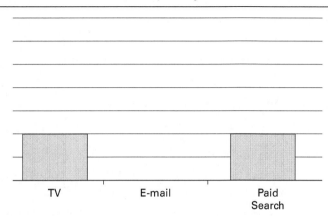

Rather than giving equal weight to all interactions, this model assumes that the interaction that originally sparked the interest and the one that finally delivered the conversion are the two important ones and the value is shared equally between them. In the example above, this would mean that TV and paid search would each be attributed 50 per cent of the conversion value.

● Time phased

FIGURE 15.7 Time phased

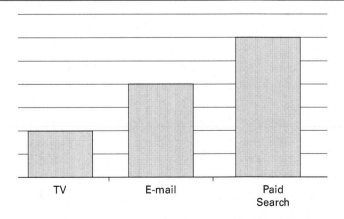

An alternative interpretation is that the interactions closer to the point of purchase are the key ones; the earlier touchpoints should be considered as simply 'shopping around' and not necessarily relevant to the conversion process. So, in the example above, the time-phased model would attribute most of the conversion value to paid search, then e-mail, then TV.

These are the most common attribution models, although there are others. If you are to build an effective and persuasive multichannel digital marketing strategy, you need to understand which attribution model is best suited to your purpose, and be able to convince your decision makers why it is relevant to your proposal.

Two more factors to consider for channel interaction are:

- conversion levels for each channel;
- the brand impact of each channel.

Do you know, for example, the ways in which a visitor from paid search behaves differently on your website compared to one from natural search? You may find that one has a lower bounce rate, visits more pages and spends longer on each, and yet has very low conversion rates, while the other simply lands, buys and leaves. It is important that you understand how on-site behaviours differ by acquisition channel, since these behaviours will impact the conversion rate and hence the effectiveness of each channel.

Brand value is notoriously difficult to quantify: in a digital marketing age where vast amounts of data are available to us, this remains one metric that defies scientific measurement. There are hints and indicators – for example, how our brand performs against competitors on the same search terms – but we will never see the full picture. But it is clear that some digital marketing channels offer better opportunities to create brand value than others, depending of course on how well they are targeted and integrated into the wider marketing mix and the quality of the creative.

Display advertising, as mentioned above, might not appear to be the best channel for driving cost-effective leads as measured by standard metrics, but it does provide a great opportunity to disseminate your message widely across a large number of relevant sites. E-mail similarly allows you great reach in getting your brand out, so when evaluating the various options it is important to recognize a channel's role in creating brand value.

Taken together, all these factors will help you to build a compelling case for your digital channel strategy, but whatever channels you use the ultimate destination of customers is your website, so it is essential that you are able to justify investment on your site when it is required.

Website

You already know, from what we have discussed above, what are the benefits and principles of creating an effective website. But how do you convince your decision makers?

The key requirements for a high-converting site are fast performance, ease of navigation, compelling content, user-focused design, SEO and analysis optimization and a strong conversion funnel. You need to be able to articulate persuasively the specific business benefits of all of these elements.

Let's imagine the objections of a particularly difficult panel of decision makers faced with your proposal to invest in the company website as part of your digital marketing strategy.

'Why do we need a website at all?'

These days, when virtually every business has a web presence, you are unlikely to hear that objection, but for those who view a website as a barely necessary evil, it is important to remind them how your customers use the internet, how digital technology, and particularly mobile, is impacting on purchasing decisions and behaviours, and of course to stress how cost-effective digital channels can be compared to their offline counterparts.

'What functionality should we invest in?'

How your website works will impact directly on how your visitors behave. You might be considering an online instant quote facility, for example, with prices generated dynamically from a link to your pricing system. If your product is very complex, however, it might be that customers convert more readily on a call, in which case a simple form on your site to capture name and contact details, or a live online chat facility, would offer a better return on investment.

Some functionality is inescapable: if you are selling products from your website you will require an e-commerce shopping basket, online payment processing and a compliant security system, for example. In each case, it is important to assess the benefits of online versus offline conversion when deciding to invest in website developments.

It is vital that you are able to explain the benefit of any investment to your decision makers. In terms of justifying your proposal, finding examples of your competitors' functionality can be useful. What is proven to work? Are there any dominant models? Can you see patterns or processes that could save you going through the time-consuming, expensive process of developing bespoke functionality?

Another useful approach to support your proposal is to build financial projections based on best-guess estimations of each metric. If you can show how your recommended approach plays out financially in different scenarios, and assuming the picture is favourable, you are much more likely to secure approval. Wherever possible use your own business's KPIs, analytics, market knowledge and supporting data, as this will be familiar to and trusted by your decision makers.

'How should it look and feel?'

The 'look and feel' of your site will of course need to reflect your unique brand values but, no matter what the design constraints or ambitions, it is vital that you consider how your creative will impact on performance.

Here is a useful checklist of points to consider when refreshing, rebranding or changing a website in any way, and each of these should be addressed in your recommendations:

- *Will it make your website faster or slower?* The faster your pages load, the easier it is to keep customers on your site and the more of them you will be able to move on to the conversion goal.

- *Will it make it easier for customers to find and buy your product?* Whatever helps steer customers in the right direction without distraction – help text, signposting, the removal of extraneous links from purchase funnels, forms that require only essential information – can create an improvement in sales.

- *Will it increase the impact of your digital marketing?* Will it increase traffic, for example by improving conversion from your key digital marketing channels or bettering your organic search performance?

- *Will it add value to your site?* If customers find your content, design or functionality valuable then the benefits are multiple: not just better SEO but also increased conversions and reduced customer service requests because visitors are able to find answers to their questions.

- *Will it increase the revenue per customer?* Adding opportunities for up-selling and cross-selling can raise CLTV by encouraging customers to buy add-ons or related products, but if handled badly it will actually reduce your conversion rate by interrupting your purchase funnel.

- *Will it give you additional insights?* Adding detailed tags to your site can allow you to gain a better understanding of customer behaviour, which can be invaluable in increasing conversions, but tagging needs to be done correctly to avoid impacting SEO performance or loading speed.

- *Does it integrate with your wider marketing?* Consistency is key: an integrated creative approach across all channels will improve conversion, because consumers who have seen one element such as a TV commercial will recognize your company when they see your marketing on a different channel, such as paid search, even if they cannot remember your name. This is not a new theory of marketing, of course, but it applies to digital as much as any other area.

Further considerations

Given below are a few more key issues that you may conceivably want to address in your proposal, although this is by no means an exhaustive list of the areas.

Trends and cycles

Every sector has its unique rhythm. Gifts sell well in the run-up to seasonal holidays. Swimwear does best in the weeks before the summer holiday season. New car sales peak when licence plates are updated. The impact that seasonal trends will have on your digital marketing is a key factor to build into your strategy proposal and the way in which it will be evaluated.

If, for example, you implement a new SEO strategy aimed at growing your website traffic, you may see what appears to be a negative result for the first few months if you launch at the end of your seasonal peak. If you have not set out this expectation clearly in your proposal you may be setting yourself up for a fall.

Figure 15.8 shows a graph that demonstrates the searches for 'vacations' and 'school uniforms' worldwide in 2014, which gives an indication of the effect of seasonal demand within different industries.

FIGURE 15.8   Seasonal trends

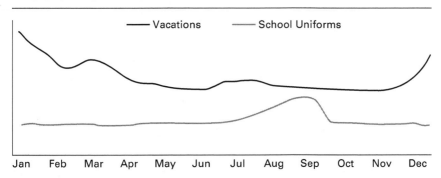

Seasonality

If your customers live a long way from where you are putting together your marketing strategy you will need to take this into account, particularly for seasonally based campaigns, and make sure your decision makers understand your thinking. You might want to ask yourself, for example:

- When is summer – August or February?
- Does it ever snow? (If not, avoid referencing snow in imagery or text.)
- What are the local holidays?
- Does the territory experience any seasonal phenomena, such as earthquakes, floods or hurricanes?

Competitor research

From commissioning a paid research agency to the savvy use of free online tools, there are many ways you can gain competitor intelligence; the better you understand your competitors' performance, the more effectively you can manage decision-makers' expectations of the results of your proposal.

Decision makers will typically be concerned above all with how your proposal will secure competitive advantage for the business. Understanding your competitors' digital strategies, by reviewing their digital activity, will allow you to demonstrate this. Even the most basic research can give you an overview of their paid search, social and natural search campaigns. If you visit their websites and make enquiries or even purchases, you will get a really detailed picture of their business model and conversion funnel. This has the side benefit that your e-mail address will be added to your competitors' e-mail database, which will continue to give you further insight into their outbound calling, SMS or e-mail strategies for months or years to come. All this data can be a powerful tool to help you shape, position and present your digital marketing strategy.

Test and learn

It is an invaluable principle of marketing in general to ensure that every campaign includes a test element, which will help you to improve future campaigns. Test elements can be focused on creative, timing, channel, landing page variations, copy, targeting and many other factors, but it is important not to combine variables in the split test, or the learnings become ambiguous.

You need to explain to your decision makers the benefits that the company will reap from this testing process; not only for improving future digital campaigns but across the whole business. It is worthwhile explaining how the test programmes will be implemented and why, and what gains they can expect to see.

Another aspect of testing is proof of concept, which may be a way to improve your chances of getting agreement from reluctant decision makers for risky strategies: if you launch your proposal as a small-scale test you limit the investment and mitigate the risk. This will, however, also reduce the impact of the project, and you need to ensure that the decision makers understand this and adjust expectations accordingly. There is also the risk that launching 'below the radar' might enable your competitors to move faster and more fully to capture the competitive advantage.

Shopping behaviour

How do your target consumers shop? Do they prefer to research online and then buy over the phone? Do they tend to stick to one company's site or do they search online across a range of brands? Do they use price comparison sites to check that they are getting the best deal? You need to factor everything you know about your customers' buying behaviour into your digital marketing proposal.

Legal and compliance

Although the internet is global, legal jurisdictions are not. Your industry may be regulated differently in other territories, and the rules governing advertising and data transfer and protection may also vary. In some countries, such as the United States and Australia, laws vary by state, and it is essential that before making your proposal you understand how these variations might impact your strategy.

Technology

Although in this book we focus on the growth of digital and emerging online trends, it is important to realize that some territories have moved faster than others. Internet access, broadband, 4G networks, smartphones and tablets are not universally available to the world's population. If you are planning to focus your strategy around mobile, for example, you need to be aware what percentage of your global consumers might be negatively affected, because this may impact your results. Including this detail in your presentation demonstrates your understanding of the issues and the thoroughness of your thinking, and creates confidence that your performance forecasts will be accurate.

In-house or agency?

Perhaps the key element of any digital marketing proposal will be the ROI: what budget and resources will be required, and what is the cost-benefit analysis? One of the main determiners of costs will be whether you use in-house resource or contract the work to an agency. As well as considering costs, you need to ensure the right balance between expertise and control. Agencies can provide highly skilled, up-to-the-minute expertise (important in this fast-moving industry), but along with the task itself you are also outsourcing full control of the individuals involved, as well as sacrificing the opportunity to build internal capability. Your proposal must address where any resource investment is best placed, as well as what the total cost will be.

With regard to cost structure, remember that agencies will charge a management fee and enforce a contract termination period, which need to be factored in to your calculations. On the other hand, you may save on salaries and overheads, and you retain flexibility of resourcing, which allows you to restructure or rescale your strategy as required.

Whichever route you take, Table 15.1 offers a quick guide to the pros and cons of outsourcing to an agency, which you can include in your proposal in order to explain your reasoning.

TABLE 15.1   Pros and cons of outsourcing to an agency

Pros	Cons
Flexible access to resource, can scale up and down as necessary	Less knowledge of/commitment to your business
Only pay when you need work done	Fee likely to be higher than in-house staff rates
Core expertise in marketing, up to date with platforms etc	Unlikely to have up-to-date expertise in your industry
Likely to have highly creative resource to dedicate to your project	Resources' priorities will not be under your control
All necessary technology and software will be in place	By outsourcing you lose opportunity to gain expertise in using this technology
Agency likely to be able to negotiate favourable media buying terms because of scale	By outsourcing you lose opportunity to build direct relationships with media contacts
All necessary relationships, eg with Google, will be in place	By outsourcing you lose opportunity to develop direct relationships

Structuring your proposal

Having clarified your objectives, identified your decision makers, considered how to source the skills you need, worked out your budget and planned the details of your channel strategy, how do you bring this all together into a compelling package that will wow your decision makers (or at least secure their approval)? How can you prepare to answer their objections?

Whatever you include in your proposal – your bullet points, evidence, graphs, summaries and so on – it must all be directed towards one end: telling a compelling story. But it is not enough simply to tell a story. The decision makers will be asking themselves: 'So what?' 'What does it mean?' 'What must we do and why?' If you rigorously hold yourself to account on these questions throughout your preparation – if you interpret the facts you are presenting into insights and recommendations – you will be better armed to answer their objections.

Let's look first at the storytelling. Hopefully, from the work you have already done in this chapter you can see your story emerging. Your story will be unique to your business and its goals, but the 6S Framework™ is a tool that you can use to shape it to best effect, ensuring that you include all the key areas in the right order.

The 6S Framework™

- **S**ynopsis: what's the answer?
  - Executive summary.
- **S**cene setting: why are we doing this?
  - Reminder of the goals and targets.
  - Background.
  - Company history.
  - Competitors.
  - Market.
  - Consumer/customer.
  - Approach.
  - Assumptions.
  - Expectations.
  - Contents and what is coming next.

- **S**tory: what are we doing and why? Should I agree?
  - Channels.
  - Website.
  - Brand impact.
  - Resource.
  - Suppliers and partners.
- **S**ums: how much does it cost?
  - Financial plans.
- **S**teps: how and when does this happen?
  - Clear action plan.
  - Timescales.
  - Responsibilities.
- **S**urprise! What about...?
  - Be prepared for questions.

We have already touched on each of the areas in the 6S Framework™, but let's just revisit each in relation to the proposal itself and the crucial 'So what?' question.

Note that you will need to tailor your approach depending on how you plan to deliver your proposal, whether it is a PowerPoint presentation; a PDF document that someone else will talk through on your behalf, or that will be read before the meeting; or some other means of communication. If you are not going to present your proposal in person you need to be doubly certain that your proposal is clear and includes all supporting data, and that you have considered and addressed all potential objections.

Even if you are planning to deliver the proposal in person it is wise to expect the unexpected. If you find your hour-long slot at the board meeting has shrunk to 10 minutes because the session beforehand overran, you need to know how you will adapt your presentation and convey the key points convincingly.

Synopsis

The executive summary is a short, clear presentation of the key takeaways and recommendations. Use bullet points and include any vital supporting data. Keep asking yourself 'So what?' as you prepare it. If the decision makers were to read only this section and nothing else, would they understand what your proposal is trying to achieve, what your recommendations are and why, and what will happen next if it is accepted?

The synopsis needs to be as short as possible, no more than one slide or a single page. Write a first draft then take a red pen to it, slashing out anything that is not absolutely essential to answer these points. Then cut it some more. Take out the detail: this should include only the essential facts, figures, actions, deliverables and deadlines. Try to clarify your message to the point where you can explain in 30 seconds all the key points to anyone who asks.

Scene setting

This is the background to your proposal. You are effectively telling your audience where you are now and why.

You can include here all the information on objectives, market, company history and budget considerations that we discussed earlier in this chapter. This will frame the proposal and give it context, explaining why you have put it together.

This section needs to include the challenges that the company is facing and how your proposal aims to address them. You can include your current performance versus that of your competitors and outline how your proposal will improve it. Make it clear that you understand how you are currently positioned in the market and what the impact of your proposal is designed to be.

This is also the place to set out any budget constraints or assumptions and outline your approach, since this is one of the first questions that the decision makers will be asking as they read. With that out of the way, you can explain to your audience how you went about putting the proposal together and why, setting out any further assumptions you have made.

End this section by making clear what you want from the decision makers. This will help them to focus on your story and pick up on all the key points as they go through the proposal.

It is useful to approach this by taking each of the points above and presenting it directly and simply, perhaps as a single question-and-answer slide, or you could talk briefly about the background on one slide then list the corresponding objectives on the next, addressing each in more detail on a dedicated slide, followed by your assumptions and expectations to frame the beginning of your story.

Story

Having set the scene, we are now ready to tell the story proper. Where do we want to go, and why? How will we get there?

Everything we have discussed in this chapter comes together in this main body of your proposal; this is where you showcase all your plans and expertise. The exact content will depend on your objectives but the principles remain the same: keep it simple and tell your story. Make sure that each slide or point follows naturally on from the one before and that each detail adds more weight to your proposal. Make sure to include detail on how the various channels you are proposing to use will interact, whether the creative will be shared or unique and so on, making your argument flow as naturally as possible.

Your proposal is certain to impact your website in some way, even if it does not involve any actual site development, so make sure that you address issues such as expected traffic increase or changes to visitor behaviour, conversion rate changes, optimization or tagging. Ensure you address that here.

You also need to demonstrate here that you understand the business impact of your proposed strategy, including the financial impact of each decision and any proposed structural or resource changes and their associated costs and risks. Will the business processes need to change and if so how? Will your brand be impacted? Are there any legal concerns? Think broadly across the whole business in order to assess the full impact of your strategy.

One way to approach this section is to use a summary box on each page accompanied by graphs, illustrations and bullet points giving the supporting detail. The summary box should include all the relevant KPIs by which this part of the strategy will be assessed, such as rate of conversion, revenue, volume of sales, acquisition costs etc. Ideally this box will contain all that a reader needs to know, even if they do not look at the accompanying detail. Make sure that the format is consistent throughout this section of your proposal so that the decision makers can quickly identify and absorb the key information.

By the end of this section, your audience should understand exactly what your plan is and what costs, benefits and risks are associated with it.

Sums

This is a key section. Now that you have communicated what you are trying to achieve, you will set out in this section both what the plan will cost and what return it will deliver.

This is perhaps the section of the proposal that will be subject to the closest scrutiny, so it is essential that your sums add up. Work through your numbers rigorously and try to identify any weak spots or gaps. Anticipate how your audience will challenge the figures and make sure you are completely confident in your calculations and can explain exactly what underpins them.

Because this section will be so rigorously interrogated, you need to be able to supply the detail alongside your high-level summary of each element so that your audience can drill down into the figures as they choose. To avoid cluttering your presentation you could supply the detail in an appendix, or simply take the detailed document into the presentation with you so that you can give it to anyone who wishes to challenge your figures. Many strategy proposals have failed because the presentation degenerated into an argument about unclear numbers. Keep things as simple and clear as possible in order to keep the focus of attention on your message, and so that each decision maker can see the benefits of your proposal.

Here is a checklist of the sorts of figures that a board will typically expect to see when they are evaluating a proposal:

- capital required;
- investment horizon;
- revenue growth;
- break-even point;
- gross profit;
- economic profit;
- internal rate of return (IRR);
- return;
- free cash flow;
- net present value (NPV);
- impact on profit and loss (P&L) – accretive or dilution;
- depreciation and amortization impact;
- source of funding – balance sheet, equity investment, debt etc.

Steps

Now that everyone is clear on what is being proposed and why, and what the financial benefits are, we are ready to focus on implementation. When will this plan be put into action, and how long will it take? What are the key steps between A and B? Who will deliver it?

This section is effectively a project plan. It needs to include a clearly formatted timeline and, alongside it, or ideally underneath it to maximize impact, a list of all the different work streams that make up the project. For example:

- Appoint an agency.
- Approach affiliates.
- Launch online shopping facility...

Each of these work streams needs its key milestones displayed. So, for example, appointing an agency might break down like this:

- Build agency objectives and KPIs.
- Produce initial tender document.
- Select agencies for tender.
- Engage agencies under non-disclosure agreement and send out tender document.
- Review initial proposals.
- Create shortlist.
- Produce detailed second-stage tender document.
- Send second-stage document to shortlisted agencies.
- Review final presentations from shortlisted agencies.
- Select preferred agency.
- Negotiate contract.
- Appointment and start date.

These milestones must be displayed clearly and simply against your project plan, and they must be realistic: keep challenging yourself as you build them to ensure you are not setting yourself up to fail by being overoptimistic.

Each work stream will need an owner, and it is important that you look at the big picture to ensure that one individual is not overloaded with simultaneous streams of activity (bearing in mind too that they will almost certainly have other work to do alongside this proposal!). Your aim is to ensure that the milestones are delivered in the timescale you have set out to ensure that your proposal meets its objectives, so make sure that they are indeed deliverable with the resource you have budgeted and in the time you have available.

Finally, think about the risks associated with the schedule and project plan you have created. Could there be other priorities, resource issues or market conditions that might impact them? You do not want to be in the position of making excuses in future if your project is derailed, so make your audience aware of these risks up front.

Surprise!

You have now delivered your proposal as convincingly as you possibly can, and it is time for the decision makers to ask their questions. The questions they ask at this stage will depend on what was omitted from or not addressed in detail in your proposal. Being aware of decision-making techniques and style, as discussed earlier in this chapter, will help you to deal with these effectively.

You will only be able to feel confident at this stage of the presentation if you know that you have presented all the relevant information comprehensively and correctly. If you have followed this structure and addressed all the points listed above then you should have answered most if not all objections already.

But it is a rare proposal that does not encounter at least one question. Make sure you are completely sure about the background to everything you are proposing, particularly the financials: you should be able to answer confidently any challenge thrown at you. The most common reason that presenters are unable to answer challenges, which often results in the failure of their proposal, is simple lack of preparation. That is completely within your control, so don't let something so basic trip you up.

Advocacy

The last point to consider is advocacy. Relationship management is one of the most important skills in any role, because if you can build excellent relationships across the entire business it ensures that you have champions to spread your messages broadly on your behalf. Both you and your proposal will benefit from others' trust networks, and the combined effect of the support of a range of trusted colleagues is incredibly powerful.

Advocacy becomes really essential, though, when you have prepared the proposal but someone else will be presenting it on your behalf. You need to ensure not only that they know everything you know about the detail of the document, but also that they share and can demonstrate your passion.

This is a challenge. If you are made responsible for driving someone else's proposal forward, you are likely to find points that you do not agree with or do not fully understand. You need to build a strong relationship, to get your colleague on your side and inspired by your vision, to ensure they can advocate effectively for you and will take responsibility for ensuring that no elements of your proposal could be misunderstood or compromised.

Summary

In order to build and present an effective proposal for your digital marketing strategy, you need to:

- *Understand your objectives.* Know what it is that your decision makers are looking for. Are they focused on growth, profit, brand value, reach, or something else? Ensure that your objectives are aligned appropriately.

- *Know your decision makers.* Make sure that you understand them as individuals, that you appreciate their unique perspectives and how they make decisions. What evidence do they need? How well do they understand digital marketing? Look at your proposal with their eyes rather than your own in order to work out how best to convince them of its merit.

- *Know the benefits.* An obvious point, but you need to be absolutely clear about the detail of the digital investment you are proposing. Make sure you understand and can explain how each digital marketing channel works, what is involved in any website developments, how the backend e-commerce and fulfilment function – you must be secure on the detail of each element, what challenges it raises and how it will be implemented.

- *Challenge yourself.* Once you have completed a first draft of your proposal, go back over it and challenge yourself rigorously. Are there any gaps or sketchy detail? Are your assumptions explicitly stated and well founded? What details are your listeners likely to take issue with?

- *Build a compelling presentation.* Don't just present your proposal: tell a story. Think about how to link your points into a smooth, logical flow, and provide summaries of all your key points. Be confident, demonstrate your grasp of both the big picture and the detail, and keep your delivery punchy and engaging. Practise, practise, practise.

- *Prepare for challenges.* The only way to prepare effectively for challenges is to know your stuff. All of it. You can build into your presentation answers to pre-empt challenges that you can foresee rather than waiting for them to be raised at the end, and make sure you have the facts at your fingertips to back up your responses. If you encounter an unforeseen objection, stay positive and avoid getting into an argument with your decision makers. Use detailed data to back up your response.

- *Advocacy.* Build a strong network of colleagues who share your vision and are passionate about your message. If someone is to present on your behalf, ensure they are fully briefed and fully in alignment with your goals – and also that they are an excellent presenter!

Chapter checklist

- Decision making ☐
- Budget ☐
- Key channel benefits ☐
- Channel interaction ☐
- Website ☐
- Further considerations ☐
- Structuring your proposal ☐
- Advocacy ☐

Further reading

- *On decision making*:
  Hardman, D (2009) *Judgment and Decision Making: Psychological perspectives*, Blackwell. This includes some fantastic insights into the psychology of this interesting field.

References

Bosomworth, D (2015) [accessed 1 November 2015] Mobile Marketing Statistics 2015, 22/07, *Smart Insights* [Online] http://www.smartinsights.com/mobile-marketing/mobile-marketing-analytics/mobile-marketing-statistics/

GSMA (2015) The Mobile Economy [Online] http://www.gsmamobileeconomy.com/GSMA_Global_Mobile_Economy_Report_2015.pdf

Kemp, S (2015) [accessed 1 November 2015] Digital, Social & Mobile Worldwide in 2015, 21/01, *We Are Social* [Online] http://wearesocial.net/tag/statistics

Bringing it all together

Throughout the book we have considered the key elements in producing your digital strategy. There are many considerations and complexities that need to be understood and factored into your final plan, but by following the processes and best practices in this book you can ensure that your strategy is robust, supported and future proofed. We have reviewed the standard deliverables of a digital strategy, including some of the core channels, user experience, analytics and also customer service. More importantly than this, however, we have also covered strategic models and wider considerations of how to align your strategy with your business.

The key message of this book is that when constructing your digital strategy it must be integrated. I would in fact go so far as to say that this applies to any marketing strategy and indeed any business strategy. Working in silos ultimately creates problems and decreases effectiveness – and so this is crucial to appreciate.

As marketing continues to evolve it is increasingly becoming an ecosystem and closer to parts of the broader organization than it has been historically. By this, I mean that marketing and customer service are now far more closely linked than they ever have been, product reviews are now often managed by marketing and consumers increasingly expect one brand at every touchpoint, which results in marketing needing to be involved at many deep levels of the business. Also, the expectation from consumers is higher than it ever has been. People are time poor and so expect fast responses; they are unwilling to accept poor service and irrelevant broadcast messaging; and indeed they will actively complain and discourage others from using a business if they are unhappy – and this feedback can be done at scale online.

None of this book is aimed at suggesting that offline marketing is dead or inferior to digital marketing. It is a mistake to believe that digital marketing will eventually destroy all offline marketing. In fact there has been a resurgence in direct mail in recent years in some parts of the world. Television advertising is still able to reach large audiences and create trust and awareness.

PR, press advertising and door drops all still have their place in specific industries. The key is to make them all work together – and so we come back to integration. 'The whole is better than the sum of its parts' is nowhere more appropriate that here. Also, the pace of technology marches on and appreciating this is vital to future proofing your strategy.

There is a further chapter of this book available online only, which looks at how digital is developing and some of the new technology that is coming soon, as well as what all of this means for your strategy. You can download it for free from: **www.koganpage.com/DigitalMarketingStrategy**.

I would strongly encourage any digital marketer to understand offline marketing in order to be able to take advantage of the integration opportunities and also to understand product, service and technology to some degree. This greatly increases your opportunity as a business to succeed. And beyond this it is essential to have good people, working together to achieve the goals. If your strategy needs to be integrated then your people need to be willing to work together to deliver a great result.

So, in summary, I hope this book gives you a structure and some insight into both the academic and practical methods of constructing your digital marketing strategy and I hope your strategy exceeds your goals. Good luck.

INDEX

Note: The index is filed in alphabetical, word-by-word order. Within main headings, numbers and the symbol '+' are filed as spelt out in full. Acronyms are filed as presented. The symbol '#' at the beginning of a heading has no filing value and the entry is filed under the first letter. Page locators in *italics* denote information contained within a Figure or Table.